A Contemporary Historiography of Economics

In recent years, historians of economics have increasingly been inspired by historians of science. This has opened up new questions regarding the utilization of sources, choice of method, narrative styles, and ethical issues, as well as a new awareness of the historian's place, role, and task.

This book brings together leading contributors to provide a methodological overview of the contemporary historiography of economics. Emphasizing the quality of the scholarship of recent decades, the book seeks to provide research tools for future historians of economic thought, as well as to any historians of social science with an interest in historiographic issues.

Till Düppe is Associate Professor of Economics at the University of Québec in Montréal, Canada.

E. Roy Weintraub is Emeritus Professor of Economics at Duke University, USA.

Routledge Studies in the History of Economics

For more information about this series, please visit www.routledge.com/series/SE0341

A Contemporary Historiography of Economics

Edited by Till Düppe and
E. Roy Weintraub

Routledge
Taylor & Francis Group

LONDON AND NEW YORK

First published 2019 by Routledge
2 Park Square, Milton Park, Abingdon, Oxon OX14 4RN
52 Vanderbilt Avenue, New York, NY 10017

First issued in paperback 2020

Routledge is an imprint of the Taylor & Francis Group, an informa business

British Library Cataloguing-in-Publication Data
A catalogue record for this book is available from the British Library

Library of Congress Cataloging-in-Publication Data
A catalog record has been requested for this book

ISBN 13: 978-0-367-66550-0 (pbk)
ISBN 13: 978-1-138-04995-6 (hbk)

Typeset in Bembo
by Swales & Willis Ltd, Exeter, Devon, UK

Contents

Contributors

E. Roy Weintraub is Emeritus Professor of Economics and Fellow of the Center for the History of Political Economy at Duke University. He is a Distinguished Fellow and past President of the History of Economics Society. His recent books include *How Economics Became a Mathematical Science* (Duke University Press, 2002) and, with Till Düppe, *Finding Equilibrium: Arrow, Debreu, McKenzie and the Problem of Scientific Credit* (Princeton, 2014), each of which won the Joseph J. Spengler Prize for the best book in the history of economics.

Till Düppe is an Associate Professor at the University of Québec in Montréal. He obtained his PhD in 2009 from the Erasmus Institute for Philosophy and Economics in Rotterdam. His main research interest is the historical epistemology of economics, inspired by phenomenological philosophy. He is the author of *The Making of the Economy: A Phenomenology of Economic Science* (Lexington, 2011), and, with E. Roy Weintraub, of *Finding Equilibrium: Arrow, Debreu, McKenzie and the Problem of Scientific Credit* (Princeton, 2014, Joseph Spengler book prize, 2014).

Dorian Jullien is a Postdoctoral Scholar at the Center for the History of Political Economy at Duke University while remaining a Research Associate at the Groupe de Recherche en Droit Economie et Gestion (Université Côte d'Azur, Nice, France). He works on the methodology, philosophy, and history of behavioral economics and rational choice theory, with an emphasis on the various roles played by the use of language by economists and economic agents.

Harro Maas is a Professor in History of Economics at the Walras-Pareto Center for the history of economic and political thought at the University of Lausanne, Switzerland. His research interests are in the historiography of the social sciences and in the role of economics in the public sphere. His recent research aims to historicize behavioral economics by historicizing the material infrastructure and practices of human deliberation. He is the author of *William Stanley Jevons and the Making of Modern Economics* (CUP, 2005), which won the Joseph J. Spengler best book award of the

History of Economics Society. With Mary S. Morgan, he edited *Observing the Economy: Historical Perspectives* (Duke University Press, 2012) and with Andrej Svorenčík *The Making of Experimental Economics: Witness Seminar on the Emergence of a Field* (Springer, 2016). He is the editor of the Cambridge series *Historical Perspectives on Modern Economics*.

François Claveau is Assistant Professor in the Department of Philosophy and Applied Ethics at the University of Sherbrooke (Canada) where he holds the Canada Research Chair in Applied Epistemology. He works on a variety of topics in the philosophy of the social sciences and in social epistemology. Recent publications include two books: *Experts, Sciences et Sociétés* (co-edited with J. Prud'homme, Presses de l'Université de Montréal, 2018) and *Do Central Banks Serve the People?* (co-authored with Peter Dietsch and Clément Fontan, Polity Press, 2018).

Catherine Herfeld is currently Assistant Professor for Social Theory and Philosophy of the Social Sciences at the University of Zurich, Switzerland. Her research concerns topics in history and philosophy of economics. She is interested in the history of rational choice theories and their uses in economics, explanation in economics, modeling in economics, and the usefulness of empirical approaches for research in history and philosophy of science, among other issues.

Andrej Svorenčík is a Postdoctoral Scholar at the Department of Economics, University of Mannheim, where he manages the local experimental economics laboratory. The overarching theme of his research is the emergence, diffusion, and reception of scientific communities, their related ideas and practices that make these epistemic groups distinct. His current book project is on the history of experimental economics. With Harro Maas he has edited *The Making of Experimental Economics: Witness Seminar on the Emergence of a Field* (Springer, 2016), which won the Best Book Prize by the European Society for History of Economic Thought in 2018.

Irwin L. Collier holds a Joint Professorship of Economics in the John-F.-Kennedy Institute of North American Studies and the Faculty of Business and Economics of Freie Universität Berlin, Germany. His blog Economics in the Rear-View Mirror (irwincollier.com) provides a regular flow of material related to the history of economics education.

Yann Giraud is an Assistant Professor of Economics at the University of Cergy-Pontoise. His research deals with the role of visual representation in producing and disseminating economic knowledge, the history of US economics education in the twentieth century, and, more recently, the relation between economics and engineering. Since 2010, he co-organizes the annual Conference on the History of Recent Economics (Hisreco).

Verena Halsmayer is a Postdoctoral Scholar at the Department of Cultural and Science Studies, University of Lucerne. She holds a PhD in the history of science (2016); in her dissertation, she worked on practices of modeling and measuring "economic growth" between the 1930s and 1970s. Her wider research interests concern the material circumstances of the making and spread of economic knowledge outside academe, and the devices and procedures of bureaucratic organization.

Tiago Mata is a Lecturer in Science and Technology Studies at University College London, United Kingdom. He has written on the history of dissent in economics, the patronage of the social sciences, and the sociology of economic expertise. In 2012–2016 he was principal investigator of a team project funded by the European Research Council, "Economics in the Public Sphere", inquiring on the origins and development of economic journalism in five countries. He occasionally writes in the popular press but most of his writings have appeared in scholarly journals in the history of economics, history of science, and science studies. His latest editorial project is an edited volume on the history of *The Economist* magazine.

Beatrice Cherrier is a CNRS researcher at the University of Cergy-Pontoise, France. She writes on the recent history of applied economics, with a focus on macroeconomics, public and urban economics, history of communities, and gender.

Introduction

E. Roy Weintraub

The origin of this book is my own self-education as an historian of economics. I am a member of the 1960s generation whose older colleagues assumed that the history of economics was part of one's general education as an economist. Although I was never trained in economics (I received a PhD in Applied Mathematics in 1969), my father was an economist trained in the 1930s when everyone read Marshall, and Jevons, and Edgeworth, and Smith, and Ricardo, and Marx, et al. He had his primary office and library at home, so I knew the brown leather binding of Böhm-Bawerk's *Capital and Interest* as well as the blue binding of the fifth edition of Gide and Rist's *Histoire des Doctrines Économiques*. The pictures on the walls of his study were decorated with photos and engravings of famous economists. I grew up with the canon at hand but unread since I studied mathematics and philosophy and literature. Coming into economics at the dissertation stage of my mathematics education, I moved over the 1970s from identifying myself as a mathematician teaching math to economists to a mathematical economist to a general equilibrium theorist.

When I arrived at Duke University in 1970, I found no senior theorists at all. I was hired into Lionel McKenzie's "theory line", open since McKenzie left in 1957, and the few junior people knew no game theory or general equilibrium theory or much mathematics. I soon met the intellectually engaging history of economics faculty – Joe Spengler, Craufurd Goodwin, and Neil De Marchi – and through the 1970s and early 1980s I gradually moved first to Lakatosian methodology of economics under the influence primarily Neil De Marchi, as well as Mark Blaug's (1980) *The Methodology of Economics*. The direct impetus for my move to history was my discomfiture with the then-current methodological appraisals of general equilibrium theory, critiques based on normative arguments based on one or another view of the right way "to do" science. I was annoyed at the appraisers' lack of knowledge of what general equilibrium theory was doing in economics, how it worked, and what its recent history consisted of. I thought that one's appraisal of modern general equilibrium theory, what I understood to be the Arrow-Debreu-McKenzie system, should be rooted in a serious historical understanding of its development so that it could function as a test case study of a successful (or if the critics were correct an unsuccessful) Lakatosian research program. The difficulty was that there was no such written history. So, I decided to write it myself. It took me four books and 35 years, while I was generally active in many other projects as well, to finish the job I began in 1982.

Looking back, my own scholarly life would have been somewhat easier had I been trained to write history. I had no models for doing oral history, or archival work, or foregrounding the context of the economics, or thinking through conflicting claims about credit. Most historians of economics were and are trained in economics. In writing history of economics, they have to find ways to keep their economics apart from their history; failure to do so often leads to anachronistic, or Whiggish, or under-researched and over-interpreted histories. As the historian of science Adrian Wilson (2017, p. 820) observed, "Whether inventing discontinuity or suppressing it . . . science invents a past for itself". Scientists, and economists, write articles in which the introduction "constructs – by selection, arrangement, validation, and so on – the past that it posits". This is called practitioner history, and such writing is part of every scientists' socialization to the profession. Economists do indeed train students how to write an economics paper, and thus economists learn how to write about an imagined past, a particular past useful for the economist's project: such a history is called a "review of the literature".

These matters are handled quite differently by historians of science, and since contemporary economics shares many characteristics with physical, biological, mathematical, statistical, engineering, and clinical sciences, can perhaps the history of science community provide some guidance for historians of economics? After all, the history of science is a well-established field of scholarship. George Sarton founded *Isis*, the journal of the History of Science Society, in 1913 even before he emigrated to the U.S in 1915, and books on the historiography of science (e.g. Kuhn 1962; Kragh 1987) are well known. With respect to the historiography of recent science, the works of Thomas Söderquist, for example *The Historiography of Contemporary Science and Technology* (1997), *The Historiography of Contemporary Science, Technology and Medicine* (with Ronald Doel, 2006), and *Science as Autobiography* (2003) illuminate a number of themes that should resonate with historians of post-World War II economics. The science studies literature, as it was employed in historical work, is also a possible guide for historians of economics. That literature is too immense to discuss here (although Golinski (1998) is helpful). The 1995 volume 10 of *Osiris*, published by the History of Science Society and edited by Arnold Thackray, was titled *Constructing Knowledge in the History of Science*, and its contributors judiciously appraised the major post-Kuhn conflicts about how to write the history of science. The absence of any how-to manual for individuals interested in writing the history of economics, the lack of any course of instruction similar to the historiography seminars routinely offered in history of science programs (e.g. at Cambridge, UK;[1] Princeton University;[2] Harvard University[3]), means that historians of economics must be autodidacts partially dependent on their mentors who themselves had no formal training in the historiography of economics.

There are only two edited volumes that carry the title *The Historiography of Economics*: the first, by Mark Blaug, appeared in 1991 and the second, compiled and edited by Roger Backhouse and Bruce Caldwell in 2014, was volume III of A. W. "Bob" Coats' collected papers. The former was a collection of previously published papers by a number of authors reflecting on the roles, the practices, and the aims of historians of economics. The latter consisted of Coats' articles on historical issues, reflections on historians' practices, and 28 of his book reviews of works in the history of economics. How then does an individual learn to write articles or books in the history of economics? If there is no course of study to follow, no certification process, no training ground, each individual scholar necessarily reads widely in the historical literatures and scavenges a bit from scholar A, a bit from B, and so on eventually forming a useful catalogue of research and writing practices suited to their own taste and sensibility. Surely though some guidance might be proffered? Surely there must be a more informed and autonomous historiography beyond the limits of economists' discourse? The present book is an intervention in this spirit.

This book has taken shape in ways very different from its original conception. It began a decade ago as an edited collection of my various papers on historiography written over a number of years. It became clear however that simple recapitulation of my earlier views was inadequate to do justice to the remarkable work being done by a new generation of historians of economics writing primarily but not exclusively on the history of contemporary economics. Subsequent to my successful collaboration with Till Düppe (2014), we began discussing ways to engage these new historiographic innovations. Could we present some of the new kinds of history-writing as exemplars for those training to be historians as well as for active historians of economics interested in expanding their toolkit of historical practices? What emerged was a plan to take advantage of the fact that many of the imaginative young scholars have been research fellows or research scholars or short-term visitors at Duke's Center for the History of Political Economy. We knew their work, and trusted their historical sensibilities. Most of these scholars have a sophisticated understanding of the historiography of science, and they are not hostile to the kinds of ideas that were mooted by Margaret Schabas in her *History of Political Economy* (*HOPE*) Minisymposium article that I long ago commissioned: "Breaking Away: History of Economics as History of Science" (1992).

Düppe and I thus organized our own mini symposium for *HOPE* (for Fall 2018) where the group of younger scholars would write short versions of their historiographic contributions for a large professional audience. Early versions of a number of those short pieces were presented in June 2017 in two sessions at the History of Economics Society meeting in Toronto. The present book then took shape in a conference at the University of Lausanne in October 2017 organized by Düppe, Harro Maas, and me. The various chapters of this volume were first presented at that conference and were significantly revised following discussion within the group. The papers were revised again with the editors' assistance. Only one of my originally proposed essays on historiography remains here, reprinted with permission of the original publisher, Cambridge University Press. And so, now in retirement, I can exit stage left.

Entering stage right are this volume's contributors. The first set of papers deals with the historiographical issues when drawing from personal memories. Following my own paper on autobiographical memory, Düppe addresses both practical and ethical issues involved in doing history in the presence of still living historical actors, where economists are seen as more than what Martin Bronfenbrenner once called desiccated robots. Next, Dorian Jullien examines the variety of uses and modes of interviews and traces the different ways oral history has been understood by historians of economics. Harro Maas presents his own case study of a witness seminar he co-directed, a new mode of examining a particular historical event or episode currently finding its way into both political history and the history of science. This meeting about experimental economics was a landmark event offering a complex reconstruction of how new work in economics came into being.

Part II presents two examples of what had been tentatively called a "quantitative turn" in the history of economics. The chapter by François Claveau and Catherine Herfeld introduces historians of economics to network analysis. Recognizing that economists are not solipsists but rather social beings who live their scientific lives in multiple communities of students, colleagues, collaborators, mentors, and competitors presents new opportunities to examine this social world by exploring the networks, the connections, of economists. Tools from statistics, graph theory, and pictorial data analysis have enabled historians of science to explore the relational character of science and the authors suggest ways in which similar approaches can open the history of economics to new sets of interesting questions. Andrej Svorenčík sets out the essential ideas of prosopography, a kind of analytic collective biography. He takes as his subject the entire American economics community as he employs a variety of metrics to suggest hierarchies and constellations of characteristics of the American economics profession.

Part III explores the historiographical issues when including the teaching of economics in our narratives. Yann Giraud examines the curious underutilization by historians of economics of textbooks in reconstructing their own scholarly projects, showing how these pedagogical devices shape historical understanding as they help to construct the economists' imagined past. Irwin ("Bud") Collier is not a youngster, except in spirit. In recent years he has been exploring, and making available to the history of economics community, economists' syllabi, course descriptions, examination questions, and other pedagogical material culled from archives around the United States. His paper here calls attention to the socialization of graduate and undergraduate economics students as a rich and mostly unexamined field for historians of economics to mine for understanding the development of economics itself.

Part IV provides three examples for what could be called "material" historiographies, which are in particularly inspired by writings rooted in the history of science. Verena Halsmayer's contribution examines economic knowledge as artefacts. Such constructs as models, graphs, pictures, metaphors etc. themselves have histories, and travel over time into different settings where they may have different uses. Following these artefacts can provide a fullness to narratives about the development of economic knowledge, and a respite from stories of disembodied thoughts untethered to anything but other thoughts. Tiago Mata's chapter explores the uses of popular histories, and popular media accounts that have economic content, showing how such accounts are in his words "history in transit", scholarly histories in the making, and are thus worth much more attention than they have hitherto received by historians of economics. In her contribution here, Beatrice Cherrier shows how the use of social media by economists – twitter feeds, blogs, and so on – creates new sources of information about economics for historians of economics, and perhaps more importantly provides historians of economics themselves with new ways to work as historians. As the history of economics community is an increasingly virtual community, its communication practices have also changed, a fact that opens new ways to "do" history of economics. Finally, Till Düppe provides a short concluding note to the collection.

The editors are pleased to acknowledge the help of a series of editors at Routledge Publishing Company who have kept the faith with this project over its many transformations and long gestation. Thank you.

Notes

1 https://www.hps.cam.ac.uk/news-events/seminars-reading-groups/graduate-seminars/aims-methods (accessed January 8, 2018).
2 "HOS 595 / HIS 595 Introduction to the Historiography of Science: An introduction for beginning graduate students to the central problems and principal literature of the history of science from the Scientific Revolution through the 20th century. The course is organized around several different methodological approaches, and readings include important works by anthropologists, sociologists and philosophers, as well as by Historians of Science".
3 The Harvard PhD Program in the History of Science requires, in the first year, "Two seminars: Historiography in History of Science (HISTSCI 303A) and Research Methods in the History of Science (HISTSCI 303B)".

References

Blaug, M. (1980). *The Methodology of Economics*. New York, Cambridge University Press.
Blaug, M. (ed.) (1991). *The Historiography of Economics*. Aldershot, Edward Elgar.
Coats, A. W. (2014). *The Historiography of Economics: The Collected Papers of A.W. Coats, Vol. III*. Compiled and Edited by Roger Backhouse and Bruce Caldwell. New York, Routledge.
Doel, R. E. and T. Söderquist, (eds) (2006). *The Historiography of Contemporary Science, Technology and Medicine*. New York, Routledge.
Düppe, T. (2012). "Gerard Debreu's Secrecy: His Life in Order and Silence." *History of Political Economy* 44(3): 413–449.

Düppe, T. and E. R. Weintraub (2014). *Finding Equilibrium: Arrow, Debreu, McKenzie and the Problem of Scientific Credit*. Princeton, Princeton University Press.

Golinski, J. (1998). *Making Natural Knowledge: Constructivism and the History of Science*. New York and Cambridge, Cambridge University Press.

Kragh, H. (1987). *An Introduction to the Historiography of Science*. New York, Cambridge University Press.

Kuhn, T. S. (1996 [1962]). *The Structure of Scientific Revolutions*. Chicago, University of Chicago Press.

Schabas, M. (1992). "Breaking Away: History of Economics as History of Science." *History of Political Economy* 24(1): 187–203.

Söderquist, T. (ed.) (1997). *The Historiography of Contemporary Science and Technology*. Amsterdam, Harwood Academic Publishers.

Söderquist, T. (2003). *Science as Autobiography*. New Haven, Yale University Press.

Thackray, A. (ed.) (1995). *Osiris Vol. 10: Constructing Knowledge in the History of Science*. Chicago, University of Chicago Press.

Wilson, A. (2017). "Science's Imagined Pasts." *Isis* 108(4): 814–826.

Part I

Memories in action

1 Autobiographical memory and the historiography of economics

E. Roy Weintraub[1]

In his autobiographical piece "A Jevonian Seditionist" Sidney Weintraub (1989 [1983], p. 50) recalled that in 1957 he sent an offprint of his paper on the microfoundations of aggregate supply to D. H. Robertson.[2] He remembered:

> Robertson generously wrote me that it was 'lucid and definitive,' and that thenceforth he would not return to the subject again. I confess that I have lost or misplaced his letter, along with the one by [Alan] Sproul,[3] in my move to Canada, though they were prized possessions.

And I have my own memory of a conversation with Sidney in which he told me that Robertson had written in that letter "If this is not what Keynes meant, it is what he should have meant".

He had, however, misremembered. After his death in 1983, I deposited his papers with the Economists Papers Project at Duke University, and in doing so I found three letters that are explanatory.[4] First, in a letter to Sidney dated 1 November 1957, Robert Clower (then at Northwestern) wrote:

> I have just finished reading with great interest (and, therefore, care) your recent EJ [*Economic Journal*] article on Agg[regate] Demand & Supply, and it seemed appropriate to let you know I found it very good. The spate of recent articles on the topic, each of which has served to muddy more water than it has cleared, should be choked off at this stage. Herewith my personal thanks for providing a reference to which I may refer future students of aggregate economics for a beautifully clear statement of what Keynes 'should have meant' if we could suppose that he was a rational being.

Second, in a letter to Sidney dated 14 January 1959, D. H. Robertson (Trinity College, Cambridge) wrote:

> I don't think I ever thanked you for sending me, a long while ago, an offprint of your AER [*American Economic Review*] article on the Theory of Wages. I think I was too exhausted at the time by my long (tho amicable)

wrangle with de Jong over the meaning of those inverse-looking D and Z curves to have much stomach for further adventure in those fields! But I have lately been reading your article with great appreciation of its clarity and thoroughness. So please accept my belated thanks.

And Sidney's reply to Robertson dated 22 February 1959 begins by saying that "it is so many years since I last heard you compliment this sometime wayward student of yours".

What had happened? It is clear that Sidney had remembered incorrectly, and had confused the Robertson letter with the Clower letter. It is not the case that there is an earlier Robertson letter since Sidney's reply denies any mail contact since 1939! Robertson would not return to the subject of aggregate supply not because of Sidney's paper, but rather because he had lost interest in the topic in his squabble with de Jong over de Jong's paper on aggregate supply. And there is a nuanced difference between the compliment "lucid and definitive" and "clarity and thoroughness".

Misremembering is not uncommon, and for historians using individuals' reminiscences to construct historical narratives, it would appear that misremembering is minimally troubling. After all, as I did with the letters that I had found, we can in some, perhaps many, cases find independent checks and confirmations of the remembrances; such "archival" materials often allow a rough validation of memory, a check on its reliability as historical evidence.

For example, in a famous paper published in *Cognition*, Ulric Neisser (1981) examined John Dean's Watergate testimony. Dean, recall, was special counsel to Richard Nixon in Nixon's second administration. Dean, in the Watergate hearings, appeared before Senator Sam Ervin's investigating panel and reported at length, from memory, the substance of conversations he had had with President Nixon and his senior staff members, particularly John Mitchell, Charles Colson, John Erlichman, and Robert Haldeman, concerning the mechanics of the cover-up following the investigation of the Watergate break-in. Dean's memory for the events was prodigious as he recounted, apparently verbatim, specific conversations on specific dates. This testimony thus implicated the president and his advisors in the Watergate cover-up, answering Senator Howard Baker's repeated question regarding Nixon: "what did he know and when did he know it?". What Dean of course did not know was that Nixon had an elaborate recording – bugging – technology in the Oval Office, and all of the conversations in which Dean took part had in fact been preserved. When the tapes of those conversations were made public, Neisser was able to compare Dean's recollections of the conversations with the transcripts of those conversations themselves.

Was Dean's recollection, his memory, accurate? The comparison of testimony with transcripts made clear that Dean had mixed up dates, made errors in attribution of remarks he recalled, and even combined separate conversations into a single one, and vice versa. Yet Neisser concludes his study of Dean's memory by noting that:

[There is a] paradoxical sense in which Dean was accurate throughout his testimony. Given the numerous errors in his reports of conversations, what did he tell the truth about? I think that he extracted the common themes that remained invariant across many conversations and many experiences, and then incorporated those themes in his testimony . . . [In] memory experiments, subjects often recall the gist of the sentence but express it in different words. Dean's consistency was deeper; he recalled the theme of a whole series of conversations, and expressed it in different events . . . [He] was wrong only in terms of isolated episodes. Episodes are not the only kind of facts. Except where the significance of his own role was at stake, Dean was right about what had really been going on in the White House.

(Neisser 1981, pp. 20–21)

There is, to my knowledge, only one serious discussion in the historiography of economics about the use of autobiography. In his recent "Biography and the History of Economics," Donald Moggridge (2003) devotes four pages, his last section, to "autobiography". Moggridge of course bases his account on the recent explosion of collections of autobiographical material. We have had the two volumes edited by Szenberg (1992, 1998), the two volume collection edited by Kregel (1989), and the two volume collection edited by Backhouse and Middleton (2000), as well as the host of autobiographically shaped interviews in such places as the *American Economist* and *Econometric Theory*. Moggridge's own count of these and a few other recent collections shows 198 such autobiographical essays. He suggests that:

The existence of this growing stock of autobiographical memoirs can play a useful role in the history of economics. In particular, given the absence of manuscript records in many universities in the U.K. (and probably elsewhere), such memoirs may prove prime supplements to university calendars in tracing the development of particular departments through most of the post war period. Their value will increase as the stock of memoirs moves beyond the heady days of the post war consolidation and 1960s expansion of economics to more recent, and more troubled times.

(Moggridge 2003, p. 599)

He makes the important connection between autobiographical writing and memory itself, and refers directly to some important work being done in cognitive psychology, by pointing out that:

Autobiographical memories are constructed out of various components, and the final construction will be 'guided by the person's goals at the time of retrieval, as well as by the goals of the time of encoding [the components, so that] changes in what is remembered should be expected' (Rubin 1995, 4).

(Moggridge 2003, p. 597)

Moggridge, looking at some of the complex evidence put forward by psychologists about autobiographical memory, focuses on the incompleteness of such memory accounts, and concludes that:

> all of this suggests that autobiographical material should be used carefully. It is useful evidence but it may not always be sound, particularly as regards to discussions of motivation or cause. Yet most collections of autobiographical essays are unreflective on their contents.
>
> (Moggridge 2003, p. 598)

Moggridge's account however is in my view somewhat incomplete. Though he wisely calls attention to the unreliability of memory, he also suggests that they may not be too unreliable for he suggests that they can usefully supplement other records by providing an independent check on some kinds of other materials. I'm not convinced they are so unproblematic.

One issue of course is separating the specifically autobiographical material from the subject's recall of past events in which the person was not so primarily engaged. That is, recalling a situation from one's own past, in which one was a witness to an event, appears to be systematically different, in its character, from a subject's recall of something that was autobiographically consequential. Memory has different characteristics from autobiographical memory.

If I ask you to recall a movie that you really liked, with a high degree of confidence I can predict that you will recall a movie that you have seen within the past few years. Performing this kind of experiment however also finds something else. The farther back in time you go from the present, the rate or density of those kinds of memories falls off. That's not surprising really, since we all tend to forget things. The surprise however comes when we ask for longer list say of movies and we will find, with some confidence, that you will also produce memories of movies from the young adulthood of your life. In study after study investigators have found that the density of memories is "double humped", as pictured in Figure 1.1.

That is, memories from early childhood are almost nonexistent, so much so that the phrase "childhood amnesia" is used by psychologists of memory. Then the density of memories per year increases through young adulthood, and then it decreases through the middle years, increasing again to the most recent years. Specifically, suppose one plots the density of memories (e.g. memories per year normalized by the total number of memories) of say 65–75 year olds vertically, and the chronological age of the person at the time of the event so recalled horizontally. It turns out that retrospective studies of such older subjects inevitably produce a curve which rises progressively to a peak somewhere in the mid to late 20s, then begins to decline to around age 45–50, and then rises again to the subject's present age. This "bump" in early adulthood is stable cross-culturally, and seems to characterize all kinds of memories: not just memories of songs, movies, individuals on baseball teams, novels, even memories of styles of clothes.[5]

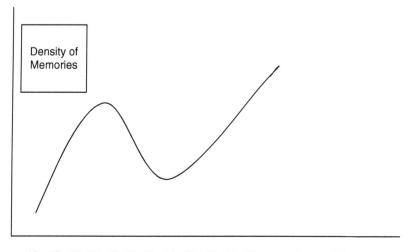

Figure 1.1 Density of memories over time

For an important class of personal/developmental memories however, the later years are not remembered as similarly consequential. We believe in our remembering, in reconstructing our own histories, that we are, as late adults, who we were by early adulthood (on average). Thus in contrast to the "double hump" curve of say "memorable reading experiences as a function of the time the book was read" (Larsen 1995, 52), the self-forming memories – memories of that which truly made me what I am today – are single peaked, with the early adulthood period apparently most important in remembrance. Such a result appears in a number of studies in the cognitive psychology literature.[6]

Since I am interested in the memories of economists as "data" for historians of economics, it is important to know whether economists are similar enough to the other groups already studied by cognitive psychologists to allow their results to inform my work. Thus in an attempt to examine whether the accounts, the autobiographical memoirs of economists, were consistent with these kinds of findings, we[7] performed a content analysis on economists' memoirs replicating the methodology in (Mackavey, Malley, and Steward 1991).[8] Specifically, we analyzed autobiographies from volumes one and two of *Recollections of Eminent Economists* (Kregel 1989).[9] Though the autobiographies used in the sample were written under broad guidelines, and though they vary somewhat in content and format, they were all written by influential economists who were at an appropriate age to reflect on their entire life experiences. Their lives in fact spanned most of the twentieth century.

Of those autobiographical essays by 24 men and one woman, several were excluded because the author did not cover the entire life span, but rather focused only on the first half of the life, or on a several-year period. We excluded auto-biographies by Giovanni Demaria, Hyman Minsky, and Nicholas Georgescu-Roegen for this reason.

The cognitive psychology literature identifies "autobiographically conse-quential memories" (ACEs) as memories which describe:

> an event, person, or set of circumstances in the individual's life that [are] remembered as having affected the unfolding of the life story in a person-ally significant way . . . this consequentiality must [be] evident through the writer's own words and [can] not be assumed . . . The memory must also [establish] a causal connection between the event or experience and the consequence.
>
> (Mackavey et al. 1991, 53)

Thus in order to qualify as an ACE, a memory needed to have had an effect on the author's psychology and outlook, and not merely on his or hers physical location or purely professional interests. Memories were identified as ACEs if they fulfilled all of the above conditions.

We also employed (but do not report here) the usual distinction between epi-sodic and non-episodic memories. As defined in the cognitive psychology litera-ture, episodic memories describe explicit events that occur over a short, distinct time period (usually a day or less), and are vivid in detail. In contrast, non-episodic memories describe in more general terms a longer period or life experience.

In order to identify ACEs reliably and consistently, initially the two inves-tigators independently analyzed several of the articles. When inconstancies appeared in the two readings, the different interpretations were discussed until the readers reached agreement. The interpretation of an ACE was refined in this way to be consistent with the earlier (Mackavey et al. 1991) model study before the larger set of articles were analyzed by the junior investigator.

Once identified, ACEs were coded for age at the time of the memory according to the following life periods: childhood: <12; adolescence: 13–17; college years: 18–22; early adulthood: 23–35; middle adulthood: 36–50; later adulthood: >50. In the rare case that the author did not provide enough infor-mation to accurately identify the age at the time of memory, the ACE was not coded. This occurred in only two cases. If an age spanned one or more periods, it was divided across the appropriate periods, hence the occurrence of x.5 ACEs in some life periods.

If an ACE was identified by the author as having occurred during the undergraduate years at college, the ACE was coded as "college years" even if the author's actual age at the time of the memory fell outside of the 18–22 period (i.e., if the memory was remembered as having occurred at the age of 17 or 23). This was for simplicity, as most college memories spanned several years and the exact age of the author could not be identified beyond that. This exception was not applied to any other life period. The results, summarized in the Table 1.1 and Figure 2.2, are clear.[10]

Table 1.1 ACEs and life stage data

Category	Age in years	ACM	% ACM	% ACM per year
Childhood	0–12	10.5	9.3	0.8
Adolescence	13–17	13.5	11.9	2.4
College	18–22	31	27.4	5.5
Early adulthood	23–34	42	37.2	3.1
Middle adulthood	35–50	14	12.4	0.8
Later adulthood	Over 50	2	1.8	0.1

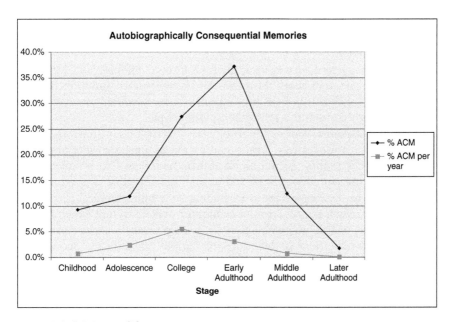

Figure 1.2 ACEs over life stages

There is a decided remembrance "bump" for the college/early adulthood period. Economists are sufficiently similar to other experimental subjects, auto-biographically, that we may place some trust in the robust results found in the cognitive psychology literature. Put another way, we can employ arguments like those developed by cognitive psychologists in assaying the autobiographical materials on offer from economists.

I wish to suggest then that the nearly 200 autobiographical memoirs of economists that Moggridge identifies are more interesting than we are accustomed to imagine. There are more interesting questions to ask of them than "are these autobiographical accounts accurate?" and "does the material support or disconfirm historical arguments drawn from other sources?". Specifically, these autobiographical memoirs themselves are documents, and are a genre of writing by economists of no less interest to an historian perhaps then econo-mists' writings on matters of high theory.[11]

I realize that this is a curious claim. We are accustomed as historians to deal with the writings, written inscriptions, of economists on weighty matters of economic science itself. The material products of these scientific communities, the scientific knowledge, appears traditionally to be our subject matter and, as historians, it has been our apparent job to reconstruct that material historically if we are of such a mind, or to reconstruct it rationally if we are unmindful of history. After all, we are supposed to think that the products of economic science are theories, analysis, examples, policy documents, etc. In traditional histories of economics the autobiographical memoirs that economists write, like their letters, like their course syllabi, like their lecture notes, are useful only (we usually argue) insofar as they contextualize the primary materials that hold our serious interest.[12]

But what happens if we step back and look at this community of economists and ask other questions about this particular class of written and spoken prod-ucts? Can we "analyze" them in any fashion? Is there anything systematic to be claimed or argued about this nearly 200-point sample?

A couple of points seem to me to be salient. First, these narratives, if read continuously in a moderately compressed period of time, are quite numbing. As literary materials they are, almost all of them, graceless. One wonders why. Perhaps it is the complex mix of author and audience that is at issue here. After all, the readers' expectations in reading an autobiographical memoir of an economist, when the reader is an economist, will be to find either a moral cautionary tale, or a shining path exemplar, to help reconstruct the narrative of the reader's own life. That is, these accounts variously describe an "economist's life script" by setting in motion various kinds of expectations about how a suc-cessful economist should conduct his or her own life: where to go to graduate school, the importance of mentors, the importance of being in the right place at the right time or the importance of not being in the right place at the right time, etc.[13] Systematically, this implies that their education, their professional training, and their early professional years will dominate the accounts they pro-vide of important issues in their lives. This isn't very surprising of course since these economists were being asked to construct autobiographical memoirs of their lives as economists, not as parents, or children, or lovers, or for the most part teachers. What we have are fairly systematic discussions of "what made me the great economist that I am, so great that you asked me to contribute my autobiographical memoir to your collection?".[14]

Second, I submit that there are real implications for the history of eco-nomics were we to take seriously results from cognitive psychology about the bump in both recall and autobiographical recall from early adulthood. We've already demonstrated that there is such a bump for ACEs in a sample of the economists' autobiographical memoirs. This suggests that economists' retro-spective personal accounts will inevitably focus on material drawn from that early adulthood period. We consumers of these memoirs are presented with an over sampling of "this is really important economics" from the memoirist's own early adulthood. This has some historiographically startling implications.

For instance, how can one explain "the years of high theory"? When Shackle (1967) wrote the book of that title, he was referring to the 1930s when all of the important theoretical work that shaped the 20th-century economics was created. Or rather, so he argued. Today, looking back on the 1930s, we see very little theory that has lasted. In his recent retrospective of macroeconomics in the 20th century, the distinguished economist Olivier Blanchard argued that the period prior to 1940 was a:

> period of exploration, where macroeconomics was not macroeconomics yet, but monetary theory on one side, business cycle theory on the other. A period during which all the right ingredients, and quite a few more, were developed. But also a period where confusion reigned, because of the lack of an integrated framework.
>
> (Blanchard 2000, p. 1376)

Keynesian ideas of aggregate demand management policies, and the economic role of governments in promoting growth, high rates of employment, and high gross national product (GNP) seemed to have survived, but what remains of the other high theories? Recall that for Shackle the other revolutionary and enduring breakthroughs from that period include imperfect competition, Sraffa and value theory (cost curves!), Myrdahl's monetary equilibrium, the formal dynamics of cycles and growth, and Leontief's input-output analysis. It is quite painful now to read Shackle's last triumphant chapter called "the landslide of invention". The claim that these years of high theory represented the break with tradition that would forever reshape economics seems quite dated, and mistaken.

But why was the claim made in the first place, and taken so seriously at the time Shackle made it? Perhaps it is that nasty bump. Ask yourself how old was Shackle (1903–1992) in those years of high theory, 1926–1939? The answer is immediate. He was a young adult, 23 in 1926, and 36 in 1939. There is something quite systematic here. It is not without reason that Paul Simon sang the line in *Bubble Boy* about "It's every generation puts its hero up the pop charts".[15] The emphasis of course in that sentence should be on the word "its" for each generation's hero is the hero of its late adolescence and early adulthood. It's not only that we can't stand the new music that the kids are listening to, since our music was much more interesting. Our music was the music of our bump. And so too with our economics. Keynes (1936, p. 384) himself wrote, in the final paragraph of *The General Theory*, that "in the field of economic and political philosophy there are not many who are influenced by new theories after they are twenty-five or thirty years of age". We 1960s' products said it another way: "Never trust anyone over 30". Don't trust anyone who's past our bump.

In other words, one problem in working with autobiographical memoirs is that what will necessarily emerge in later years is a systematic emphasis on the events and categories of the memoirist's young adult period. A large number of autobiographical accounts penned by the heroic generation of economists who came of age intellectually between the late 1930s and the late 1940s focus on how economics was transformed as a professional discipline in precisely that period. They gave us, and told us about, the econometrics revolution, the Keynesian revolution, and the game theory revolution. They told us stories about a time when giants walked the earth.[16]

Historiographically, we have not understood these kinds of arguments to be systematic in a structural sense. That is, we do spend a great deal of time arguing about whether economics really really was transformed by the probabilistic revolution in econometrics, or whether general equilibrium theory, or that beast called formalism, really really was transformatory of economics in the early 1950s. Mark Blaug's concern with the formalist revolution of the early 1950s,[17] which I (Weintraub 2002) have argued never really happened, appears to reflect exactly and precisely his own concerns with the important issues of his own early adulthood. And so too with much of our historical writing. I am not of course here attempting to dismiss Blaug's and other historians' concerns with "it's merely the bump talking". Rather I want to recommend caution in our use of autobiographical materials, especially when those materials can be construed as projecting an individual's history onto a larger historical narrative. It is not simply a matter that the materials may be unreliable in accidental or systematic ways. It is that the structure and nature of these kinds of auto-biographical memoirs are not unproblematic documents. They are written to some purpose we often do not understand, for an audience of non-historians. And they reflect a number of different issues from both the personal and cultural life scripts which they illuminate and which in turn shape and reflectively are shaped by exactly these kinds of accounts. As a consequence we historians of economics understand too little of the autobiographical impulse and have too impoverished a vocabulary to provide interesting, let alone compelling, appraisals of its products. Scholars in history, psychology, sociology, literature, and medicine have begun to address these issues. I submit that we historians of economics have a lot of interesting work left to do.

Notes

1 This chapter is a slightly edited version of an article of the same title that appeared in the *Journal of the History of Economic Thought* (2005), 27(2): 1–11. It is reprinted here with the permission of Cambridge University Press. David Rubin, my Duke colleague, is a cognitive psychologist who has devoted his career to understanding autobiographical memory. I am pleased to have had his guidance as I sought some partial understanding of these complex matters, and as usual my friend and colleague Neil DeMarchi provided much-needed criticism of various drafts. With the usual disclaimer, I am appreciative of their help.

2 "Dennis Holme Robertson (1890–1963), Fellow of Trinity College 1914–38, 44–63; Lecturer in economics at Cambridge University 1920–28; Girdlers' lecturer 1928–30; Reader at Cambridge University 1930–38; Professor of Economics at University of London 1939–44; Professor of Political Economy at Cambridge

University 1944–57; adviser to the Treasury 1939–44" (http://cepa.newschool.edu/het/, accessed 14 October, 2003).

3 Sproul was then president of the New York Federal Reserve Bank.

4 Sidney Weintraub Papers, Rare Book, Manuscript, and Special Collection Library, Duke University, Box: Correspondence 1939–1963, folders 1957 and 1959. I also found two letters from Sproul in that 1957 folder.

5 The power function for retention was first identified by Crovitz and Schiffman (1974). Rubin, Wetzler, and Nebes (1986) found the "bump". A fairly large literature developed from that paper, a literature nicely surveyed in (Rubin, Rahhal, and Poon 1998). It was Galton though who did the first age distribution with about four categories similar to the one I have used.

6 Constructing an adequate theory of these varied components of autobiographical memory is difficult. Recent availability of functional magnetic resonance imaging technologies has opened new connections across the field however; for one set of attempts to integrate these partial theorizations, see (Rubin 1998) and (Greenberg and Rubin 2003).

7 A then Duke undergraduate, Mr Bogdan Albu, was my collaborator in spring 2003 in this content coding project.

8 That study, "Remembering Autobiographically Consequential Events: content analysis of psychologists' accounts of their lives" appeared in *Psychology and Aging* in 1991, and reported on recall phenomenon in autobiographical accounts written by distinguished psychologists. Those autobiographical accounts, similar to the kinds of autobiographical memoirs that we economists are accustomed to use, were scored and analyzed for content. That is, 49 eminent psychologists' accounts were scored for ACEs in order to examine their density across the lifecycle. The finding was that "memories were concentrated during the college and early adult years" (p. 50): they found the now usual bump.

9 As Kregel stated in the foreword to volume one, these essays were originally printed, starting in 1979, in the *Quarterly Review* published by the Banca Nazionale del Lavoro, and in the Italian-language version of that journal, *Moneta e Credito*. These publications are described as economic journals "addressed to an international readership", and as "an international market-place for the ideas of economists throughout the world" (1989, vol. 1, p. xi).

"Frequent contributors" to the journal, as well as "other eminent economists", were asked, beginning in 1979, "to reflect on their personal activities and experiences in the process of the development of their research work in economics". Furthermore, "no particular constraint or format was placed on these contributions" (1989, vol. 1, p. xi).

10 I am pleased to acknowledge the assistance of Dr Cathleen McHugh in the preparation of the Table 1.1 and Figure 1.2.

11 Of course, what is of interest to an historian is not necessarily of any interest to an economist.

12 George Stigler once wrote: "[B]iography distorts rather than illuminates the understanding of scientific work" (Stigler 1970, p. 426).

13 This matter of constructing, and employing, what sociologists call "life scripts" in autobiographical narratives is not simply understood. The process of autobiographical remembering itself is intertwined with those scripts (Rubin and Berntsen 2003). We have no historical studies of evolving life scripts of individuals identified as "economists" over time, or space. For instance, what were the changed expectations of a professional life for the members of the European émigré generation, and how did those brutally changed scripts affect narrative memory?

14 Sometimes of course these memoirs do touch on other kinds of events where the author is able to contextualize the economist's life with important kinds of world events that help shape the professional career. Wars, revolutions, immigrations, are all to be found and are often judged to be explanatory by the memoirs.

15 I am of course fully aware that my near total recall of Paul Simon lyrics is from my "bump". This is precisely the kind of evidence on generations or eras brought forward by Jerome R. Sehulster (1996), who not entirely facetiously asked who was your host of the "Tonight Show", who was your James Bond, and who were your Tristan and Isolde?

16 One of the consequent issues here of course is the notion of an "era" or a "generation". This concept seems perfectly understandable, and indeed it finds its way into everything from journalistic practices, to marketing strategies. It is, however, slippery to identify a generation "objectively". The idea seems to be attributable to Karl Mannheim (1952 [1928]), and has been reconstructed and analyzed in useful ways in (Schuman and Scott 1989), a paper which should be better known among historians of economics.

17 Blaug was born in 1927, and received his PhD in 1955.

References

Backhouse, R. E. and R. Middleton (eds) (2000). *Exemplary Economists, Volumes 1 and 2*. Northampton, Edward Elgar.

Blanchard, O. (2000). "What Do We Know About Macroeconomics That Fisher And Wicksell Did Not?" *Quarterly Journal of Economics* (November): 1375–1409.

Crovitz, H. F. and H. Schiffman (1974). "Frequency of Episodic Memories as a Function of their Age." *Bulletin of the Psychonomic Society* 4: 517–518.

Greenberg, D. L. and D. C. Rubin (2003). "The Neuropsychology of Autobiographical Memory." *Cortex* 39(4–5): 687–728,

Keynes, J. M. (1936). *The General Theory of Employment, Interest, and Money*. New York, Harcourt Brace.

Kregel, J. A. (ed.) (1989). *Recollections of Eminent Economists, Volumes 1 and 2*. New York, New York University Press.

Larsen, S. F. (1995). "Memorable Books: Recall of Reading and its Personal Context." In *Empirical Approaches to Literature and Aesthetics*. M. S. MacNealy and R. Kreuz (eds). Norwood, Ablex: 52.

Mackavey, W., J. E. Malley, and A. J. Steward (1991). "Remembering Autobiographically Consequential Experiences: Content Analysis of Psychologists' Accounts of Their Lives." *Psychology and Aging* 6(1): 50–59.

Mannheim, K. (1952 [1928]). *The Problem of Generations. Essays on the Sociology of Knowledge*. London, Routledge and Kegan Paul.

Moggridge, D. E. (2003). "Biography and the History of Economics." In *A Companion to the History of Economic Thought*. W. J. Samuels, J. E. Biddle and J. B. Davis (eds). Malden and Oxford, Blackwell: 588–605.

Neisser, U. (1981). "John Dean's Memory: A case study." *Cognition* 9: 1–22.

Rubin, D. C. (1998). "Beginnings of a Theory of Autobiographical Remembering". In *Autobiographical Memory: Theoretical and Applied Perspectives*. C. P. Thompson, D. J. Herrmann, D. Bruce et al. (eds). Mahwah and London, Lawrence Erlbaum Associates: 47–67.

Rubin, D. C. and D. Berntsen (2003). "Life Scripts Help to Maintain Autobiographical Memories of Highly Positive, But Not Highly Negative, Events." *Memory & Cognition* 31(1): 1–14.

Rubin, D. C., S. E. Wetzler, and R. D. Nebes (1986). "Autobiographical Memory Across the Lifespan." In *Autobiographical Memory*. D. C. Rubin (ed.). Cambridge and New York, Cambridge University Press: 202–221.

Rubin, D. C., T. A. Rahhal, and L. D. Poon (1998). "Things Learned in Early Adulthood Are Remembered Best." *Memory & Cognition* 26(1): 3–19.

Schuman, H. and J. Scott (1989). "Generations and Collective Memory." *American Sociological Review* 54(3): 359–381.

Sehulster, J. R. (1996). "In My Era: Evidence for the Perception of a Special Period of the Past." *Memory* 4(2): 145–158.

Shackle, G. L. S. (1967). *The Years of High Theory: Invention and Tradition in Economic Thought 1926–1939*. Cambridge, Cambridge University Press.

Simon, P. (1986). "Bubble Boy." *Graceland*. Warner Brothers. Released 28 August, 1986.

Stigler, G. (1970). "Review of Robbins's *The Evolution of Economic Theory*." *Economica, New Series* 37(148): 425–426.

Szenberg, M. (ed.) (1992). *Eminent Economists: Their Life Philosophies*. New York and Cambridge, Cambridge University Press.

Szenberg, M. (ed.) (1998). *Passion and Craft: Economists at Work*. Ann Arbor, University of Michigan Press.

Weintraub, E. R. (2002). *How Economics Became a Mathematical Science*. Durham, Duke University Press.

Weintraub, S. (1989). "A Jevonian Seditionist: A Mutiny to Enhance the Economic Bounty?" In *Recollections of Eminent Economists, Volume 1*. J. A. Kregel (ed.), New York, New York University Press, 1: 37–56.

2 Dealing with the personal in the contemporary history of economics

Till Düppe

Introduction

Contemporary history, as a field, emerged in the post-War period in response to the experience of the 20th century as one of "extremes" (Rothfels 1953; Catterall 1997). It is that branch of history that deals with the past that is still remembered by living persons. Contemporary history, *Zeitgeschichte* in German, is history that is still "time" – that is, lived memory that is not yet, and may never be, settled in clean facts of documentation. More than other periods, contemporary history is marked by open wounds, deliberate distortions, unsettled conflicts, anxieties of oblivion, oppressed memories, disappointments, and grief, but also by pride, gratitude, honor, and other feelings attached to the personal past of our parents' and grandparents' generations. It is history that concerns us. While historiographical issues of preceding periods mainly involve how and in what terms we can bring back a past that is foreign to us today, contemporary history has to deal with these sentiments and negotiate them between generations.

And so does the history of contemporary science. As difficult as the relationship might be between modern masters of knowledge and the ephemeral stream of time, scientists must also rely on being remembered. And as elsewhere, emotions run high when negotiating what will be forgotten and what will endure. In fact, the very struggle over truth, in practice, comes down to a struggle over what is remembered in science. It is in the midst of this struggle that the historian of contemporary science adds his contribution to the production of collective memory. The presence of those living persons relevant to contemporary science can be as virtual as an imagined reader – such as Robert Lucas, who hardly engages historians' accounts of the representative agent – or as intimate as E. Roy Weintraub writing about his father (2002). In any event, it is unavoidable. All practical questions at each point of one's research – the choice of sources, the way texts are read, the style of writing, the kinds of arguments, the choice of contexts, but also the way to respond to referees and to communicate results – are not only scholarly but also personal and, furthermore, moral choices. Whose interests will my history serve? How do I relate to those who were witnesses, who took part, and may still have an axe to grind? Shall I ignore them, confirm them, or shall I blame or even provoke them? History of economics becomes a matter of you and me, of them and us. While historical distance often requires the historian to simply translate ideas for today's readers, historical vicinity forces us to think about our *ethos* and self-consciously demarcate the historian's voice. In the following, I will reflect on the historiographical questions related to the fact that we write the history of that which is still remembered by persons living among us.

Contemporary history is historically specific. In classical historiography, say that of the 19th century historical school of the Rankean kind, historical vicinity was perceived as threatening to the professional codes of proper documents, reinforced by the doubt that eyewitnesses are not reliable historical sources as they are tainted by interests (Vierhaus 1957). Historiographical debates since this period have been overshadowed by the question of whether the use of personal memories causes a *bias* in historical writings, and if the historian becomes an accomplice or in any sense instrumental to current power struggles. The experience that forced Western historians to nevertheless enter contemporary history was the 20th century as a time of extremes – referring initially to the disaster of the two World Wars, which then resulted in a renewed sense of historical responsibility when thinking about the present. The field thus emerged from a *sense of urgency*, an immediate "need of self-articulation" (Rothfels 1953, p. 5) caused by the lack of understanding between cultures, people, and generations that are separated by their extreme experiences. And the sciences, economics in particular, having gone fairly blindly through major transformations in the 20th century, have made their contribution to the lack of comprehension of how we ended up with the world we live in today. The sciences are a *symptom* of the 20th century.

Responding to this sense of urgency, this chapter provides a historiography of the contemporary that fully embraces the presence of the personal in science. I begin by presenting a theoretical framework for writing histories of the scientific self – a concept at the center of what I call *lived epistemology*.[1] Writing such histories, in practical terms, raises questions of harmony and conflicts of interest in the history of science. I argue that the question of bias that overshadows the historiography of the contemporary is a *Scheinproblem* that appears if one avoids underlying ethical questions when assuming the personal.

Lived epistemology

If contemporary science requires a discussion different from ancient science, knowledge seems to have a historical nature. This in itself is a contentious claim. In the history of philosophy, reflections on the historical nature of knowledge grew out of dissatisfaction with the conceived, specifically Kantian, contrast between that which is known and that which is ephemeral. For Kant, time is merely a form of apperception (*Anschauung*) but not one of cognition (*Verstand*). He also placed time awkwardly as the "scheme" or pattern of imagination (*Einbildungskraft*): that which renders intuitive categories of cognition (such as causality, unity, or necessity) when applied to what is presented to our senses. It was only at the beginning of the 20th century that our sense of before and after became a central concern in the context of neo-Kantian epistemology when scholars like Wilhelm Dilthey, Ernst Cassirer, and Edmund Husserl tried to spell out how cognition is enacted in concrete and how knowledge, and science in particular, results from historical life (see Rheinberger 2010). Time and history, for them, were central to what it means to be an understanding being. This same post-Kantian desire is at work when, for example, Lorraine Daston describes her work as a "history that would pose transcendental questions in a highly particularistic mode" (2000, p. ix).

Consider, for example, Edmund Husserl. The starting point of his historicized epistemology was the "subjectivity that accomplishes science" (1970, p. 295; see also Hyder and Rheinberger 2010). To speak of the subjective accomplishment of science is to focus on the necessity of someone to carry out knowledge: someone needs to keep track of, has to be with, and has to go through the reasoning, the evidence, the judgment, the research material, etc. Even the most general or abstract theory is the result of a unique and concrete course of *efforts* required to accomplish it. This is not only a matter of "practices" that can be described in a behavioral fashion (Stapleford 2017), but requires a distinct attitude (*wissenschaftliche Einstellung*) that brings about a different way of experiencing oneself. Knowledge is not only a set of justified beliefs representing something, but an experience for the subject carrying out this knowledge. Science can be viewed as a way of feeling, viewing, and relating to oneself, others, and our surroundings. In this way, science can be described as any other experience through which we come to understand the seat of science in life, as Husserl said. Or, to quote a more recent historian of science: "Just as we have social histories of eating, dying, breeding, and getting and spending, so too we can have a social history of truth making" (Shapin 1994, p. xxiii).

Husserl spoke of such analysis as a "regression to the life-world", and as the "digging out of buried sense-accomplishments" (*Ausgraben verschütteter Sinnesleitungen*). What must have already been accomplished in our life for a scientific interest to emerge within us? What is the "act of meaning formative for the experience of scientific thinking"? (Dodd 2004, p. 7) The history of these buried accomplishments is what he calls, in contrast to the history of facts, the *history of sense*, the writing of which is the "tremendous task of a true and genuine philosophy of science" (Husserl 1970, p. 398). In the context of the mathematization of the natural sciences, he asks:

> Where is that huge piece of method . . . that leads from the intuitively given surrounding world to the idealization of mathematics and to the interpretation of these idealizations as objective being? . . . How formulae in general, how mathematical objectification in general, receive meaning on the foundation of life and the intuitively given surrounding world – of this we learn nothing.
>
> (Husserl 1970, p. 296)

This huge piece of method is particularly daunting when considering 20th-century economics. What remains as its "residual", its body of knowledge, are some vague intuitions – "doing the best", "scarcity", "waste", "tastes", "markets" – treated with formally defined theoretical concepts – equilibrium, aggregation, mechanisms, sunspots – that are treated by a set of techniques – graphs, functional analysis, axioms, regressions, calibrations, simulations – which are some of the ingredients of what are called models. Now think of the 20th century: two wars that exceeded what the world had seen before, atomic destruction, genocide, growing inequality, the space race, the rapid development of communication technologies, and what not. How did it come that *this* 20th century created the conditions of *that* kind of knowledge to prevail over other forms of economic knowledge? The last century was a time of historical ruptures that made many silence, paper over, and oppress memories, leaving us with incomprehension between people, cultures, and generations. 20th-century science has contributed to this great incomprehension, insofar as it tells us little about its origins. The halls of economics offered a place to live in the harassed world of 20th-century man, but economists tell us what made this place attractive. This is how I came to understand Husserl's notion that science "lacks the knowledge of what gives meaning to it".

Heidegger also had something similar in mind when he mentioned, without elaborating, an existential, in contrast to a logical, concept of science (1962 [1927], p. §69b). According to the logical concept, science is viewed in terms of its results; that is, "something established on the interconnection of true propositions". According to the existential concept of science, instead, he asked what were the "existentially necessary [conditions] for the possibility of Dasein's existing in the way of scientific research" (p. 408). Science is, in his words, a "mode of Being-in-the-world", a "way of existence". The distinction between the personal and the scientific is, in this case, a "privative mode", as Heidegger would have said, of a more intimate connection between the two. Modes of reasoning, modeling techniques, can be understood as attitudes we adopt toward our experiences and concerns, thus a kind of "self".[2] Scientific claims not only result in anonymous truths that may or may not be the case; the question of truth, rather, refers back to the state of being able to make a truth claim. Truth is, first of all, a "claim on me". Science in this sense, as Söderqvist boldly claimed about the case of Niels Jern, is like writing a diary (2003). In the words of one of the commentators of Husserl:

> Thus to reflect on the possibility of making the claim myself, in my own voice, not only brings the truth of a proposition into question, but it also brings myself into question as well – for the question here takes the form: what would it mean, to be the one who would make such a claim.
>
> (Dodd 2004, p. 9)

With this in view, the questions to be answered are thus: What kind of person do I need to be to lend my voice to this or that scientific truth? What moral identity is induced by doing so? From which existential project is economic knowledge the result? How is it to speak as an economist? Which attitude must one to adopt to form an interest in economic science? How does one get to see oneself as an economist, and how do others come to support this self-perception? One might call this theory of knowledge, in resemblance with the notion of lived experience, *lived epistemology*. In lived epistemology, we view knowledge not as a cognitive activity but as an experience that happens to someone.

***

Clearly, this understanding of science is *critical* to the extent that science itself tells us little about its experience. Science is presented as a representation of what is, and speaking about oneself is limited to the language of the rules of conduct – to methods. Science is "selfless" insofar as its truth is independent of whether someone is interested in it. It requires, in Galison's words, the "right way of self-abnegation" (2015). It is as if scientists, watching a mirror, believes they are behind the mirror. Or, in Husserl's words: "Merely fact-minded sciences make merely fact-minded people" (1970: 6). Instead, in lived epistemology, science is not considered a representation of the world, but a *response* to it; it tells us from attempts and failures to find one's place in a historical situation. It is this critical element that renders lived epistemology a non-trivial task. The impersonality of scientific expression, reinforced by the degree of technicality, creates a *complex*, or better, a historically contingent relationship between "life" and "work". It is not obvious from Debreu's work that he preferred mathematical rigor to economic chit-chat because he inherited a basic *Angst* from his broken family (Düppe 2012); it is not obvious from Krelle's publications that he wished to modernize German economics out of feelings of guilt that he, rather than his comrades in the trenches next to him, survived the war (Düppe 2018b).

Several topics can be addressed when writing histories of the scientific self. One of them is what has been called the *scientific personae*; that is, the character the scientific community or society associates with the scientist and which an individual aspires to (Daston and Sibum 2003). In contrast to a mere professional activity, being a scientist is to adopt a social role, a calling, an ethos, or in any event an aspiration to identify with. Scientific personae are historically specific, as one might sketch with a big brush: the ancient scholar, the medieval learned, the Renaissance instrument maker, the early modern traveler, the natural philosopher of the enlightenment, the 20th-century intellectual, today's experts, etc. (for an overview, see Lightman 2016). In all these cases, being a scientist requires committing to specific *epistemic virtues* – such as precision, patience, or moderation, but also radicalism, purism, or perseverance – that not only discipline thought but also offer a moral identity – such as seriousness, honesty, courage, dedication, selflessness, or responsibility. As Steven Shapin took as a precept of his *Social History of Truth*:

> What we know of comets, icebergs, and neutrons irreducibly contains what we know of those people who speak for and about these things, just

as what we know about the virtues of people is informed by their speech about things.

(Shapin 1994, p. xxvi)

Note that we do not require that these epistemic virtues ever be fully realized. They do, however, provide the scientific experience with a teleological frame. The scientific personae is, as Daston and Sibum (2003) argued, located between the individual biography and the social institutions of science. It is a "mask" providing a social identity. While social epistemology can categorize them, and historical epistemology can describe their transformation, in lived epistemology we spell out the life path that is subject to these virtues. Why is it that a certain scientific personae is attractive as a life choice for this or that person in this or that time? And which historical situations bring about the conditions under which these virtues become attractive models of life?

Aspiration is one source of the scientific self; another is the *psychological need* these aspirations respond to. What are the psychological conditions of the possibility of feeling and acting like a scientist? Due to an age-old *intrinsic value* of knowledge as if it is a basic instinct of mankind, stylized by epistemic virtues such as selflessness, we have a very poor understanding of this need. However, considering that a large part of mankind lives without scientific ambitions, and considering the costs of a scientific career – long periods of education, higher mobility, lower social bonds, small markets due to high specialization – it is not at all obvious why someone develops such a degree of commitment. We might look in vain for a general theory of these needs as they are, like the scientific personae, historically contingent.[3] But we can observe individual cases: insofar as academia allows for solitude, it might attract those who react against attachment (as Shapin (1990) has shown for 17th-century scholars); insofar as emotions are left out of scientific discourse, it might attract those with emotional disorders (John Nash being a well-known example); insofar as scientific principles promise to anchor what is otherwise felt as being uncontrollable, it might attract those needing to deal with anxiety (as Leonard (1998) has shown for Carl Menger in the tumults of Vienna of the interwar period); insofar as science is only hypothetically related to reality, it can provide consolation for suffering, as for the Russian mathematician Sofja W. Kowalewskaja after witnessing the death of her sister: "At such moments mathematics are a relief. It is such a comfort to feel that there is another world outside one's self" (in Koblitz 1993, p. 202); or, to go yet further, insofar as scientific objects promise immutability, their aesthetics might attract a death instinct as the daughter of the mathematician Claude Chevalley said about her father:

The way my father worked – it seems that this was what counted most – was the production of an object which then became inert; dead, really. It was no longer to be altered or transformed. Not that there was any negative connotation to this . . . [My father] thought of mathematics as a way to put objects to death for esthetic reasons.

(in Senechal 1998, p. 26)

In all these cases, it is the experience of knowledge and not its representational content that explains its meaning for the scientist.

Epistemic virtues as well as epistemic needs usually do not come in isolation but are manifold and can be in conflict or in harmony with other virtues. Selves, in contrast to academic compartments, are not neatly limited. How is science integrated into the rest of one's life? The precision, dedication, and patience needed for building a large-scale macro-econometric model, for example, can be in surprising harmony with nationalist sentiments and Protestant virtues of hard labor (Düppe 2018b); the virtue of communitarianism, to mention one of Merton's classic norms of science, can come into conflict with the ambitions induced by the reward system of science (Düppe and Weintraub 2014); the very desire for individual happiness can be compromised by the devotion and "monomania" needed for achieving a certain degree of intellectual depth (Daston 2008); and the need to feel relevant is consistently frustrated by various standards for scientificity, a repeatedly lamented source of scientific pessimism and cynicism in the heterodox critique of economics (Colander and Klamer 1987). The same question can be posed on a more global level: Do the values of science match those of the rest of society? Such was the big question of Mertonian norms in the face of World War II, a question that was formative for of the very field of science and technology studies (Merton 1942). While in social epistemology one can observe and state these conflicts, it is in lived epistemology that their experience is described.

To be sure, the scientific self can be a topic of individual life-writing, but it can also be the subject of a larger, *cultural history of science*. What kind of science is brought about by witnessing the French Revolution, the October Revolution, the Holocaust, the atomic bomb? Two examples: the general mistrust in economic affairs, during mercantilism, for example, can explain why visions of social structures at which this mistrust is neutralized, are attractive to those who are subject to this mistrust, merchants (Düppe 2011); the general feeling of anxiety during the first years of the Cold War can explain the rise of the protocol-based notion of scientific rationality (Erickson, Klein, Daston, Lemov, Sturm, and Gordin 2013). Such more-speculative histories allow us to understand the culture of science in a twofold sense of science constituting its own culture and of our culture being determined by science – two facts that surprisingly often do *not* form a contradiction. As hard as 20th-century scientists tried to express themselves differently from other forms of cultural expression (literature, art, and even religion), they understood little of how much they were caught by them.

If we cannot expect a general theory resulting from lived epistemology, then what is its purpose? While it presumes a shared sensibility for life stories, it is not a form of voyeurism. Scientists, though very reflective when it comes to justifying their practices, have little means to think about themselves in other than the terms provided by their methodologies. If one has not independently acquired a language from art or literature, one has no means for thinking about the meaning of one's profession. Lived epistemology can provide such language through examples. Just as art can intensify the visual experience of forms and objects, so can lived epistemology intensify the intellectual experience of knowledge. Lived epistemology aims at intriguing and intimidating the scientist to evoke a sense of self and thus of responsibility. This might be best compared with what *parables* do: describe moral dilemmas, questionable decisions, and the consequences of these decisions. Παραβολη means to "walk aside"; histories of scientists' selves can be apologues that transmit a moral question in an indirect, but nevertheless concrete way. In this sense, life-writing in science can then indeed be called an "edifying genre", as Söderqvist has called it (1996).

Coming back to the contemporary, these topics of histories of the scientific self are, in principle, not limited to a specific period. Lived epistemology can rely on sources that are not limited to the contemporary such as diaries, letters, and personal notes – anything that helps in getting to know someone. But for two reasons the contemporary lends itself to lived epistemology. First, historical vicinity makes it easier to get to know someone as we can actually meet him or her. Second, today's specific regime of knowledge of economics favors abstraction over description, which increases the urgency of drawing back this form of knowledge into economists' life-world.

Conflicts of interests

When applied to contemporary history, this research program pushes the limits of what is considered "the private sphere" – which has its own history and cultures. If archives impose a 30-year limit for legal reasons – a criminal record would otherwise not be a historical but a legal document – and the access to living persons gets around this limit, contemporary history runs the risk of violating privacy laws. When the limits between the personal and the representational in science are trespassed, questions of interests impose themselves. In this section, I reflect on these questions.

The root of the problem is that historical work is only one minor source of the production of collective memory. Economists themselves fondly remember, and express their feelings through review articles, science prizes, honorary doctorates, theorem tagging, journalism, and blogging, but also in person when one meets and talks to them. History is a strategic realm in which several interests are negotiated among those who have access to it. And if one does not want to be a popularizer of their ideas, a caricature of their self-display, or a product of one's reactionary feelings against them, questions of conflict and harmony of interests must be negotiated, as well as reflected in historical work. Before publication, one is often asked to assure that there are no potential conflicts of interests, and one might push doubts aside because of the pressure of publication. But the lack of self-interrogation in this respect is a serious problem in the recent history of economics. So what are the sources of harmony and conflicts of interests?

Consider the following correspondence I received in response to a commissioned work on the history of the economics department in Bonn at the occasion of a university anniversary (Düppe 2018a). The circumstances are telling: while all other faculties had internal authors, some retired professor who is considered as having sufficient knowledge of the department's past, there was no elderly economist who was deemed to have had enough expertise about their own history – one example of the cultural ruptures typical of the 20th century, in this case the rupture between generations of literary economists such as Arthur Spiethoff, Erwin von Beckerath, and Joseph Schumpeter, and a younger generation of technical economists such as Wilhelm Krelle, Werner Hildenbrand, and Reinhard Selten. After the work was done and the internal refereeing process was finalized, the higher faculty positions changed, and I received the following message:

> As a [high rank faculty member] of the Faculty of Law and Economics at the University of Bonn, I would like to thank you very much for your beautiful draft of the history of our department . . . May I make a cordial request? There are two passages that I beg you to consider critically . . . [One] concerns Mister Krelle: The description of his family situation seems to me . . . not that which readers expect from a department history published by the university . . . I would be very pleased if you could consider my concerns when preparing the final version.
>
> (email to the author)

What happened? And how to respond?

There is harmony of interest insofar as the field of history is considered a source of scientific *credit*. The history of economics, at its best, is perceived as a selection process of that which is worth preserving. Whether one is supposed to add to already-given credit, or, like a lender of last resort, grant credit that had been refused, the hope is that we *feed their ego* (or that of their deceased mentor). Many economists, often incapable of distinguishing personal admiration for their teachers from gratitude for the career opportunities they offered, think of history as a form of worship. The power to grant credit thus makes contemporary history vulnerable to the attempts of censorship (Cantor 2006). Economists cooperate with historians because they wish to *influence* the first sediments of history. When writing about those who have been already credited, one is not supposed to deviate from the official terms; or, when writing about those who have *not* been credited, one is equally supposed to undo past injustice, like lawyers of the forgotten. The role of the historian as a *scholar* in explaining scientific performance that is nevertheless *instrumental* for the reward system constitutive of this very performance is thus deeply precarious. You might have received similar messages as this:

> You proclaim that the development of the department was essentially the result of a game of power of different networks, in which nationalism, if not Nazism, and the desire to find the connection to the USA were the driving forces. You are free to hold this opinion, but I consider it wrong

and not well-founded . . . You do not see that the very great success of the
department was essentially due to the scientific quality brought about here.
(email from famous German economist to author)

Clearly, the issue goes further than the choice between an "internalist" and
an "externalist" account. It concerns the historian's identity with respect to
economists. One way out is to appeal to the shared scholarly ethos by claiming
the right to "set the historical record right", thus hiding behind facts. I used this
rhetorical move when responding to the message cited at the beginning of this
section: "The background of the family was well-known in the department,
and is therefore a historical fact of the faculty . . . To ignore this fact would
mean to be caught by history of the department instead of reporting about it".

Evidently, the matter was not to point to the fact of there being a fact – as
if there was only one way of writing history, which is the very denial of the
historicity of human life. Instead, it was to undermine the feeling that family
information is inappropriate as presentism. Reference to facts in contemporary history easily begs the moral issues looming behind the noble motive of
setting the record right. It is to play down conflicts without facing them. Note
also that it is only after one reduces the writing of history to the reporting of
facts that the question of bias can be posed. This question is thus a derivative
of an attitude that tries to avoid questions on how to relate, as a person, to
those who are concerned by the stories one tells.

Another source of cooperation, next to the power to grant credit, is the
anonymity that the halls of modern knowledge provide. Whatever the historian writes, a model or a proof stands. Because nobody would see the value of
a great theorem diminished by what kind of person the discoverer is, technical
economists speak more easily about themselves. Mathematicians often lead an
aloof life which is reflected in a rather liberal attitude, flirting with the scientific
personae of an eccentric non-conformist. Having asked Monique Florenzano
if she wondered why Gérard Debreu stuck out as a person, she replied: "No
I did not. In this profession, people are crazy anyway, and he was not weirder
than others" (personal conversation).

However, the person matters in economics more than in other sciences insofar as the discipline always travels under a cloud of *ad hominem* arguments and
ideological suspicion (see Chapter 3 in this volume). This was a specific challenge to my work with *socialist economists* in East Germany (Düppe 2017). They
were trained to show utmost professional dedication, and to personally represent
their work, and thus had a strong work ethos to defend and to communicate.
However, their professional dedication was a political duty, controlled ultimately by the secret police, such that they learned to hide or control the display
of personal matters. Also, they clearly suspected that I, born in West Germany,
embraced the winner's version of history and treated them as mere dogmatists.
General respect for historical truthfulness was largely burdened under the tenets
of dialectical materialism, where historical memory is but a symptom of power
relations. Cooperation stood and fell ultimately with their own coordination.

They acted as a "collective", though the interviews were conducted individually. They might have coordinated what to reveal and what to hide, which made their memories no less interesting. Even if their commitment to the party line was of varying degrees, it turned out that all of them were similarly critical about the political limits imposed on them, and they shared very similar biographical memories. The solution was to write on a "generation", which allowed me to put distance from any claims about individuals.

Another group that can be an important source for contemporary historians are those who suffered from the intellectual obsession of their fellows and their elevated ego brought about by the academic reward system: family members and friends. Adding their voices fulfills the genuine purpose of oral history "from below" to give voice to minorities otherwise unheard. Some might be protective of the self-display of their close fellow, but others are also willing to correct it and to share what happened behind the scenes of representational ideas and referential truth. Talking to them is to learn about the lived struggle for ideas without knowing these ideas. Mindful of the difficulty of confronting family past, I never push, and let the participant decide how far to engage. While I try to find a way around censorship from those who wish to maintain the given credit status, it is from them that I accept changes. It is also their applause that I seek because it is for them that my work can make an actual difference in their personal lives. Regarding the same family content that colleagues wished to omit, the daughter responded:

> Thank you for sending us the first draft, which . . . I have read several times carefully. It is a good detailed work on our father and our family. Many tears run . . . I think you did very well in doing justice to the character of my father. I am very happy for my father. I thank you cordially.

The troubled private life of her father, unknown to the public, difficult to be reminded of for the family, and yet, when exposed in an academic journal, the daughter is grateful *for him*. What more could we expect from our work than helping to live through grief and sorrow.

When facing open wounds and conflicts among those concerned, *balance* is certainly an epistemic virtue of historical work. What is historical memory good for if it does not provide inclusion, agreement, and some form of reconciliation, even if this too often means revealing conflicts that are withdrawn from the public? Debreu's daughter repeatedly referred to her father as manic depressive, though he was never diagnosed. Since this judgment hardly played a role in Debreu's life (he saw a psychologist only a few times) I did not use the word. The reader might draw such judgment from my narrative but it should not be its presupposition. One sign of having found balanced language is that those who disagree about their past, those who still live through ongoing conflicts, can agree on the way the narrative is presented. Another, equally important, sign is that, as an author, one has no wish to blame or to accuse, which is, to no longer reproduce our parents' and grandparents' feelings, to cease their struggle with their past. In contemporary debates, we argue about actions and beliefs. In contemporary history, we come to understand them.

Potential conflicts can be, and should be, prevented by being as transparent as is necessary and by securing prior agreement. Practices in our community differ widely, which one might take as a sign of pluralism but also of a lack of professionalism (see Chapter 3 by Jullien). Some historians of economics of an older generation, when conversing with economists, use no form of agreement, do not record, and do not ask for approval when (indirectly) quoting the conversation, such that readers are left with good faith in the author's memory and truthfulness. The trade-off is clear: when being more formal, one gains security of agreement but puts potential conflicts on the table, which might be a reason for withholding information or even withdrawing from participation. Considering the precariousness of our field discussed above, however, presenting myself as one of them who, presumably, shares the same interest would be a straight lie. Full transparency is certainly impossible and also not necessary, but I learned to ask for ethics approval from my university, and use agreement forms to sign, record, and grant the possibility of, but avoid *ex post*, approval of direct citations. There is no recipe for best practice, and I experienced several failures: I had interviews interrupted, statements changed *ex post*, and imposed self-censorship in anticipation of future approval. Fortunately, it never happened that disagreements took a legal form, the ultimate failure of having dealt badly with conflicts of interest. After all, it comes down to the person's trust, which is an entirely personal question.

Another source of conflicts of interest that needs to be mentioned is unrelated to the trespassing of the private sphere and the credit system in science, but is related to commercial or political interests. Do historians who inquire into the strictures of economists with business and political lobby groups have no other possibility than to keep economists at a safe arm's length? When Mirowski writes about the Mont Pelerin Society or the Nobel Prize, we would not expect members of the Mont Pelerin Society or the Swedish Academy to agree on his account. The nature of such histories, on the contrary, is to evoke disagreement of those one writes about. These narratives are so enmeshed in the negotiations of interests that the reader tends to learn more of Mirowski's interests than about the historical actors. However, when we involve actors with commercial and political interests – which might touch on state or business secrets – we do not necessarily become their accomplice. For next to balance, *subtlety* should be considered an epistemic virtue in the historiography of contemporary economics. It is the subtlety of narratives that lend them an exposing flavour that does not threaten the professional integrity of actors.

But the most important strategy in dealing with potential conflicts of interest for my work is the appeal to the human. The history of contemporary economics can provide the inclusion of economics into human memory – which knows no taboos but understanding between generations. The instinct of the older generation to share with the younger generation is very basic. Without it, memories would be no more than melancholy of an irrevocable past. In response to the message cited at the beginning, I wrote:

The interest for the person of Krelle is so great that an essay like this must react to it. There will be readers who will read the essay only to see how the military past is represented. And the family background shows that as a scientist Krelle did not only remain an officer, but also a human being. Readers of department histories are also human beings, and therefore will not be offended by the human aspects of such a story. This applies to all of my research.

I received no response.

There is no general recipe for dealing with potential conflicts between economists and historians. If one does not reflect on them, however, one might end up being caught by them. The quality of our work depends on how we individually find balance between conflicting and harmonious interests. And the more we know the personal implications of our work, the better we can deal with them.

Notes

1 History and theory being exclusive of each other in 19th-century discussions, the meaning of the term "historical theory" is not obvious. The notion of "historiography" might indeed be considered a placeholder for topics regarding the conceptual framework (theory) and the methodology (practical tools) in historical research. Among historians of economics, only certain highlights in historical theory are known (Popper, Kuhn, or Foucault). In the history of science, I consider "theory" to refer to the epistemological question of what is the historical nature of knowledge, to the historical topics that follow from it, and to its intended results. Together with the discussion of the practical questions related to applying this theory in the second section, this chapter presents a historiographical approach, if not a research program.
2 The notion of the scientific self figures prominently in the works of Galison (e.g. 2004), and also in Daston and Galison (2007). Galison associates it with the idea that "changes in the self (are) necessary for certain scientific procedures, and . . . certain scientific procedures became training exercises . . . that cultivated a certain kind of self" (2015, p. 95). He specifically contrasts the 19th century will-based self in the Kantian tradition and the will-to-willness that describes the current scientific self. He relates this notion to the Foucauldian project of the history of the self, but acknowledges its roots in the phenomenological tradition (p. 100).
3 There are surprisingly few attempts that have ventured a psychology of science. A small field journal in the *Psychology of Science and Technology* has been launched by Gregory Feist. It is limited to statistical surveys of pre-defined measures, such as personality tests (Feist 2008). Another, epistemologically more profound attempt, is still the classic study of Gaston Bachelard published in 1938, *The Formation of the Scientific Mind* (2002[1938]), which, in a modernist spirit, tries to explain scientific progress.

References

Bachelard, Gaston (2002 [1938]). *The Formation of the Scientific Mind*. Manchester, Clinamen Press.
Cantor, David (2006). "The Politics of Commissioned Histories (Revisited)." In Ronald E. Doel and Thomas Söderqvist (eds), *The Historiography of Contemporary*

Science, Technology, and Medicine: Writing Recent Science. New York, Routledge: 45–66.

Catterall, Peter (1997). "What (if anything) Is Distinctive about Contemporary History?" *Journal of Contemporary History* 32(4): 441–452.

Colander, David, and Arjo Klamer (1987). "The Making of an Economist." *The Journal of Economic Perspectives* 2: 95–111.

Daston, Lorraine (ed.) 2000. *Biographies of Scientific Objects*. Chicago, University of Chicago Press.

Daston, Lorraine (2008). "Monomanie in der Wissenschaft." In Heinrich Meier (ed.), *Über das Glück*. Munich, Piper: 221–252.

Daston, Lorraine, and Peter Galison (2007). *Objectivity*. New York: Zone Books.

Daston, L., and Sibum, H. (2003). "Introduction: Scientific Personae and Their Histories." *Science in Context* 16(1–2), 1–8.

Dodd, James (2004). *Crisis and Reflection: An Essay on Husserl's 'Crisis of the European Sciences.'* Dordrecht, Kluwer.

Düppe, Till (2011). *The Making of the Economy: A Phenomenology of Economic Science*. Lanham, Lexington.

Düppe, Till (2012). "Gerard Debreu's Secrecy: His Life in Order and Silence." *History of Political Economy* 44 (3): 413–449.

Düppe, Till (2017). "The Generation of the GDR: Economists at the Humboldt University of Berlin Caught between Loyalty and Relevance." *History of the Human Sciences* 30(3): 50–85

Düppe, Till (2018a). "Der Bonner Wandel der deutschen Volkswirtschaftslehre"; anniversary chronicle of the University of Bonn.

Düppe, Till (2018b). "War after War: Wilhelm Krelle, 1916–2005", working paper.

Düppe, Till, and E. Roy Weintraub (2014). *Finding Equilibrium: Arrow, Debreu, McKenzie and the Problem of Scientific Credit*. Princeton, Princeton University Press.

Erickson, Paul, Judy L. Klein, Lorraine Daston, Rebecca Lemov, Thomas Sturm, and Michael D. Gordin (2013). *How Reason Almost Lost Its Mind: The Strange Career of Cold War Rationality*. Chicago, University of Chicago Press.

Feist, Gregory J. (2008). The Psychology of Science and the Origins of the Scientific Mind. New Haven, Yale University Press.

Galison, Peter (2004). "Image of Self." In Lorraine Daston (ed.), *Things That Talk: Object Lessons from Art and Science*. Brooklyn, Zone Books.

Galison, Peter (2015). "From Objectivity to the Scientific Self: A Conversation with Peter Galison (Interview with Jason de Stefano)." *Qui Parle* 23(2): 89–114.

Heidegger, Martin (1962 [1927]). *Being and Time*. Hoboken, Blackwell.

Husserl, Edmund (1970). *The Crisis of European Science and Transcendental Phenomenology. (Die Krisis der europäischen Wissenschaften und die transzendentale Phänomenologie: Eine Einleitung in die phänomenologische Philosophie*. Den Haag, Nijhoff. Translated by David Carr. Evanston, Northwestern University Press.

Hyder, Davis and Hans-Jörg Rheinberger (eds) (2010). *Science and the Life-World: Essays on Husserl's 'Crisis of European Science.'* Stanford, Stanford University Press.

Koblitz, Ann Hibner (1993). *A Convergence of Lives. Sofia Kovalevskaia: Scientist, Writer, Revolutionary*. New Brunswick, Rutgers University Press.

Leonard, Robert J. (1998). "Ethics and the Excluded Middle: Karl Menger and Social Science in Interwar Vienna." *Isis* 89(1): 1–26.

Lightman, Bernard (ed.) (2016). *A Companion to the History of Science*. Chichester, John Wiley.

Merton, Robert K. (1942). "Science and Technology in a Democratic Order." *Journal of Legal and Political Sociology* 1: 115–126 (later published as "The Normative Structure of Science").

Rheinberger, H.-J. (2010). *On Historicizing Epistemology: An Essay*. Stanford, Stanford University Press.

Rothfels, Hans (1953). "Zeitgeschichte als Aufgabe." *Vierteljahreshefte für Zeitgeschichte* 1: 1–8.

Shapin, Steven (1990). "'The Mind Is Its Own Place': Science and Solitude in Seventeenth-Century England." *Science in Context* 4(1): 191–218.

Shapin, Steven (1994). *A Social History of Truth: Civility and Science in Seventeenth-Century England*. Chicago, University of Chicago Press.

Senechal, M. (1998). "The Continuing Silence of Bourbaki: An Interview with Pierre Cartier." *The Mathematical Intelligencer* 1: 22–28.

Söderqvist, Thomas (1996). "Existential Projects and Existential Choice in Science: Science Biography as an Edifying Genre." In Michael Shortland and Richard Yeo (eds), *Telling Lives: Studies of Scientific Biography*, Cambridge, Cambridge University Press: 45–84.

Söderqvist, Thomas (2003). *Science as Autobiography: The Troubled Life of Niels Jerne*. New Haven, Yale University Press.

Stapleford, Thomas A. (2017). "Historical Epistemology and the History of Economics: Views Through the Lens of Practice." *Research in the History of Economic Thought and Methodology* 35A: 113–145.

Vierhaus, Rudolf (1957). *Ranke und die soziale Welt*. Münster, Aschendorff.

Weintraub, E. Roy (2002). *How Economics Became a Mathematical Science*. Durham and London, Duke University Press.

3 Interviews

Some methodological and historiographical issues of oral sources

Dorian Jullien[1]

Introduction

The interview, as an exchange between an interviewer and an interviewee, is a type of interaction that takes many forms and pervades our contemporary society. We have all been interviewed for a job and some readers might have also interviewed job applicants. In the media, we often come across a journalist, a columnist, a television or radio host interviewing a politician, an artist, an athlete, a scientist, an ordinary citizen, and so on. Some sociologists even argue that we live in the "interview society", where the interview is seen as an accepted mean of getting information and as a privileged way of disclosing authentic subjectivity (see Atkinson and Silverman 1997; Holstein and Gubrium 2004; Gubrium and Holstein 2012). Medicine, psychology, the social sciences, and the humanities, they argue, are active participants in the interview society. Indeed, these fields have produced a profuse and diverse amount of methodological and historiographical writings about the interview – in its multiple manifestations (for a representative sample of this diversity, see Fielding 2009).

How does the history of contemporary economics fit in this picture? Restricted to the most common form of interview encountered in other disciplines, i.e., the oral (usually face-to-face) interview, a quick search reveals more than 100 papers and a dozen books over the last 40 years where historians of economics have used interviews.[2] This number includes papers that either make use of someone else's interviews as sources (which roughly represents about 60 percent of these contributions) or the use of interviews conducted by the historian for her or his work. Only a few of these contributions offer comments on the specificity of using interviews and on the conditions of production of the interviews. Less than ten contributions (not necessarily using interviews themselves) propose methodological and historiographical reflections informed by other disciplines about using interviews in the history of contemporary economics (Mata 2005, Appendix; Weintraub 2007; Mata and Lee 2007; Emmett 2007; Freedman 2010; Cherrier 2011; Svorenčík 2015, Appendix). These reflections are valuable but they are either quite brief or focused on a narrow object (usually a set of interviews conducted by the author).

The goal of this chapter is to broaden the scope of these reflections in two directions, both of which aim at better characterizing the practices of using interviews in the history of contemporary economics. First, the chapter covers a greater number of contributions in the history of economics to show how the similarities and differences in these practices bear on a specific historiographical issue, namely that the research project for which interviews are used might be perceived by some scientists (i.e., the ones that are interviewed or other members of the community) as involving a potential threat to scientific legitimacy. Second, the chapter puts these practices in perspective with a larger diversity of methodological and historiographical contributions from other disciplines using interviews, sometimes suggesting further developments.

The goal of this chapter is not to provide a list of "dos and don'ts" regarding the use of interviews for historians of economics. Indeed, there seems to be no consensus among scholars who have written on the methodology and historiography of interviews regarding good practices, which are highly dependent on context (including the personalities of the interviewer and interviewees) and epistemological positions. Instead, the goals are to emphasize issues to be mindful of when using interviews as oral sources as opposed to more traditional written ones, as well as to highlight the interaction and interdependence between oral and written sources.

Practices of using interviews in the history of economics and potential threats to scientific legitimacy

A historical research project that uses interviews might be perceived by some scientists as involving a *potential* threat to their scientific credit, scientific reputation, or even to the scientific legitimacy of their discipline. This comes from the broader issue that the history of contemporary science (including economics) can produce historical narratives that challenge scientists' self-produced historical narratives, and history is one source for the establishment of scientific credit and legitimacy (see, e.g., Klamer 1983, p. 250; Söderqvist 1997; Weintraub 2007; Düppe and Weintraub 2014, preface; Wilson 2017). Indeed, pointing out the importance of institutional, social, or technological factors for a given result can be taken as reducing the scientific credit scientists deserve for that result. Similarly, pointing out the cultural or ideological ladenness of the meaning of scientific results can be taken as reducing the scientific legitimacy of a discipline. This section explains how historians of economics make different uses of interviews that can involve the perception of a threat to scientific reputation, credit, or legitimacy – and how they did (or could) manage this issue. It is organized around a number of representative examples that reflects an evolution in the history of economics. In a certain chronological order, three broad types of interview topics have emerged as particularly relevant for the members of the discipline: economists and policy-making, economists and the content of their academic work, and the careers and lives of economists.

Economists and policy-making

In 1978, A. W. Coats encouraged historians of economics to study the role of practicing economists in policy-making institutions. He argued that "special attention must be given to the opportunity, at least for recent periods, to interview economists about their working experiences" (Coats 1978, p. 313). His main justification for the use of interviews was that they allow one to get information that could otherwise not be obtained from written documents due to confidentiality restrictions.

In an earlier paper, Coats acknowledged making use of documents traced by "many government officials" as well as of "a number of valuable interviews with senior agricultural economists in Whitehall and in the Universities" (Coats 1976, p. 381). Coats used the documents – which do not seem to be confidential – explicitly (p. 383) to argue that the UK's Ministry of Agriculture shaped British agricultural economics as a professional sub-field. However, the interviews were neither cited nor mentioned anywhere in the paper (besides the acknowledgment footnote). By contrast, Coats briefly gave voice to an interviewee in another paper on the role of economists in the British government to illustrate an argument: "a lone economist has been imported into a department because a minister or senior official had the vague notion that it might be helpful 'to have a tame pundit around the place' [fn57: "This is an actual quotation from an interview"]" (Coats 1981, p. 391).

This paper was part of a special issue of the journal *History Of Political Economy* responding to Coats's 1978 call, in which issue five papers (including Coats's) out of ten used interviews. The interviewees in S. Ambirajan (1981), P. R. Haddad (1981) and A. Petridis (1981) articles were anonymous as in Coats's papers and are barely given voices. Instead, their interviews were mentioned either to give general impressions from the field, to better interpret statistical data or to fill some gaps in these data. William Barber (1981), by contrast, used an interview from the oral history project on President Truman to provide an anecdotal illustration of politicians' tactics to make economists' reports sound less neutral and more in agreement with the Administration's line:

> Murphy [Legal Counsel to Truman] has observed that 'we found out along about midnight that Dr. Nourse [first president of the *Council of Economic Advisers*] would begin to agree to anything. So we'd do most of the work after midnight.' Oral History Interview with Charles S. Murphy, Harry S. Truman Library, p. 122.
>
> (Barber 1981, fn18, p. 523)[3]

In sum, interviews are a means for Coats and the others to get access to places where elites make decisions that impact economics or involve economists. What they are after is information about that decision-making process.[4]

The interaction between the political and the scientific domains, i.e., between a country's political environment, its science policies and the activities of scientists, is a research theme that can easily generate a perceived threat to scientific credit and legitimacy from the scientist (see, e.g., Gaudillère 1997, pp. 122–124). The anonymity of the interview citations, their scarce use, and the use of interviews conducted by other scholars might mitigate this perception. Yet it can be argued that the way by which the potentially perceived threat is most reduced is by the very research goals behind the use of interviews. With the exception of Coats (1976), the goal is to understand conflicts between economists in policy-making institutions and other politicians. Hence economists are not interviewed *qua* academic economists, which undermine potential threats to their scientific credibility. Furthermore, these conflicts, as they are described in the papers, threaten the reputation of politicians much more than the reputation of economists – because economists are described as doing the best they can while remaining unheard by politicians. Finally, the self-produced historical narratives of economists are typically silent on their role in policy-making institutions, which greatly limits the possibility of a clash with the historians' historical narrative.

Economists and their academic work

Compared to these contributions on economists and policy-making, a radically different set of practices regarding the use of interviews was introduced in a book by Arjo Klamer (1983). His interviewees were not anonymous: they were famous macroeconomists such as Robert Lucas or Thomas Sargent. Their voices were not silenced: they constituted the core of the book as every chapter except the first and last ones were transcripts of the interviews. Furthermore, Klamer interviewed economists *qua* academic economists.

More precisely, Klamer was defending that economics is a rhetorical activity where theoretical and empirical arguments are not the most important elements of persuasion among economists. He used interviews as a means to push economists into an argument, into justifying their approaches to economics, i.e., as a means to observe how economists verbally behave in controversies. One implication that is fairly rare compared to other uses of interviews (in history of economics and beyond) is the incisive and improvised ways by which Klamer introduced his own opinions about, or counter examples to, the interviewee's narrative. Sometimes he did so by suggesting his own interpretation – as when he let Lucas know that he (Klamer) found some terms used in a paper with Sargent to be "*very strong*" or "*quite strong*" (p. 34). At some other times he did it through others' interpretations – as in this exchange: "[Lucas:] Everybody likes the idea of rational expectations. It's hardly controversial. [Klamer:] *But if you talk with Post-Keynesian economists they think it's a lot of nonsense*" (p. 35). Note that Klamer's interviews also had a historical dimension in two senses: 1) they were carefully put into historical context by both the introduction and the first questions in each of the interviews and, more trivially, 2) they were historically situated (i.e., in the early 1980s). As such, they can be used by historians of macroeconomics (e.g., Sent 1998; Rancan 2017, p. 169).

Compared with Klamer, other historians of economics who have used interviews for a similar purpose tend to let economists tell their narratives without intervening too much into it (e.g., Snowdon and Vane 1999; Colander, Holt, and Rosser 2004). These contributions do not provide an equivalent to Klamer's concluding essay where the historian interprets the interviews and argues what can be made explicit from them. That is left to the reader – or to another historian, e.g., to Mark Blaug in Brian Snowdon and Howard Vane (1999, pp. 314–333). There are however some contributions that are in Klamer's spirit and that even bring some innovations to his practices. One example is the book by Esther-Mirjam Sent (1998) on the role of Sargent in the history of rational expectations. Her last chapter before the conclusion is an interview with Sargent, in which she confronts him with the methodological and historical points made in the preceding chapters. Another example is Verena Halsmayer (2014), who conducted an interview with Solow while she was working on methodological and historical dimensions of his modeling practice. Without publishing the transcript, Solow's retrospective description of his practice as "engineer in the design sense" (p. 231) opened the door for further methodological and historical characterization by Halsmayer.

The historians who have implicitly or explicitly followed part of Klamer's interviewing practices are less worried about the perception of a threat to scientific legitimacy, either because what they want is a personified account of the historical narrative self-produced by economists or because they engage in an explicitly more collaborative way with their interviewee as in the case of Sent and Halsmayer. Such collaboration takes a very scholarly form in Halsmayer's case by Solow's providing comments on an earlier draft of her paper (2014, p. 229). By contrast, the historical narrative produced by Klamer suggests that political beliefs and other potentially "nonrational" (1983, p. 238) elements of persuasion are more important than empirical and theoretical arguments in macroeconomics – or that the nonrational elements influence the empirical and theoretical arguments. Hence Klamer's use of interviews can obviously generate a perceived threat to the scientific credit of macroeconomists or to the scientific legitimacy of macroeconomics. For the ideal of a value-free science is usually part of the historical narrative self-produced by most economists (see, e.g., Hands 2012). Indeed, when questioned directly about this theme, Klamer's interviewees usually deny any political motivation in their contributions to economics (e.g., Sargent, p. 80) or express the belief that a requirement for the scientific legitimacy of economics is that normative considerations about the economy ought not influence theoretical and empirical propositions (though the other way around is acceptable) (e.g., Lucas, p. 52). How does Klamer manage the possible perception of a threat to scientific credit or legitimacy in his practice? First, the explicit purpose of the interviews is not presented to the interviewees as being the production of a counter-narrative to the ones self-produced by economists. Second, Klamer is successful in establishing a good rapport through some biographical questions and only then, tackling controversial topics head on. In this practice, what seems most relevant is Klamer's conversational skills.[5]

The contributions discussed here strongly highlight the role of the interviewer in the outcome of the interview. Most of the practices discussed here involve a conversational tone in the interviews and the production of narratives. That is not usually the case in other interviews of economists conducted by scholars who are not (at least primarily) historians of economics. For instance the interviews conducted by George Feiwel (1987a, 1987b) with or about Kenneth Arrow have a structure that is closer to a "question and answer" (Q&A) session one can observe at the keynote speech of a conference. The answers are however more reflective than in an actual Q&A session and hence are often valuable for methodologists and philosophers of economics. The same applies for interviews of economists by economists periodically published in, e.g., *Econometric Theory, Macroeconomic Dynamics* or *Social Choice and Welfare*.[6]

The careers and lives of economists

Another set of practices of using interviews in history of economics emerged at the end of the 1980s, with historians of economics focusing more on the lives and careers of economists – and other scholars related to economics – as historical contexts in which the meanings of their academic work can be enriched. An early instance of this practice was Earlene Craver's (1986) historical account of the intellectual milieu of economists in Vienna from the 1920s to their emigration in the 1930s. Her account was based on interviews with 12 economists (e.g., Friedrich von Hayek, Oskar Morgenstern) and two mathematicians (Franz Alt and Karl Menger) who took part in this emigration. Craver used the interviewees' voices to give vivid illustrations of how scholars judged each other on personal and intellectual dimensions, of the institutional locations of various communities, and of experiences of anti-Semitism.

In another example, Robert Leonard's (1992) account of the development of game theory was partly based on interviews he conducted with mathematicians who worked at the RAND Corporation in the late 1940s. Although the voices of his interviewees are heard in his later 2010 book, they do not surface in the 1992 paper. Instead, the interviews are noted as sources to support claims about matters such as mathematicians discovering game theory well after John von Neumann and Oskar Morgenstern's book (Leonard 1992, p. 59) or about RAND's internal organization (p. 67).

In yet another fashion, E. Roy Weintraub conducted an interview with Gérard Debreu in 1992 and used it in subsequent publications to illustrate a part of the origins of the change in mathematical economics around the 1950s. In these uses, the voice of Debreu recounting moments of his education is given equal footing to the one of Weintraub commenting on it (2002, pp. 115–117). The interview, which is fully transcribed (pp. 125–154), focused on the role of mathematics through Debreu's education and professional career. But it still delivered information about other people and institutions because Weintraub probed in that direction when possible. Till Düppe (2012) complemented this approach with information about Debreu's personal life and subjectivity, notably obtained by interviewing acquaintances of Debreu, including his widow and his daughter. Düppe and Weintraub (2014) show how such information can further our understanding of an episode of the history of general equilibrium theory, notably by showing how different motivations and interpretations of the existence proofs can be understood through the different personalities and lives of Debreu, Arrow, and Lionel McKenzie.

None of the historians of economics discussed so far in this chapter has written reflections on her or his own practice, i.e., on the specificity of constructing or using oral sources.[7] By contrast, Tiago Mata (2005, Appendix) provided methodological and historiographical reasons for the 16 interviews he conducted with radical economists about whom he wrote a history of the social context that shaped their work. For instance, he explains that his goals were to explore how economists from a specific group share the same (present) sense of the past and to get an understanding of this sense that would guide him into the written literature. He explains how these goals lead him to choose, among the different methods of interviews available across disciplines, the life story interview from the discipline of oral history. In that kind of interview, the interviewee recounts his or her life under minor guidance from the interviewer and following a more or less chronological order. Mata also explains how he had to tailor a semi-structured guide for the single two-hour sessions and how he made summary transcripts (instead of full ones) that helped him get a better understanding of his historical object (see also Mata and Lee (2007) for further reflections).[8]

Ross Emmett (2007) also furnishes a reflection on the process of his oral history project on the Chicago School of economics. One of his goals behind his interview project is to give voices to the people who do not leave many written traces and are absent from histories focused on eminent economists. The interview with Marianne Ferber, one of the rare women to obtain a PhD in economics at Chicago in the beginning of the postwar period (1954), was the closest he considered he got in achieving this goal. Furthermore, Emmett explains how he was interested in the fact she did not self-identify with Chicago economics, which allowed him to provide multiple perspectives on the Chicago Department of Economics. One very concrete methodological choice discussed by Emmett is his decision to send questions in advance to the interviewees. This is worth noting because it allows to highlight the underlying continuum of possibilities, from setting up the interview so that the interviewees can reflectively construct their discourse, to setting it up as a spontaneous conversation where the interviewees have less control over what they say.

Finally, Andrej Svorenčík (2015, Appendix) provides a discussion of the methodological and historiographical issues raised by the more than 50 interviews he conducted with experimental economists and used to reconstruct a history of experimental economics. He explains that, unlike Mata, his interviews were "not traditional oral interviews in the sense of deeply personal accounts" (Svorenčík 2015, p. 246). Yet his "mixed focus . . . on the social history of experimental economics, the interviewee's perspective and participation in it, and their intellectual trajectories" (p. 246) greatly overlaps with the focuses of the other historians of economics discussed in this section. He also used the opportunity of the interviews to convince experimental economists to deposit their papers in archives and (explicitly) to gather materials in view of a subsequent witness seminar (see Svorenčík and Maas 2016; Chapter 4 by Maas in this volume). His main historiographical problem is to avoid the potential biases he might have created as a historian interviewer to carry over to the historical narrative he constructed. To avoid that risk, he tried to cross-check information with archives and across interviews, and gave priority to written archival sources, when available, to establish a point in his narrative. Finally, he emphasized how establishing and maintaining trust with his interviewees in even the tiniest social interactions was a crucial issue.

The potentially perceived threats to scientific reputation, credit, or legitimacy in these contributions here is minimal because the focus of the interviews is not primarily on the content of scientific contributions. If any threat is perceived in the final narrative of the historian, it is more likely to be due to interpretations of written sources (especially when archives are involved). However, by contrast with the interviews in the previous subsections, there is a greater potentially perceived threat to personal integrity and individual reputation that the historian has to subtly manage (Chapter 2 by Düppe in this volume).

As oral historians (whose work is discussed in the next section) often argue, the very format of life story or career story interviews, in which interviewees tell a more or less chronological self-narrative, provides a natural way of managing the potentially perceived threat to integrity or reputation (see Descamps 2005, Part II, Chap. 3, §23).[9] In the beginning of the interview, apparently trivial questions about childhood or education create a dynamics of reciprocity whereby the interviewee progressively opens up by giving away elements of his or her life and the interviewer gives back some help for the reconstruction of a life or a career (ibid.). Once that dynamics is established, it is easier to explore in depth potentially more delicate themes with minimal potentially perceived threat (ibid.).

Methodological and historiographical issues of oral sources

This section further characterizes the three families of practices identified in the previous section by analyzing the relation between oral and written sources more closely and by drawing more substantially on insights from other disciplines using interviews. It focuses on how oral sources are used in written contributions and how that implies different conceptions of oral sources. Special attention is given to oral history, which consists in historians conducting interviews and using them according to a number of more or less consensual rules (see Oral History Association 2009). Illustrations of these rules and how they are (implicitly or explicitly) violated or not by historians of economics are provided throughout the section. It should be noted at the outset that not many historians of economics use interviews in the way oral historians (or practitioners in other disciplines using interviews) do. This section is not a criticism of this state of affairs. It takes practices from outside of the history of economics as sources of inspiration rather than constraints – which also explains why the disciplinary origins of the interviewing practices discussed in the section are not systematically detailed.[10]

Specificities of orality and uses in writing

Oral speech can express meaningful contents that are proper to orality, in the sense that they can only be indicated in a written transcript but not reproduced as some words can: "silences, sighing and respiration, laughs . . . changes of tonality . . . hesitations", all of which constitute the rhythm of the speech (Descamps 2005, Part III, Chap. 1, §24). Furthermore, a proper relation between the historian and the interviewee confers to orality the virtue of expressing certain themes better than it would (if at all) have been done in written: "the invisible, the collective unconscious, the imperishable, the secret, the desire, the anxious" (Part I, Chap. 4, §57). How are such specificities involved in the practices of using interviews by historians of economics?[11]

The capacity of orality to express what falls under the theme of *the secret* seems to play a main role in the practices of those who study the relation between economists and policy-making. Interviews allow historians to "break in the cultures of secrecy that surround the exercise of power and sovereignty" (Part IV, Chap. 1, §4). Hence it is not surprising that the uses of the interviews are in a large part invisible in the written texts on economists and policy-making: no comments on their contexts and contents (only brief acknowledgments of their existence), anonymity of the interviewees, and few verbatim quotes giving voices to them. The few cases when we do "hear" the interviewees are restricted to an "illustrative" (or "ornamental") type of use of oral sources in oral historian Florence Descamps's sense (Part III, Chap. 2, sect. 1). This means that the content of the quote brings some life and gives some flesh to an argument in the text but does not contribute much to the force of that argument – most of which comes from other evidence and reasoning that are independent of the quote. In sum, even though the interviews are crucial in the research process and in shaping the historical narrative, they are nearly invisible in that narrative.

It can be argued that the capacity of orality to express that which falls under the theme of *the invisible* plays a main role in the practices of historians who study the content of economists' academic work. However, the existence of reflexive essays on scientific contributions by scientists and historians alike suggests that written expression can make the implicit explicit just as well. A non-trivial difference is that what is made explicit in an interview is not the result of either the scientist or the historian alone, but of their conversation, i.e., of a concrete human interaction that goes beyond the reading of one another. Indeed, some anthropology-minded sociologists argue that the intonations, body language, facial expressions, and the like of even the most careful interviewer will always leak interpretations influencing the interviewee's responses (Holstein and Gubrium 2004; Gubrium and Holstein 2012). One implication, they argue, is that interviewers should embrace more "active" styles of interviewing, which roughly correspond to Klamer's. Most oral historians and historians of science using interviews (e.g., Chadarevian, 1997) share this premise. However, only historians of science, as some like to point out (esp. Hoddeson, 2006), tend to follow its implication in terms of interviewing style.

This issue of more or less intervention from the interviewer carries over to the type of use of oral sources made by the historian. How we "hear" the interviewee's voice is not merely "illustrative" (or "ornamental") in Descamps's sense. It is rather one of the two other types she identifies. An "expressive" (or "restitutive") use of oral sources consists mostly in long quotes with very little contextualization and very little critical perspective on the content of these quotes (Descamps 2005, Part III, Chap. 2, sect. 2). Historians who present interview transcripts as book chapters, which is akin to a very long quote, do usually provide some information to better understand the content of the interview, but not much, if at all, to get a sense of its context: a few elements about locations, time, and date are usually offered but nothing is provided on the relation between the interviewer and interviewee, e.g., about the presentation of the goals behind the historian's research project. Descamps (Part III, Chap. 2, sect. 3) favors another type of use of oral sources that she labels the "in-depth use". This use is very demanding in terms of the analysis and critique of content to end up in a balanced interplay between quotes and comments from the historians – Klamer's (1983, Chap. 13) concluding essay roughly fits this description.

The very publication of interview transcripts as chapters can be interpreted as partially meeting oral historian's rule regarding the archiving of interviews. On the one hand, such chapters undeniably constitute sources that other historians can check or work on – even though oral historians usually archive their transcripts in specific institutions often hosted in university libraries. On the other hand, however, oral historians usually insist that, in principle, proper archiving requires the conservation of the audio or video recordings along with meta-data about the relation between the interviewer and the interviewee. The reason is that without such meta-data it is difficult, if not impossible, to proceed to a scholarly critic of oral sources. The historians of economics interested in economists and policy-making do not provide access to recordings or transcripts and the meta-data are nonexistent to the extent that the reader does not even know whether the interviews were audio recorded or if references to the interviews come from historians' memories or written notes taken during or after the interview. Those interviewing economists about the content of their academic work, by contrast, do provide an access to the transcripts but not to the recording, and not much, if at all, to any kinds of meta-data. It should be noted that, in practice, oral historians (and of course scholars from other disciplines using interviews) also break these rules, which are in any case more akin to guiding principles than to strict procedures.[12]

Nevertheless, if the goal of an interview is to make explicit what is implicit in discourses because specific oral characteristics such as tonality, silence, laughs (and eventually body language in video recordings), then recordings and meta-data could be very helpful for interpretation. Notice here the complicated relation between the written and the oral. The use of an interview is first motivated by an issue with written contributions, namely that they contain too much implicit elements to fully understand the intellectual dynamics behind them. Whether or not the oral conversation makes the implicit explicit, the end result is again a written text (interview transcripts and their interpretations), on which both the interviewer and more problematically (Weintraub 2007, p. 3) the interviewee have intervened *ex post* by means of written expression, i.e., transcripts are usually edited by interviewees before being archived or published. Note also that a strong standard of sharing interviews, e.g., imposing their disclosure to referees in a publication process, might seem unfair – hence discouraging – in the history of economics as this is usually not required for written private correspondence (e.g., through email).[13]

Finally, the specificity of orality to express a range of themes from *the collective unconscious* to *the intimate* (Descamps 2005, Part I, Chap. 1, §29) draws historians interested in the lives and careers of economists. Depending on the goals of the historians, oral discourse can compensate for the lack of expressions in written sources about social relations, institutional contexts, and personal matters, which the interviewee cannot – or does not naturally – put in print. These goals result in an in-depth use of oral sources: either in Descamps's sense of a balanced use of quotes and the historians' comments (sometimes even with explicit critical scrutiny of the content, e.g., in the work of Svorenčík) or in the sense of the historian impregnating herself or himself "in-depth" with the interviews in order to influence the historical narrative produced – e.g., Mata performing "repeated listening [of] the recordings" (2005, p. 289).

It should be noted that some of the historians of economics working on the lives and careers of economists have archived the transcripts and some-times even the recordings of their interviews. For instance, most of Craver's interviews were conducted by her or her husband Axel Leijonhufvud as part of an oral history project at the University of California, Los Angeles' Center for Oral History. Two of the transcripts are available there and those two can be found online.[14] Weintraub also archived in his papers at the Rubeinstein Library of Duke University both the tape and the transcript of his interview with Debreu. The main historiographical issue raised by this common practice in oral history is that if the goal of the interview is to capture the intimate then the fact that the record of the conversation might be public or semi-public can constrain the interviewee to open up (see Chapters 2 (Düppe) and 4 (Maas) in this volume; Descamps, Part II, Chap. 2, §55). One traditional way of dealing with this limitation is to emphasize that the recording can be stopped at any moment to allow for off-record statements or that any sequence can be deleted *ex post* from the archival record. In that case these information can still impregnate the historian's narrative but they cannot legally figure explicitly within it.

Indeed, it is usually under-appreciated that (at least in France and in the US) the interviewee is the legal owner of the interview and should sign a release form (besides the inform consent) to transfer his property rights to the interviewer (see, e.g., Descamps, 2005, Part II, Chap. 4, sect. 2). Nevertheless, that procedure does not dispense the historian of the moral choices that need to be made when information about one's privacy are turned into public discourse, which is obviously an ethical problem (see Chapter 2 by in this volume).

Different conceptions of oral sources depending on research goals

The initial motif of historians interested in economists and policy-making (e.g., Coats) for using interviews, i.e., to bypass legal confidentiality restrictions on written material, is a classical justification in political history (see Descamps, 2005, Part IV, Chap.1, sect. 1) and history of contemporary science (Chadarevian 1997). The main reason is, Descamps (ibid.) explains, that the law is not as clear on the oral communicability of confidential information as it is on written communicability. In the papers on the history of economists and policy-making, the reader however is left in ignorance as to what exactly was supposed to be confidential. Indeed, the very status of the information as confidential makes it hard to explicitly disclose it as such and might further inhibit the historians of economics to explicitly comment on the contexts and contents of the interviews.

Here, the underlying conception of the oral source is the traditional one in oral history, as a "palliative source" (ibid., §2) for written documents to which the historian lacks accessibility or for impressions and information that simply do not exist in any written document (e.g., the impressions from the field or Murphy's anecdote about Nourse). Indeed, that the interview process tends to lead to other non-confidential documents (in Coats's case) is another classical justification for the use of interviews by historians of science (see Söderqvist 1997, p. 8; Hoddeson 2006, p. 187).

In this set of practices, the only case of a non-anonymous interviewee, Murphy, does not involve the historian, Barber, as an interviewer. Barber uses instead an interview done by professional oral historians. That interviewees should not, as far as possible, be anonymous is indeed one of oral historians' rules. It can however be argued that the status of the interviewees with respect to the object of study here is likely to warrant anonymity for oral historians as well. Using anonymous interviews has nevertheless raised criticisms by (at least one) historians of economics who argued that not knowing who speaks prevents the reader from assessing the reliability of the speech (Tribe 2011, p. 621).[15]

The historians of economics interested in the content of economists' academic work can be thought of as displaying a variant of the palliative conception (as characterized by Descamps) for the scientific domain. Recall that these historians use interviews to uncover information that is implicit in the written sources but not directly accessible to the reader (especially when the reader is not part of the subculture). The main goal behind their interviews is akin to the main goal behind the use of interviews by most anthropologists (e.g., Spradley 1979, Chap. 1) and some historians of science (see Doel 2003, p. 358): making explicit what is tacit, i.e., taken-for-granted, in a given culture or subculture. For instance, most of the elements of persuasion identified by Klamer (1983) are not explicit in the written texts of his interviewees. These elements are nonetheless necessary for a non-member of the subculture of academic macroeconomics to understand the dynamics of written intellectual exchange in that subculture.

In contrast with the previous two research goals, a common aim behind all the apparently diverse interview practices of those who study the lives and careers of economists can be identified by contrast with the previous two research goals: to get a better sense of the "personal and social factors" that Klamer (1983, pp. 254–251) admitted to have left in the background of his interviews. That goal is indeed shared with most historians of science inspired by the field of science and technology studies who have used interviews or commented on their potential (Doel 2003, pp. 357–363).

The underlying conception of oral sources here goes beyond the traditional palliative one in Descamps's sense and is better characterized by either one or both of the other two conceptions that she distinguishes: oral sources as a basis for enriched biographies and socio-biographies (2005, Part III, Chap. 2) and oral sources as a basis for histories of organizations (ibid., Chap. 3). The difference can be understood as a matter of degree: information elicited under the conception of oral sources as a basis for enriched (socio-)biographies and histories of organizations takes a more narrative form (temporally organized sequences of events and impressions) than information elicited under the palliative conception. Furthermore, interviews can be a means of saving time for the collection of either biographical or organizational information that could be found in the archives – or at least as a guide for what to look for in the archives. But most importantly it can be the only means to gather personal impressions and psychological feelings that are harder to find in the archives – hence enriching a biography or socio-biography based on written sources only. One risk looming larger on these conceptions of oral sources than on the other (palliative) conception is that the interviewer is only going to get well rehearsed myths and (self-)narratives from the interviewers. Most methodological and historiographical advises one can find about how to avoid this risk are usually very pragmatic, e.g., be well documented on such well-known myths or narratives and use your conversational skills to get something new. Some historians also recommend bringing written documents (e.g., archives) that contradict the myths or standard narratives to the interview. The idea is to eventually expose these documents to the interviewees and engage in a discussion about their meanings (see Hoddeson (2006) for an illustration in the history of science). In a sense this partly turns the individual critical work that historians are supposed to perform when using oral sources in-depth (e.g., the triangulation with archival and published written sources done by Svorenčík) into a collective endeavor with the interviewee.

Notice that, by using interviews as guides to explore the published record, Mata (2005) is in a sense displaying a conception of oral source in opposition to the palliative one, i.e., not because there are too little written documents but too many. This argument is also a classical justification from historians of science to deal with the "documentary overload" (Söderqvist 1997, p. 4) characteristic of the contemporary period (see Chadarevian 1997; Hoddeson 2006). This very function of interviews makes them more akin to be guides for existing written sources (including archives) or generators of leads for one's research rather than sources in themselves. In a sense conducting oral interviews for this purpose is not so different from more traditional written interviews whereby historians of economics correspond with economists – and acknowledge or eventually quote such correspondence in the final written research output. For instance, such written exchanges were part of the initial historical work on general equilibrium by Weintraub (1983), who later used interviews for another purpose as we have seen.[16]

By using interviews to hear the voices of non-eminent economists, Emmett is employing the traditional palliative use but from social rather than political history, i.e., capturing non-elites' voices from those who leave no written traces instead of capturing elites' voices to complete the written records. However, oral historians in social history could still consider intellectuals such as Ferber, a prominent feminist economist who left plenty of written sources, as an elite member. Relevant for historians of economics and potentially considered as non-elites interviewees could be the secretaries, research engineers, technicians, and the like (Doel 2003, p. 359) hints in that direction, though he seems to want to get information about their roles not necessarily by interviewing them).

Conclusion

By way of conclusion, a key issue already raised by Weintraub (2007) is worth re-emphasizing here: historians of economics could be inspired by historians of physics who are running a large-scale oral history project whereby they share recordings and transcripts of interviews online. This institutionalized oral history project is hosted by the *American Institute of Physics*, which helps historians "gain the confidence of physicists" (Weart 1990, p.39), i.e., reduces the potentially perceived threat to scientific credit and legitimacy. One can hope for an equivalent initiative sponsored by the *American Economic Association* or another similar institution (maybe in Europe). There are more ways to embed such a project in the so-called digital humanities than the historians of physics' project, i.e., taking full advantages of the combination of digital technologies with the Internet to build interactive video archives. There are already good guides to do it. This idea corresponds to the last paradigm shift in oral history according to Alistair Thomson (2007) and is also well discussed by Douglas Boyd (2016 [2014]). This might help the whole field to grow as there is an increasing amount of grant opportunities focused on the constitution of archives and the digital humanities.[17]

Notes

1 I thank the participants to the Max Weber seminar, the Historiography of Contemporary Economics conference and the Center for the History of Political Economy lunch seminar who have offered many useful oral comments on previous versions of this chapter, along with E. Roy Weintraub, Till Düppe, Verena Halsmayer, Nicolas Brisset, Erich Pinzón Fuchs, Thomas Delcey, Margarita Fajardo, and especially Tiago Mata for useful written comments. I also thank David Colander, Robert Leonard, Ross Emmett, Andrej Svorenčík, Tiago Mata, Verena Halsmayer, Arjo Klamer, Béatrice Cherrier, Hodson Thornber, Paul Burnett, Sara Seten Berghausen, and especially Catherine Herfeld, Muriel Gilardone, and Antoinette Baujard for having shared their experiences on different dimensions of the status of interviews in the history of economics (some of which have found their ways into the endnotes of this chapter).

2 The quick search used the keywords "interview", "conversation", and "personal communication" and their French equivalents in several history of economics journals (online); the papers were then read to figure out whether the keywords were indeed used in the sense of an oral face-to-face exchange. The standard case is with one interviewer and one interviewee, although there can be a few cases where there are two interviewers or two interviewees. Cases with more than two interviewees are usually not considered as interviews *per se* in the literature, but as focus groups or witness seminars (on the latter, see Chapter 4 by Maas in this volume).

3 Most Presidential Libraries contain oral history interviews with some economists who were involved in policy recommendations, usually in the Council of Economic Advisers. These interviews represent a good part of historians of economics' uses of interviews conducted by someone else. For more information on the Presidential Libraries regarding the history of economics or oral history, see (respectively) James Cochrane (1976) and Regina Greenwell (1997).

4 An earlier paper that somewhat shares some of these practices of using interviews is William Allen (1977), who profusely cites a number of non-anonymous interviewees, including famous economists (James Tobin, Charles Kindleberger), about their experiences in policy-making institutions. Later papers that fit this first set of practice include William Yohe (1990), Verónica Montecinos (1996), Judy Klein (2001), Ivo Maes (2011), Rob Roy McGregor and Warren Young (2013), Pedro Teixeira (2017).

5 In a personal communication, Klamer pointed out that for the interview to have a sincere conversational tone, one needs to be careful about pre-interview conversations, i.e., try not to talk too much about the issues that are supposed to be covered in the interview.

6 It should be noted that some of these interviews involve as interviewers scholars who are recurrent contributors to history or methodology of economics journals, e.g., Mary S. Morgan (and Jan R. Magnus) interviewed Jan Tinbergen for *Econometric Theory* (Magnus and Morgan 1987), David Colander (1999) interviewed James Tobins and Robert J. Shiller for *Macroeconomic Dynamics* and Antoinette Baujard and Muriel Gilardone (with Maurice Salles) interviewed Amartya Sen for *Social Choice and Welfare* (Baujard, Gilardone, and Salles, forthcoming). Baujard and Gilardonne remarked in a personal communication that biographical questions were regarded as not suitable by economists of the journal who were in charge of validating the themes of the interview. Indeed, it seems that the use of interviews is naturally related to questions pertaining to the status and limits of biographies in the history of economics as witnessed by the frequent discussions of interviews in the 2007 annual supplement to *History of Political Economy* on economists' lives (Weintraub and Forget 2007).

7 This remark is not intended as a criticism. It is meant to highlight how natural interviewing seems when doing history of *contemporary* economics. Craig Freedman (2010) discusses how unprepared he was when engaging, in the late 1990s, on an oral history project about George Stigler.

8 Among the other details present in the methodological and historiographical discussion are how the social encounter of the interview afforded him access to some archives; or how he prepared himself for the interview, notably by reading other interviews, especially Klamer's. See also the video oral history on Craufurd Goodwin by Tiago Mata and Harro Maas about the birth of history of economics as a sub-field: https://www.youtube.com/watch?v=uLjmq3BFWV4 (last consulted on 10 June 2017).

9 Florence Descamps's book on oral sources is the main resource in oral history from which this chapter draws. It is written in French and all translations are mine. The numbered paragraphs correspond to the ones that are explicitly indicated in the online edition.

10 It should also be noted that "oral history" is notoriously polysemic as it can be used to refer to an academic discipline (this is the only sense in which it is used in this chapter), to an interview conducted according to some rules formalized in that discipline, to the transcript of such interviews, or to written productions from that discipline (e.g., books or academic papers by oral historians).

11 A nice illustration of the argumentative power of orality is provided by Baujard and Gilardone (2017), who argue (against some claims made in the literature on the capability approach) that Sen is not a capability theorist, notably by starting their paper with the following extract from their interview with Sen: "I have to rescue myself by saying [thumping table] 'I'm not a capability theorist! For god's sake, I'm not a capability theorist'". This extract goes with a link to the relevant part of the video recording of the interview (i.e., at 20'20") which can be checked online by the reader at www.unicaen.fr/recherche/mrsh/forge/262 (last consulted on 23 February 2018).

12 Svorenčík and Maas (2016, Chap. 1) and Maas (Chapter 4, this volume) offer a thorough and innovative discussion of the transcription process and the necessary choices one has to make in this process (they are discussing this regarding witness seminars but their points apply just as well to interviews).

13 Catherine Herfeld, who conducted interviews with economists and philosophers (about their contributions to and critical engagement with rational choice theories) that are forthcoming in a book, pointed out in a personal communication that interviewees' written interventions heavily depend on their personalities, from those who make substantial changes so that the outcome would have been achievable through email exchanges, to those who don't even want to have a look at the transcript before its publication.

14 See for instance Hayek's transcript: https://archive.org/details/nobelprizewinnin00 haye (last consulted on 6 December 2017). The recordings and transcripts of Emmett's interviews are available in the archives of the University of Chicago. In personal a communication, Andrej Svorenčík mentioned that he would like to make his interviews available in some archives in the future but he has not yet secured permission to do so from his interviewees.

15 It should be noted that Keith Tribe's target is a book by sociologist Marion Fourcade (2009), which can indeed be taken as a contribution to the history of economics but not by a self-identified historian of economics. Including books and articles by scholars such as Fourcade in this chapter would have taken too much space and would not have added substantially different practices of using interviews from the

ones already discussed, hence the decision to narrow the scope on self-identified historians of economics.

16 Scholars in other disciplines characterize more precisely the concreteness of the human interaction in face-to-face interviews as a synchronous communication in both time and place – by contrast with the synchronous communication in time but asynchronous communication in place characteristic of telephone interviews and online instant messengers, and the asynchronous communication in both time and place characteristic of email interviews (see, e.g., Opdenakker 2006). Written interviews, especially online through emails, are increasingly discussed as a proper research tool by scholars in other disciplines (see, e.g., Meho, 2006). A historian of economics sending a couple of questions by email to an economist and then using (or just acknowledging) the answers in a contribution can qualify as using (written) interviews. This chapter does not focus on this set of practices, although many of the reflections apply to them too.

17 On the American Institute of Physics oral history project, see https://www.aip.org/history-programs/niels-bohr-library/oral-histories (last consulted on 13 June 2017). Regarding economics, a project in the same spirit – albeit narrower in the sense of being restricted to a specific set of economists, namely from the Chicago School – is the Economist Life Stories Project hosted by the Oral History Center at the University of Berkley, see hwww.lib.berkeley.edu/libraries/bancroft-library/oral-history-center/economist-life-stories-project (last consulted on 24 February 2018). Hodson Thornber, one of the founders of this project, remarked in a personal communication that he intended a broader project (beyond the Chicago School), but has yet to find enough institutional support for that within the profession. Also, Paul Burnett, the oral historian in charge of the interviews for this project, remarked in a personal communication that he was greatly helped by historians of economics (along with political and cultural historians) in the preparation process (especially for the first interview). He also mentioned that the online versions of the interviews are going to be redesigned to allow for synchronized streaming of audio, video, and transcript text (along with search across collection), i.e., in the fashion of the digital humanities. More generally on this last dimension, the Oral History in the Digital Age project is an invaluable resource (with plenty of practical advice on every stage of an interview process) to see the potential of digital technologies for oral history and get some training to take advantage of it: http://ohda.matrix.msu.edu/ (last consulted on 10 June 2017).

References

Allen, W. R. (1977). "Economics, Economists, and Economic Policy: Modern American Experiences." *History of Political Economy* 9(1): 48–88.

Ambirajan, S. (1981). "India: The Aftermath of Empire." *History of Political Economy* 13(3): 436–470.

Atkinson, P. and Silverman, D. (1997). "Kundera's Immortality: The Interview Society and the Invention of the Self." *Qualitative Inquiry* 3(3): 304–325.

Barber, W. J. (1981). "The United States: Economists in a Pluralistic Polity." *History of Political Economy* 13(3): 513–547.

Baujard, A. and Gilardone, M. (2017). "Sen Is Not a Capability Theorist." *Journal of Economic Methodology* 24(1): 1–19

Baujard, A., Gilardone, M., and Salles, M. (forthcoming). "A Conversation with Amartya Sen." *Social Choice and Welfare.*

Boyd, D. A. (2016 [2014]). "'I Just Want to Click on it to Listen': Oral History Archives, Orality and Usability." In Perks, R. and Thomson, A. (ed), *The Oral History Reader*. Third Edition., London and New York, Routledge: 117–134.

Chadarevian (de), S. (1997). "Using Interviews to Write the History of Science." In Söderqvist, T. (ed.), *The Historiography of Contemporary Science and Technology*. Amsterdam, Harwood Academic Publishers: 51–70.

Cherrier, B. (2011). "The Impossible Art of Oral History." Available at: https://history ofeconomics.wordpress.com/2011/02/23/the-impossible-art-of-oral-history/ (consulted on 06/26/18).

Coats, A. W. (1976). "The Development of the Agricultural Economics Profession in England." *Journal of Agricultural Economics* 27(3): 381–392.

Coats, A. W. (1978). "Economists in Government: A Research Field for the Historian of Economics." *History of Political Economy* 10(2): 298–314.

Coats, A. W. (1981). "Conclusions." *History of Political Economy* 13(3): 681–692.

Cochrane, J. L. (1976). "The U.S. Presidential Libraries and the History of Political Economy." *History of Political Economy* 8(3): 412–427.

Colander, D. (1999). "Conversations with James Tobin and Robert Shiller on the 'Yale Tradition' in Macroeconomics." *Macroeconomic Dynamics* 3(1): 116–146.

Colander, D., Holt, R. P. F., and Rosser, J. B. (2004). *The Changing Face of Economics: Conversations with Cutting Edge Economists*. Ann Arbor, University of Michigan Press.

Craver, E. (1986). "The Emigration of the Austrian Economists." *History of Political Economy* 18(1): 1–32.

Descamps, F. (2005). *L'historien, l'archiviste et le magnétophone: de la constitution de la source orale à son exploitation*. Institut de la gestion publique et du développement économique, Comité pour l'histoire économique et financière de la France, Paris.

Doel, R. E. (2003). "Oral History of American Science: A Forty-Year Review." *History of Science* 41(4): 349–378.

Düppe, T. (2012). "Gerard Debreu's Secrecy: His Life in Order and Silence." *History of Political Economy* 44(3): 413–449.

Düppe, T. and Weintraub, R. E. (2014). *Finding Equilibrium: Arrow, Debreu, McKenzie and The Problem of Scientific Credit*. Princeton and Oxford, Princeton University Press.

Emmett, R. (2007). "Oral History and the Historical Reconstruction of Chicago Economics." *History of Political Economy* 39(Suppl 1): 172–192.

Feiwel, G. R. (ed.) (1987a). *Arrow and the Ascent of Modern Economic Theory*. London, Macmillan Press.

Feiwel, G. R. (ed.) (1987b). *Arrow and the Foundations of the Theory of Economic Policy*. London, Macmillan Press.

Fielding, N. G. (2009). *Interviewing II (Four Volume Set)*. London, Sage Publications.

Fourcade, M. (2009). *Economists and Societies*. Princeton, rinceton University Press.

Freedman, C. (2010). "South Side Blues: An Oral History of the Chicago School." *Journal of the History of Economic Thought* 32(4): 495–530.

Gaudillière, J.-P. (1997). "The Living Scientist Syndrome: Memory and History of Molecular Regulation." In Söderqvist, T. (ed.), *The Historiography of Contemporary Science and Technology*. Amsterdam, Harwood Academic Publishers: 109–128.

Greenwell, R. (1997). "The Oral History Collections of the Presidential Libraries." *The Journal of American History* 84(2): 596–603.

Gubrium, J. F. and Holstein, J. A. (2012). "Narrative Practice and the Transformation of Interview Subjectivity." In Gubrium, J. F., Holstein, J. A., Maravasti, A. B., and McKinney, K. D. (eds), *The SAGE Handbood of Interview Research. The Complexity of the Craft*. London, Sage: 27–44.

Haddad, P. R. (1981). "Brazil: Economists in a Bureaucratic-Authoritarian System." *History of Political Economy* 13(3): 656–680.

Halsmayer, V. (2014). "From Exploratory Modeling to Technical Expertise: Solow's Growth Model as a Multipurpose Design." *History of Political Economy* 46(Annual Supp.): 229–251.

Hands, W. D. (2012). "The Positive-Normative Dichotomy and Economics." In Mäki, U. (ed.), *Handbook of the Philosophy of Science, Vol.5: Philosophy of Economics*. Oxford, Elsevier: 219–239

Hoddeson, L. (2006). "The Conflict of Memories and Documents: Dilemmas and Pragmatics of Oral History." In Söderqvist, T. (ed.), *The Historiography of Contemporary Science, Technology, and Medicine: Writing Recent Science*. Abingdon, Routledge: 187–200.

Holstein, J. A. and Gubrium, J. F. (2004). "The Active Interview." In Silverman, D. (ed.), *Qualitative Research. Theory, Method and Practice*. London, Sage: 140–161.

Klamer, A. (1983). *Conversations with Economists*. Totowa, Rawman and Allenheld.

Klein, J. L. (2001). "Economics for a Client: The Case of Statistical Quality Control and Sequential Analysis." *History of Political Economy* 32(Annual Supp.): 25–70.

Leonard, R. J. (1992). "Creating a Context for Game Theory." *History of Political Economy* 24(Annual Supp.): 29–76.

Leonard, R. J. (2010). *Von Neumann, Morgenstern, and the Creation of Game Theory: From Chess to Social Science, 1900–1960*. New York, Cambridge University Press.

Maes, I. (2011). "Alexandre Lamfalussy et les tentatives de la BRI pour éviter un endettement excessif en Amérique Latine dans les années 1970." *Histoire, économie & société* 30(4): 59–77.

Magnus, J. and Morgan, M. (1987). "The ET Interview: Professor J. Tinbergen." *Econometric Theory* 3(1): 117–142.

Mata, T. (2005). "Dissent in Economics: Making Radical Political Economists and Post Keynesian Economics, 1960–1980." PhD Dissertation, London School of Economics and Political Science.

Mata, T. and Lee, F. S. (2007). "The Role of Oral History in the Historiography of Heterodox Economics." *History of Political Economy* 39(Suppl 1): 154–171.

McGregor, R. R. and Young, W. (2013). "Federal Reserve Bank Presidents as Public Intellectuals." *History of Political Economy* 45(Annual Supp.): 166–190.

Meho, L. I. (2006). "E-mail Interviewing in Qualitative Research: A Methodological Discussion." *Journal of the Association for Information Science and Technology* 57(10): 1284–1295.

Montecinos, V. (1996). "Economists in Political and Policy Elites in Latin America." *History of Political Economy* 28(Annual Supp.): 279–300.

Opdenakker, R. (2006). "Advantages and Disadvantages of Four Interview Techniques in Qualitative Research." *Forum Qualitative Sozialforschung/Forum: Qualitative Social Research* 7(4), available at: www.qualitative-research.net/index.php/fqs/article/view/175/391 (consulted on 06/26/18).

Oral History Association (2009). "Principles and Best Practices", available at: www.oralhistory.org/about/principles-and-practices/ (consulted on 06/26/18).

Petridis, A. (1981). "Australia: Economists in a Federal System." *History of Political Economy* 13(3): 405–435.

Rancan, A. (2017). "The Wage-Employment Relationship in Modigliani's 1944 Article." *The European Journal of the History of Economic Thought* 24(1): 143–174.

Sent, E.-M. (1998). *The Evolving Rationality of Rational Expectations*. Cambridge, Cambridge University Press.

Snowdon, B. and Vane, H. R. (1999). *Conversations with Leading Economists: Interpreting Modern Macroeconomics*. Cheltenham and Northampton, Edward Elgar.

Söderqvist, T. (1997). "Who Will Sort Out the Hundred or More Paul Ehrlichs? Remarks on the Historiography of Recent Contemporary Technoscience." In Söderqvist, T. (ed.), *The Historiography of Contemporary Science and Technology*. Amsterdam, Harwood Academic Publishers: 1–10.

Spradley, J. P. (1979). *The Ethnographic Interview*. Fort Worth, Hartcourt Brace Jovanovich College Publishers.

Svorenčík, A. (2015). "The Experimental Turn in Economics: A History of Experimental Economics." PhD Dissertation, University of Utrecht.

Svorenčík, A. and Maas, H. (2016). *The Making of Experimental Economics: Witness Seminar on the Emergence of a Field*. Heidelberg, Springer.

Teixeira, P. N. (2017). "Economic Beliefs and Institutional Politics: Human Capital Theory and the Changing Views of the World Bank About Education (1950–1985)." *The European Journal of the History of Economic Thought* 24(3): 465–492.

Thomson, A. (2007). "Four Paradigm Transformation in Oral History." *The Oral History Review* 34(1): 49–70.

Tribe, K. (2011). "Book Review of Economists and Societies by Mario Fourcade." *History of Political Economy* 43(3): 620–623.

Weart, S. R. (1990). "Preserving and Making Known the History of Physics: The American Institute of Physics Center for History of Physics." In Roche, J. (ed.), *Physicists Look Back: Studies in the History of Physics*. Bristol and New York, Adam Hilger: 29–43

Weintraub, E. R. and Forget, E. L. (eds) (2007). *Economists' Lives: Biography and Autobiography in the History of Economics*. Annual Supplement to Volume 39 of *History of Political Economy*. Durham and London, Duke University Press.

Weintraub, R. E. (1983). "On the Existence of a Competitive Equilibrium: 1930–1954." *Journal of Economic Literature* XXI: 1–39.

Weintraub, R. E. (2002). *How Economics Became a Mathematical Science*. Durham and London, Duke University Press.

Weintraub, R. E. (2005). "2004 HES Presidential Address: Autobiographical Memory and the Historiography of Economics." *Journal of the History of Economic Thought* 27(1): 1–11.

Weintraub, R. E. (2007). "Economists Talking with Economists: An Historian's Perspective." In Samuelson, P. A. and Barnett, W. (eds), *Inside the Economist's Mind: Conversations with Eminent Economists*. Malden, Blackwell: 1–11.

Wilson, A. (2017). "Viewpoint: Science's Imagined Pasts." *Isis* 108(4): 814–826

Yohe, W. P. (1990). "The Intellectual Milieu at the Federal Reserve Board in the 1920s." *History of Political Economy* 22(3): 465–488.

4 The witness seminar

Method, results, and implications

Harro Maas[1]

What is a witness seminar?

On May 28–29, 2010, 12 experimental economists gathered at the Dutch Royal Academy of Arts and Sciences in Amsterdam for a witness seminar on the history of the experiment in economics. The event was organized as part of a grant for research on the history of observational practices in economics, on which I was working with two PhD students.[2] One of them, Andrej Svorenčík, concentrated on economic experiments in a laboratory setting; such experiments had gained widespread acceptance in the economics profession from the end of the 1980s onward but have a history that goes back at least to the early 1940s. Though the witness seminar is used as an oral method of research in contemporary history and in the history of medicine and technology, the method had not been tried in this form in the history of economics. My contribution examines the witness seminar as a method of oral history, its merits and pitfalls, using our own witness seminar as a nonrepresentative sample.

A witness seminar is a moderated group conversation that was introduced as a method of historical inquiry almost simultaneously at the Wellcome History of Twentieth Century Medicine Group (Wellcome Group) and the Institute for Contemporary British History (ICBH) in the early 1990s.[3] A witness seminar aims to bring together key participants of a specific historical event or episode to obtain a mix of different perspectives that may clash or coincide but preferably lead to an exchange of memories that feed upon one another in interesting and unexpected ways. Participation does not necessarily need to be restricted to elite individuals – Nobel laureates, politicians, senior administrators – as it will depend on the topic under discussion who is "key" or not. A historical understanding of an experiment at CERN depends as much on the work of Nobel laureate theoretical physicists as on technicians, programmers, and institutional funding agents who collaborated to construct the large hadron collider and to keep it in operation (see, e.g., Galison 1997). Similarly, in the history of economics, the topic of the witness seminar will determine which participants will make the most relevant contribution. Understanding the construction and impact of the MIT (Massachusetts Institute of Technology)-Penn monetary model or of Dynamic Stochastic General Equilibrium (DSGE) modeling on central banking will need a different cast of characters than an investigation into the effect of the rise of Vector Auto-Regression (VAR) modeling on econometrics. Individuals who are accustomed to media exposure will relate an almost scripted version of past events, which makes their contribution run the risk of hardly going beyond what is already known from other (published) sources. The interaction at a witness seminar may help destabilize such scripted versions and encourage the exploration of otherwise untouched topics (Tansey 2006).

Witness seminars run by the ICBH have been devoted to strictly circumscribed events in time and place but also to events that span several decades. Examples of the first are "The Winter of Discontent in 1978–1979" (1987) or "Let Us Face the Future: The 1945 Labour General Election Victory 5" (1995). An example of the second is "The Bretton-Woods Exchange Rate System, 1944–72" (1994).[4] E. M. Tansey, the driving force behind the witness seminars run by the Wellcome Group, has emphasized the focus on specific events, but this did not prevent the organization of seminars devoted to events that span several decades. Examples are "Ashes to Ashes: The History of Smoking and Health" (1995), "Clinical Research in Britain, 1950–1980" (1998), and "Beyond the Asylum: Anti-psychiatry and Care in the Community" (2003).[5] The Royal Institute for Technology in Stockholm conducted more than 160 interviews and almost 50 witness seminars as part of a large-scale project to write the history of IT in Sweden (Lundin 2009, 2012).[6]

Witness seminars are moderated events, but the level of structuring differs from a fixed set of questions prepared by the organizers to a more open format in which participants can raise whatever issues they think relevant to the event under discussion. Whatever format is chosen, a careful preparation of the seminar and a careful choice of the moderator are key to its success. As part of its preparations, the ICBH regularly commissions position papers intended to sensitize participants to specific issues (e.g., the role of specific individuals, technologies, events, institutions). Participants are sometimes encouraged and sometimes explicitly discouraged to bring with them objects related to the topic of the seminar and talk about their importance. An audience may or may not be present, and if one is present, it may or may not participate. Obviously, all these issues have consequences for how the seminar will evolve and for its results.

To my knowledge, the witness seminar on the history of the experiment in economics is the most extensive seminar pursued in the history of economics so far, but there have been events with similar features. Kevin Hoover and Warren Young, for example, organized and moderated a panel discussion at the annual conference of the Allied Social Sciences Association (ASSA) on January 7, 2011, on the occasion of the 50th anniversary of John Muth's famous 1961 paper in *Econometrica*, "Rational Expectations and the Theory of Price Movements." This paper is commonly considered to have initiated the advent of rational expectations in macroeconomic modeling. Earlier, Frank den Butter and Mary Morgan (2000) organized a moderated conversation about the role of macroeconomic modeling (institutes) in economic policy preparation. Another example is a session on the historiography of econometrics organized by Marcel Boumans and Mary Morgan as part of a History of Political Economy conference on the history of econometrics (Boumans and Dupont-Kieffer 2011). They made charts in advance, linking conferences, individuals, and events, that structured the discussion during the session. Because of this, Boumans referred to the session as a "chart session" instead of a witness seminar.

In his introduction to the panel on rational expectations, Hoover explained to the panelists and audience that the format of the panel was a "group interview or witness seminar" intended to "remember and reflect" on the "integration of rational expectations in to economics" (Hoover and Young 2013, p. 1171). The panelists, amongst who were Robert Lucas and Robert Shiller, both winners of the Nobel Memorial Prize in Economics, were chosen because they were "witnesses" – contributors – to this important episode in the history of macroeconomic modeling. Hoover and Young had prepared questions in advance that were targeted at individual participants, but they encouraged others on the panel to jump in the conversation.[7] The transcript, published in 2013 in *Macroeconomic Dynamics*, a journal that regularly includes interviews with economists, gives a good sense of what a witness seminar aims at: reflecting on an event by building on participants' memories. The following fragment, which also raises questions about transcripts that I will come back to, may serve as an example:

Shiller:	I have a question: I have absolutely no connection to Carnegie-Mellon, but I did go to graduate school at MIT [Massachusetts Institute of Technology]. Carnegie Mellon used to be Carnegie Institute of Technology. In my experience at MIT, another institute of technology, we were surrounded by scientists, and I kind of incorporated that in my thinking – I felt like a scientist too – and I just wonder if there is a broader sense like that at Carnegie Mellon[?] Also, you were not in a regular business school but in something different: . . . at Carnegie Tech it was called Industrial Management . . .
Lucas:	. . . and we didn't give an MBA; we gave an MS, a Master of Science.
[Dale] Mortensen:	That's because you had to have a math background to get in.
Shiller:	You had to have a math background to get in. So, there is something scientific behind the rational expectations revolution, and it comes from weather forecasters and oceanographers . . . The question is, is there a broader Carnegie culture that you can reminisce about, and where did it come from?
Hoover:	That's the question we were trying to ask earlier.

(Hoover and Young 2013, p. 1178)

Both examples indicate that what counts as a witness seminar and how it should be organized are fluid. Indeed, even today, there is no standardized way to conduct a witness seminar. But building on participants' memories is perhaps its most important unifying feature.

Why a witness seminar?

In the history of science, technology, and medicine, witness seminars have been used to improve the understanding of scientific discoveries, technological or institutional innovations that may span several years if not decades, or as a tool to uncover untapped archival resources, in particular the recording of memories that otherwise will be lost. These goals are nonexclusive. The first witness seminar organized by the Wellcome Group was about the discovery of monoclonal antibodies for which César Milstein, an Argentinian-born scientist, and Georges Köhler, his German postdoctoral fellow, received the Nobel Prize in Physiology and Medicine in 1984 (together with Niels Jerne). The seminar was especially organized to uncover the context around their conscious and controversial decision not to patent their invention (Tansey 2006). Clearly, the presence of these two key participants was crucial for the success of the seminar and turned out to be even more so as both died within a few years after the seminar took place.

In our case, getting access to additional archival materials was an important reason to organize the seminar. Participation in a witness seminar may make participants aware of the historical importance of materials in their possession and encourage them to provide access to these sources, because of the questions asked by the moderator or as a result of the seminar interaction. Our seminar made participants realize they had to preserve first versions of papers, correspondence, and notebooks that they had considered of little or no importance. Thanks to the seminar and follow-up work by Andrej Svorenčík, these materials became available to him for his thesis work; some participants even donated their materials archival collections, such as the Economists' Papers Archive at Duke University, for preservation. For contemporary history writing, a witness seminar may thus not only function as an entry to archival sources but may also help to build an infrastructure for historical research. The shaping of such an infrastructure clearly has implications for future research, because it affects the kind of questions that can be posed by future historians. The witness seminar method thus also bears on discussions among historians on how to extend source materials beyond published and archival sources.[8]

A witness seminar runs the risk of favoring stories of success instead of failure. Well known are the objections to oral history-writing about biased and distorted memories, and such objections may hold even more for witness seminars. Implicit or explicit hierarchies between participants may inhibit participants from speaking out on specific issues, concealing instead of revealing issues that were at stake. The very fact that participants are part of a collective conversation may enforce biases and tunnel visions. It is less likely that Nobel laureates such as Robert Lucas and Robert Shiller would have participated in the panel on rational expectations if the subject had been advertised as a complete failure or dead end in economics. Historians thus should be aware of the risk of bias or of making themselves accomplices to the stories of success that primary actors wish to hear and tell.

This is a danger not only for the collective form of oral history that are witness seminars but for oral history more generally. Philip Mirowski refused to interview some of the key figures of his postwar history of economics in *Machine Dreams* (2002); similarly, Edward Nik-Khah (2006, 2008) relied on secondary sources instead of interviews in his history of the Federal Communications Commission (FCC) auction to keep primary actors at arm's length. But interviews can serve critical purposes as well. Indeed, oral history originally emerged to give voice to those who were traditionally excluded from the historical record because they made no contribution to the written record (the poor and the oppressed).[9] This social activist stance associated with the writing of "history from below" may have vanished in the United States in the postwar period, but it is still visible, for example in Ross Emmett's large-scale oral history project on the Chicago School.[10] Emmett interviewed not only elite staff members but also members of the support staff (such as secretaries) and students who dropped out of the graduate program to attain a more balanced account of the Chicago School's successes and failures. In my view, the important thing is to be aware of the fine line between becoming an accomplice and preserving distance and to be explicit that the purposes of the historian may be quite different from those of primary agents.

Written sources can be equally biased. Archives are sometimes demonstrably incomplete or provide an image of events that hinges on the ordering of the archive and so runs the same risks as oral sources. The reordering of the Alfred Marshall archives at Cambridge University also reordered the man and his work. The same holds for the editions of the complete works of David Ricardo, John Stuart Mill, and John Maynard Keynes, which created the persons as much as they conserved them. If an archive of a prominent economist enters special collections fully catalogued – as was the case with Paul Samuelson's papers at Duke University – that should be a source of worry for the historian. It takes an almost heroic effort to lift oneself above the ordering provided to see things in another light. In short, bias in historiography should not be concealed but confronted productively. It can even be argued that "bias" is not the right way to frame the choices involved, because it wrongly suggests that historical writing can stand as an unbiased statistical estimator of historical data. That itself is a biased view of what history writing is about.[11]

It should be clear, then, that a witness seminar is not intended to establish "the truth" or "what really happened" at a specific juncture of time or with regard to a specific event. Results may even stand at odds with published or unpublished (archival) materials. As Hoddeson (2006) rightly argues, tensions between oral and written sources do not count against oral histories but can be used as clues for revising existing interpretations and as encouragement for new research.

The witness seminar on the experiment in economics

As already stated, the lack of archival sources was a major reason to try the method of the witness seminar for our project. At the time, Vernon Smith's donation of part of his papers to the Economists' Papers Archive at Duke University was the most important archival source on experimental economics available, and thesis work relying on archival sources thus naturally took Vernon Smith's work as its focus.[12] For his detailed case study on the FCC auction, Francesco Guala interviewed key experimentalists and game theorists at Caltech and elsewhere. His widely acclaimed book on the methodology of experimental economics in 2005 opened up a new and still growing independent field of philosophical and methodological reflections on economic experimentation (Guala 2005).[13] But Guala was well aware that his book addressed an audience of philosophers and methodologists and lacked a proper history of laboratory experimentation in economics.

Even though our interests overlapped with methodological concerns, we were not so much interested in normative questions about the justification of experimental research but in descriptive questions of how the laboratory as a dedicated site of research had produced changes in economists' research practices, in terms of the kind of actors involved, their skills, and the nature of data produced.

Using some of the more pertinent texts on experimentation and the experimental method in the history and sociology of science, we identified four themes for discussion: community building, funding, skills and techniques, and the laboratory as a research site.[14] These themes and a rough timeline from the early 1950s until the founding of the Economic Science Association (ESA), the Society of Experimental Economics established in 1986, and its journal *Experimental Economics* served as a loose grid to choose our cast of characters: participants should for example have been in charge of the design of a laboratory or of the development of dedicated software; there should be sensible relations between participants in terms of pioneers, first-generation PhD students, early presidents of the ESA, the first editor of the journal, economists on National Science Foundation (NSF) committees, and experimentalists from outside of the United States.[15]

In consultation with Frans van Winden, the founder of the experimental laboratory of the economics faculty at the University of Amsterdam, we narrowed an initial list of 25 names to the 12 individuals we invited to the seminar. This list, and our reasons for inviting them, reflects our own rudimentary understanding of the history of experimental economics at the time.[16] We asked Chris Starmer, an experimental and behavioral economist from Nottingham, to moderate the event. Starmer had taught economic history at Nottingham with one of the leading British historians of economics, the late Bob Coats, which assured us of his historical sensibilities. Because our choice of timeline excluded the separate trajectory of the emergence of the experiment in Britain, Starmer seemed also a good choice from that perspective. Starmer agreed on the condition that a sufficient number on our selected list would agree to participate, somewhat assuming, as he told us afterward, that this would never happen. We first invited Vernon Smith, Charles Plott, and Reinhard Selten, and after they had committed proceeded with the rest. Within a few days all but one had accepted our invitation. We clearly hit upon something our invitees considered important, not least because they had important and different stakes in this history.[17] Werner Güth, best known for developing the ultimatum game, declined because he was not convinced a witness seminar was the right format for the complex issues we wanted to address.

Preparation of the seminar

We followed several tracks to prepare for the seminar. We asked experimental economist Andreas Ortmann to write a short essay on a few "museum pieces" of experimentation in economics that also introduced the four themes of interest. This was sent to the participants a few weeks before the seminar. During the year preceding the seminar, Andrej Svorenčík conducted in-depth interviews with all participants individually. He also interviewed experimental and other economists who were close to our invitees in relevant ways (as co-authors, supervisors, students, etc.). By the time of the witness seminar, all participants had been interviewed at least once, with each interview lasting on average two hours.

These interviews were crucially important in the preparation of the seminar itself. They enabled us to create "thick" CVs that showed the particular strengths of the individual participants, points of contact with the other participants, and moments and events in their careers pertaining to the four themes of interest. We provided each participant with a copy at the seminar to flip through if necessary. Starmer used this information in preparation, however, without making a list of ready-made questions. Instead, and in consultation with us, the CVs served to make an informal list of fallback options to which he could take recourse once a topic was, or seemed, prematurely exhausted.

There were a great many practical issues that in fact are quite important for a successful seminar. In advance of the seminar we asked all participants to sign an agreement that the original audiotape and videotape and a transcript could be made available for scholarly purposes. The choice of venue for the seminar, the seating arrangement, and the recording technology are nontrivial: they affect not only the quality of the end result but also the cost of the project. Because we flew in most participants from the United States, it became a high-cost event. A half a year in advance of the seminar, we invited Chris Starmer to go through practical matters on site and to discuss the best way to physically organize the seminar. We divided the seminar itself into six sessions to allow a smooth transition from one topic to another and to incorporate sufficient flexibility to expand on one of them if that seemed appropriate from the unfolding discussion. During the seminar breaks, we consulted with Starmer on topics that could be explored more in depth.

We arranged for one video camera and a separate audio recording. Penny wise, pound foolish. For public distribution purposes and use in teaching, one camera is a clear mistake because at least two cameras are needed for a video recording that can follow the pace of the conversation. This recording was, however, helpful in making the transcript, for example, in case we lost track of who was speaking.

We discussed at great length whether to allow an audience at the seminar and eventually chose against it. In this choice we diverged from the established practices at the Wellcome Group and the ICBH, which generally allow for an audience who can also ask questions. We considered an audience a hindrance for an open exchange between the participants; we also thought an audience would encourage scripted versions of past events, especially because the audience would have consisted of experimental colleagues of the experimental economics center in Amsterdam, CREED. We somewhat compromised by allowing Andreas Ortmann and our historian and philosopher of economics colleague Marcel Boumans in the room – Ortmann, because he wrote the position paper, Boumans, because we wanted to have feedback on the event from a colleague in the history of economics community. We did not allow them to take notes to ensure that the participants would feel their privacy was secured. Clearly, this is an issue on which one can take a different stance, but as mentioned earlier, whichever route is taken will influence the seminar and its result.

The seminar and its results

Although we sometimes discussed the witness seminar as if it were an "experiment", a witness seminar intentionally lacks control. The choice of topics, and the advance preparation with Chris Starmer, set limits to but did not control (within those limits) what participants could discuss. This doesn't mean that we, as organizers, did not intervene in the unfolding of the witness seminar itself. Starmer remembers our emphasis on the use of surprise in asking questions, such as, for example, asking about examples of *failed* experiments and telling something about them. This led to now seemingly trivial but highly consequential observations from our 12 participants about the need to ensure that experimental subjects understand instructions and thus, for example, read tables in the right manner or read carefully the information on computer screens before pressing any buttons. Such experiences had made experimenters tighten their protocols but also adjust the architecture of the laboratories themselves, so as to ensure, for example, that instructions could be read from different angles of the room.

Surprise also was an important consideration in how we planned the start of the seminar. We considered it imperative that the first question would not be posed to Vernon Smith. This was not just because he might give a scripted answer but also because it could confirm other participants' expectations about the seminar. We instructed Starmer to pose the first question to Jim Friedman, which would most likely come as a surprise to all and thus, we hoped, unsettle expectations. On Tjalling Koopmans's suggestion, Friedman had written a thesis with Martin Shubik in the early 1960s in which he had used experiments to study oligopolies. But Friedman had turned away from experiments in the early 1970s, to turn into a "pure theorist", a self-perception he had cherished from his early days of study. Shortly before the first session, we informed Friedman that the first question would be about his decision to use experiments in his thesis. Chris would then proceed with a similar question to Reinhard Selten and only then to Vernon Smith. Afterward the floor would be opened to all participants.

As already indicated, the seminar helped to tap into a wealth of private resources, some of which are now in public as well as private library collections, in the Economists' Papers Archive at Duke University in particular. Among the papers deposited there due to the witness seminar (and Svorenčík's persistence) are now the papers of Alvin Roth and Jim Friedman. Archives of several other experimentalists are still being negotiated. There are personal collections of papers we were granted access to that are or will be deposited elsewhere, as in the case of Elizabeth Hoffman. In addition, the witness seminar pointed us to unexpected actors such as Austin C. Hoggatt, whose laboratory at Berkeley turned out to be an important reference point for Reinhard Selten and Vernon Smith, as well as important for Jim Friedman's experimental work. Finally, the witness seminar made the community of experimental economists aware of its own history and this has led to some activity at international conferences.[18]

As an example, let me expand on Austin ("Auggie") Hoggatt's computerized laboratory of the early 1960s at Berkeley. Its importance for the rise of laboratory experimentation clearly emerged from the conversation, even though Hoggatt's lab can be largely considered as a very expensive failure. Originally trained as an engineer, Hoggatt was a professor at the Berkeley Haas School of Business who received a million-dollar grant in the early 1960s to build a fully equipped computerized laboratory to run economic experiments. Only few experiments were performed, and the laboratory was discontinued in the early 1970s and reconfigured into office space. Friedman's early collaboration with Hoggatt made him abandon experimentation. In contrast, Hoggatt's laboratory served as a source of inspiration for Reinhard Selten's laboratory in Bonn, Germany, and equally for the first laboratory built by Bill Starbuck at Purdue when Vernon Smith was about to leave for the University of Arizona. Charles Plott remained at Purdue for another few years but never performed any experiments there.

The discussion about Hoggatt's laboratory made it clear that a state-of-the-art technological infrastructure was not enough, and not even a precondition, for the emergence of an experimental culture. A laboratory is more than its physical infrastructure; it needs people to feed it. As Vernon Smith remarked, "Berkeley invested in infrastructure and not in people. And people would have actually used it [Hoggatt's lab] and be an integral part of that process. That's the thing. But it was the kind of thing that had to be learned" (Svorenčík and Maas 2016, p. 165). But it was not only a social infrastructure that was needed to get laboratory experimentation going. It was also *which* social infra-structure. Van Winden explained the links between summer schools, annual workshops, invited external fellows, and pilot runs that had helped to establish an experimental culture at the CREED center in Amsterdam. Commenting on the transcript, Plott added that Starbuck's effort to build something similar to Hoggatt's laboratory at Purdue was also ignored by economists because they considered it as a psychology laboratory: "It was a psychology laboratory. No economic experiments were done there during my period at Purdue at least to my knowledge" (Svorenčík and Maas 2016, p. 233).

The seminar made it clear how important it is to pay attention to the exact timing of events. While two pioneers of laboratory experimentation were present at Purdue when Starbuck's laboratory was built, Vernon Smith and Charles Plott, they did not use the facility. This did not mean that there were no economic experiments performed at Purdue. Smith, John Ledyard, John Kagel, and Plott are all connected via Purdue, but when Kagel came there at the end of the 1960s, Smith had already left, and there was no institutional memory of Smith's classroom experiments of the early 1960s. Even during John Ledyard's studies at Purdue in the mid-1960s he did not encounter experiments at all.

Another issue that emerged was the very different trajectories that participants attributed to the same source of inspiration. Both Kagel and Smith acknowledged inspiration from the psychologist Sidney Siegel for their experimental practice, but their actual inroads into experimental economics were very different (Svorenčík 2015b). Friedman, Smith, and Selten are all three connected to Hoggatt, but whereas Friedman's experiences with Hoggatt made him give up on experiments, Smith and Selten in contrast were inspired by Hoggatt's laboratory and adjusted his example to their own needs once they had the opportunity (and felt the need) to build a lab of their own. Game theory was important for some but not for all participants to become infected with the "experimental bug", as Plott put it.

The above points to the importance of specific institutional settings. Both Purdue and Caltech were important sites for the emergence of the experiment in economics. However, the fact that Purdue and Caltech were not like traditional economics departments divided into separate groups (macro, micro, labor, etc.; Caltech does not have a separate program in economics but a joint program with the other social sciences) appeared an important enabling condition for experimenting with experimentation. Carnegie Mellon, commonly less associated with experimental economics, offered Friedman a job,[19] Holt studied there, and Ledyard went there after graduating from Purdue. Just as at Purdue and Caltech, there was openness to new ways of doing research not found at traditional economics departments, thus confirming studies in history and sociology that show that scientific innovation in a great many cases comes from the (relative) fringes of a discipline, where there is an openness to experiment with methods, theories, and data in ways not found at centers of vested interests.

This should not lead one to conclude that the economic mainstream was explicitly hostile to the experiment. On the contrary, the early experiences of Jim Friedman or Alvin Roth in getting their first experimental paper published in journals such as *Econometrica* and *Management Science*, or in receiving research funding (as in Friedman's case), gave them the illusion that their academic lives would be easy. This seemingly contrasts with the shared sense among the first generation of PhDs trained in experimental economics not to advertise themselves as such in the job market – seemingly, because at the time there was no sustained separate teaching in experimental economics, and job interviews followed *Journal of Economic Literature* (*JEL*) code classifications in which experiments until the mid-1980s did not figure at all. At conferences, experimental papers were placed in educational sessions, which did not contribute to their standing. Publication seemed to become more difficult once the "experimental bug" had spread more widely in the economics community and referee reports began to become much more sophisticated than the "this is an experiment, that's interesting, let's publish it" experience of Roth. The *JEL* codes now have experimental research as a subcategory of mathematical and quantitative methods. Such experiences and changes almost cry for further research.[20]

As documented in Svorenčík's subsequent work, acceptance and rejection policies in mainstream journals turn out to be a far more complex story, but it is exactly such further research that, we hope, will be prompted by this witness seminar (Svorenčík 2015a, Chap. 5 in particular). Again, institutional constraints as seemingly trivial as the lack of a proper *JEL* code may prevent new techniques and methods from catching on; *JEL* codes for education do not earn PhD candidates a position on one of the major economics faculties. Institutional support, from NSF administrators such as Dan Newlon, market-sensitive editors of major presses, or contract research for companies searching for solutions to concrete problems, provided the necessary funding for subject payments as well as personal and technological infrastructure for the method to survive, stabilize, and grow.

The transcript

The most important public outcome of a witness seminar is its transcript. Ours has now been published by Springer (Svorenčík and Maas 2016). If one rereads the short fragment from Hoover and Young's panel on rational expectations, it is clear that one is not reading the words that were actually spoken. In the raw transcript we read that Shiller did not "have a question"; rather, he had a question "it was probably not worth getting up for". Such qualifiers color the ensuing conversation, and it is unclear why they should be suppressed. However, there will inevitably be a difference between the spoken and the published text. A verbatim transcript is literally unreadable.

Let me concentrate here on how we proceeded with the transcript of our seminar. A rough first transcript was made by a professional company after we sampled several agencies, which differed substantially in performance. Once we had a rough transcript, Svorenčík listened again to the tapes, watched the videos, and revised the text accordingly. He then further edited the transcript by adding extensive footnotes and asking questions for clarification to participants where he deemed it necessary. This version of the transcript was then sent to the participants, not to revise or edit what they were represented as saying but for approval and further comments, comments that were added as a separate set of endnotes to the transcript. Approval only meant that participants agreed with the transcription, even though they might have, given the chance, phrased things differently on second thought. Any second-thought remarks were likewise added as endnotes to the transcript. For the book publication, we asked for separate permission from the participants.

Moving from the final transcript to a book manuscript meant another round of editing, which introduced substantial interpretive elements from us as editors. We deleted time markers and added subject headings, increasingly moving away from the audiotapes. Because the printed version will become the text of reference, it is important to acknowledge the historiographical choices this process entailed. For example, we summarized parts of the conversation with labels such as "The Experiment as Interface for Arguments", "Anything You Change Can Make a Difference", and "Designing an Experiment Is a Joint Effort"; the substance of those labels will raise certain expectations in readers – prime them, as it were, just as the other labels will prime them. In sum, we must acknowledge that our own editorial interventions can manipulate one's experience of the transcript. But that comes with the territory. Though the text is a collectively created document in which first-person participants jointly reflected on a major event in the economics discipline, our edits enforce only one specific story.

Concluding remarks

Witness seminars can be useful tools in contemporary history writing. To make them work, careful preparation is imperative. This is a time-consuming but potentially rewarding endeavor. One needs to think well in advance about the event or theme to be explored and what one expects as a result. This will help organizers select the right participants, who also need to be well instructed about the purpose of the witness seminar and about the organizers' expectations. This makes a witness seminar inevitably a method that co-opts its subjects of inquiry into the process. It is a process of mutual trust that may open untapped resources for inquiry and point to unexpected avenues that one would not have had access to otherwise, or only in roundabout ways.

The choices we made in organizing our witness seminar helped build an infrastructure for future research that is enabling and constraining at the same time. The questions asked, the persons invited, the seminar itself was colored by our present concerns and demands, which will inevitably differ from those of other and future researchers. Our seminar thus serves as an entry to a specific understanding of this episode in the history of economics, but it should function as an incentive to create other stories to be told.

Notes

1 Centre Walras-Pareto for economic and political science, IEPHI/Bâtiment Geopolis, Bureau 5224, Université de Lausanne, 1015 Lausanne (Suisse), email: harro.maas@unil.ch

2 The project was funded by the Dutch Science Foundation and concerned a history of observational practices of economists. It consisted of three subprojects that took sites of observing as their starting point: the observatory, the laboratory, and the armchair. On the observatory as a site of observing, see D'Onofrio (2012) and Porter (2007). On the armchair, see Maas (2011). On the laboratory, see Svorenčík (2015a). See also Maas and Morgan (2012).

3 See Tansey (2006, 2008) for useful accounts of the method of the witness seminar. E. M. Tansey initiated and organized (and still does so) the witness seminars at the Wellcome History of Twentieth Century Medicine Group.

4 For the complete list of witness seminars organized by the Institute for Contemporary British History at King's College, see https://www.kcl.ac.uk/sspp/departments/icbh/witness/WitSemscomplete.aspx. The Winter of Discontent was a very cold winter in which Britain was haunted by a sustained period of strikes that eventually brought Margaret Thatcher to power. The name refers to Shakespeare's *Richard III*: "Now is the winter of our discontent/Made glorious summer by this son of York". See also Hay (2010).

5 The first two were published as Lock, Reynolds, and Tansey (1998), and Reynolds and Tansey (2000). The third is accessible at the online Wellcome Library.

6 Lundin (2012) provides an excellent overview of the arguments pro and con on the use of oral methods in historical research.

7 The session organized by den Butter and Morgan on macroeconomic modeling and policy preparation also had a list of set questions. See den Butter and Morgan (2000).

8 For perceptive essays on the problems and issues surrounding the writing of "the history of now", see Doel and Söderqvist (2006) and Söderqvist (1997). See also Cortada (2016); Weintraub (2005, 2007, 2010); and Weintraub and Forget (2007).

9 Paul Thompson (1978) highlighted oral history's emancipatory origins in what has been called "history from below". This changed when Allan Nevins at the end of the 1940s turned his attention from marginalized groups to leaders in business, political, and social life for a large-scale oral history project at the University of Columbia. Nevins also coined the term "oral history".

10 See Emmett (2007) for a description.

11 I thank Till Düppe for helping me clarify this point.

12 See, e.g., Lee (2004).

13 See, e.g., Bardsley, Cubitt, Loomes, Moffatt, Starmer, and Sugden (2010) and Santos (2009). Also, issues of *Economics and Philosophy* and the *Journal of Economic Methodology* are peppered with contributions on the methodological questions posed by the experiment in economics.

14 Histories of the experiment and the laboratory have focused on the natural sciences, medicine, and psychology. The literature is too vast to cover here. Classic references are Collins (1985); Galison (1987, 1997); Knorr Cetina (1999); Latour and Woolgar (1986); and Shapin and Schaffer (1985). For a recent reflection on histories of the laboratory, see Kohler (2008) and subsequent articles in that focus section of *Isis*.

15 Our focus on the introduction of the experiment in economics made us refrain from engaging with the now currently misnamed opposition between experimental and behavioral economists. We wanted to have a conversation about the method of the experiment, not about the existence, yes or no, of a fully rational agent.

16 Listed in order of year of birth, these were Vernon Smith (1927), Reinhard Tietz (1928), Reinhard Selten (1930), Jim Friedman (1936), Charlie Plott (1938), John Ledyard (1940), John Kagel (1942), Elizabeth Hoffman (1946), Frans van Winden (1946), Charlie Holt (1948), Stephen J. Rassenti (1949), and Alvin Roth (1951). Jim Friedman died on February 17, 2016, Reinhard Selten, on August 23, 2016. Only Reinhard Tietz had to cancel because of a short-term illness a few days before the seminar. Unfortunately, that reduced the number of European participants to two, turning the seminar into a largely US affair.

17 One participant flew business class at his own expense and never asked to be reimbursed for any part of his fare. Because of budget constraints, we could reimburse in full only economy, nonrefundable fares.

18 There was a joint session at the ASSA of the History of Economics Society and the ESA on the 25th anniversary of the ESA (2012), and a similar session organized by the ESA itself (2012). Sessions on experimental economics' history at the ASSA (2013) and the relationship between economics and psychology at the ASSA (2015) were also attended by experimental economists.

19 Friedman's Yale classmate F. Trenery Dolbear, who also wrote an experimental thesis, was offered a job at Carnegie as well, but unlike Friedman he took it.

20 On the development of the *JEL* codes, including the one for experimental economics, see Cherrier (2017).

References

Bardsley, Nick, Robin Cubitt, Graham Loomes, Peter Moffatt, Chris Starmer, and Robert Sugden (2010). *Experimental Economics: Rethinking the Rules*. Princeton, Princeton University Press.

Boumans, Marcel, and Ariane Dupont-Kieffer (2011). "A History of the Histories of Econometrics." *History of Political Economy* 43 (supplement): 5–31.

Cherrier, Beatrice (2017). "Classifying Economics: A History of the *JEL* Codes." *Journal of Economic Literature* 55(2): 545–579. DOI: 10.1257/jel.20151296.

Collins, Harry M (1985). *Changing Order: Replication and Induction in Scientific Practice*. London, Sage.

Cortada, J. W. (2016). "Studying History as It Unfolds, Part 2: Tooling Up the Historians." *IEEE Annals of the History of Computing* 38(1): 48–59.

den Butter, Frank, and Mary S. Morgan (2000). *Empirical Models and Policy Making: Interaction and Institutions*. London, Routledge.

Doel, Ronald Edmund, and Thomas Söderqvist (2006). *The Historiography of Contemporary Science, Technology, and Medicine: Writing Recent Science*. London, Routledge.

D'Onofrio, F. (2012). "Making Variety Simple: Agricultural Economists in Southern Italy, 1906–9." *History of Political Economy* 44 (supplement): 93–113.

Emmett, Ross B. (2007). "Oral History and the Historical Reconstruction of Chicago Economics." *History of Political Economy* 39 (supplement): 172–194.

Galison, Peter (1987). *How Experiments End*. Chicago, University of Chicago Press.

Galison, Peter (1997). *Image & Logic: A Material Culture of Microphysics*. Chicago, University of Chicago Press.

Guala, Francesco (2005). *The Methodology of Experimental Economics*. Cambridge, Cambridge University Press.

Hay, Colin (2010). "Chronicles of a Death Foretold: The Winter of Discontent and Construction of the Crisis of British Keynesianism." *Parliamentary Affairs* 63(3): 446–470.

Hoddeson, L. (2006). "The Conflict of Memories and Documents: Dilemmas and Pragmatics of Oral History." In Ronald Edmund Doel and Thomas Söderqvist (eds), *The Historiography of Contemporary Science, Technology, and Medicine: Writing Recent Science*. London, Routledge.

Hoover, Kevin, and Warren Young (2013). "Rational Expectations: Retrospect and Prospect; A Panel Discussion with Michael Lovell, Robert Lucas, Dale Mortensen, Robert Shiller, and Neil Wallace." *Macroeconomic Dynamics* 17(5): 1169–1192.

Knorr Cetina, Karin (1999). *Epistemic Cultures: How the Sciences Make Knowledge*. Cambridge, Harvard University Press.

Kohler, Robert E. (2008). "Lab History: Reflections." *Isis* 99(4): 761–768.

Latour, Bruno, and Steve Woolgar (1986). *Laboratory Life: The Construction of Scientific Facts*. Princeton, Princeton University Press.

Lee, Kyu Sang (2004). "Rationality, Minds, and Machines in the Laboratory: A Thematic History of Vernon Smith's Experimental Economics." PhD diss., University of Notre Dame.

Lock, Stephen, Lois A. Reynolds, and E. M. Tansey (1998). *Ashes to Ashes: The History of Smoking and Health*. Clio Medica 46. Atlanta, Rodopi.

Lundin, Per (2009). "From Computing Machines to IT: Collecting, Documenting, and Preserving Source Material on Swedish IT-History." *History of Nordic Computing* 2: 21–23.

Lundin, Per (2012). *Computers in Swedish Society: Documenting Early Use and Trends*. Heidelberg, Springer.

Maas, Harro (2011). "Sorting Things Out: The Economist as an Armchair Observer." In Lorraine Daston and Elizabeth Lunbeck (eds), *Histories of Scientific Observation*. Chicago, University of Chicago Press: 206–229.

Maas, Harro, and Mary S. Morgan (eds) (2012). *Observing the Economy: Historical Perspectives*. Durham, Duke University Press.

Mirowski, Philip (2002). *Machine Dreams: Economics Becomes a Cyborg Science*. Cambridge, Cambridge University Press.

Muth, John F. (1961). "Rational Expectations and the Theory of Price Movements." *Econometrica: Journal of the Econometric Society*: 315–335.

Nik-Khah, Edward (2006). "What the FCC Auctions Can Tell Us about the Performativity Thesis." *Economic Sociology–European Electronic Newsletter* 7(2): 15–21.

Nik-Khah, Edward (2008). "A Tale of Two Auctions." *Journal of Institutional Economics* 4(1): 73–97.

Porter, Theodore M. (2007). "Introduction: The Statistical Office as a Social Observatory." *Centaurus* 49(4): 258–260.

Reynolds, L. A., and E. M. Tansey (eds) (2000) *Clinical Research in Britain, 1950–1980*. Wellcome Witnesses to Twentieth Century Medicine 7. London, Wellcome Trust.

Santos, Ana Cordeiro dos (2009). *The Social Epistemology of Experimental Economics*. London, Routledge.

Shapin, Steven, and Simon Schaffe (1985). *Leviathan and the Air-Pump: Hobbes, Boyle, and the Experimental Life*. Princeton, Princeton University Press.

Söderqvist, Thomas (1997). *The Historiography of Contemporary Science and Technology*. Amsterdam, Harwood Academic.

Svorenčík, Andrej (2015a). "The Experimental Turn: A History of Experimental Economics." PhD diss., University of Utrecht.

Svorenčík, Andrej (2015b). "The Sidney Siegel Tradition in Experimental Economics: The Divergence of Behavioral and Experimental Economics at the End of the 1980s." *History of Political Economy* 48 (supplement): 270–294.

Svorenčík, Andrej, and Harro Maas (2016). *The Making of Experimental Economics.* Heidelberg, Springer.

Tansey, E. M. (2006). "Witnessing the Witnesses: Pitfalls and Potentials of the Witness Seminar in Twentieth Century Medicine." In R. E. Doel and T. Söderqvist (eds), *The Historiography of Contemporary Science, Technology, and Medicine: Writing Recent Science.* London, Routledge: 260–278.

Tansey, E. M. (2008). "The Witness Seminar Technique in Modern Medical History." In H. J. Cook, A. Hardy, and S. Bhattacharya (eds), *History of the Social Determinants of Health: Global Histories, Contemporary Debates.* Hyderabad, Orient Blackswan: 279–295.

Thompson, Paul (1978). *The Voice of the Past: Oral History.* Oxford, Oxford University Press.

Weintraub, E. Roy (2005). "Autobiographical Memory and the Historiography of Economics." *Journal of the History of Economic Thought* 27(1): 1–11.

Weintraub, E. Roy (2007). "Economists Talking with Economists: An Historian's Perspective." In P. A. Samuelson and W. A. Barnett (eds), *Inside the Economist's Mind: Conversations with Eminent Economists.* Malden, Blackwell: 1–11.

Weintraub, E. Roy (2010). Review of *Lives of the Laureates: Twenty-Three Nobel Economists*, edited by William Breit and Barry T. Hirsch. *History of Political Economy* 42(4): 779–82.

Weintraub, E. Roy, and Evelyn L. Forget (eds) (2007). *Economists' Lives: Biography and Autobiography in the History of Economics.* Durham, Duke University Press.

Part II

Quantitative histories of economics

5 Social network analysis

A complementary method of discovery for the history of economics

François Claveau and Catherine Herfeld[1]

Introduction

Relations of various kinds have always been part of the subject matter of the historian in general and the historian of economics in particular. They are a major factor in scientific knowledge production. Economists collaborate, use similar methods, and share their results. Science as a social enterprise has instantiated mechanisms for feedback on research and allow for critical discourse, all features that emphasize the relational character of science. And as in any other discipline, albeit to different degrees, it holds also for economics that the process of knowledge production takes place in a setting that can be characterized largely by way of such varied relations. Understanding relations and their impact is therefore essential for any historian of economics.

Network analysis is increasingly used in history. It allows for studying multiple types of relations and how they operate (Borgatti, Mehra, Brass, and Labianca 2009, Düring and Keyserlingk 2015; Lemercier 2015; Whetherell 1998). More specifically, network analysis encompasses a set of innovative theoretical, mathematical, statistical, and computational tools for analyzing, modeling, and understanding networks. The main task of *social* network analysis (SNA) is to study relations between social entities, be they individual actors, organizations, or groups of people (Wassermann and Faust 1994, p. 3). It can also be applied to study relations among non-human entities, such as publications, organizational affiliations, institutional structures, and many others. In either case, (social) network analysis allows to systematically analyze relational and attribute data in order to better understand latent structures and hidden patterns.

Applied to the history of science, SNA offers a distinctive perspective on knowledge production by systematically treating relationships among interacting scientists as relevant (i.e., explanatory) factor. Moreover, the unit of analysis is usually not the single scientist but rather a whole set of entities and the relations between them. As SNA presupposes that those relationships have a non-arbitrary effect on how knowledge is produced, relations play an explanatory role in understanding knowledge production. Furthermore, SNA allows for a formalization and systematic characterization of those relations and the entities connected in virtue of those relationships. Besides capturing the most basic idea of the existence or non-existence of a relation, SNA allows us, among other things, to study: 1) the intensity and closeness of a relationship; 2) the centrality of an entity, for instance, of an actor or various actors in a group; 3) the structural positions that entities can occupy in the larger context of their network; and 4) the temporal changes of those relations.

So far, SNA has been rarely used in history of economics. One exception is an extensive study of the emergence of subfields within the discipline of economics since the second half of the 20th century (Claveau and Gingras 2016). Another paper has studied the diffusion of rational choice theories within economics and across the social and behavioral sciences from the 1940s onwards (Herfeld and Doehne 2018). Again, another study has analyzed a network of Viennese scholars in the early 1920s (Wright 2016). These three papers already indicate that SNA can tackle a diversity of historical issues. To us, the wealth of SNA in the broader literature in history and historical sociology demonstrates that we have only scratched the surface of the potential applications of the method in the history of economics.

Our aim in this article is to discuss the usefulness of SNA for the history of economics. While we acknowledge that SNA confronts a range of limitations, we argue that it is a promising method for the field. We make two main points about SNA. First, contrary to what is sometimes assumed, it is not primarily a method of data representation, but foremost a method of discovery and confirmation. It is as such a promising method that should be added to the toolbox of the historian of economics. Second, to be meaningfully applied in history, SNA must be complemented with historical knowledge gained by other means and often by more traditional, mostly qualitative, methods. It should therefore be viewed as a method that complements rather than replaces more established approaches in the history of economics.

Network analysis as a method of discovery and confirmation

While this chapter is not meant as a detailed introduction to SNA, the following terminology sets the conceptual ground for what follows. SNA tries to analyze 1) a phenomenon that either possesses relational properties or can be modelled from a relational perspective. The researcher produces what we call 2) "network structures" to model some of those properties of the phenomenon. In its simplest form, a network structure, or for short a network, is "a collection of points joined together in pairs by lines" (Newman 2010, p. 1). It includes a set of nodes and a set of edges (or ties) connecting some or all of the nodes. Nodes and edges also have attributes such as identifiers, weights, or more substantive attributes such as variables for socioeconomic status. A network consisting of such nodes and edges can be stored in various formats. Small networks can be written down on a piece of paper or even stored in someone's mind. Networks are however typically stored on computers in form of matrices of nodes and edges, with their respective attributes. Network structures can also be visualized as graphical representations (often called sociograms). To produce what we call 3) a "network representation", some of the attributes of nodes and edges must be mapped onto visual properties such as colors, diameter of circles, thickness of lines, etc. Other visual properties must be added such as, most notably, the positioning of the nodes in space.[2]

A research project can produce a network representation of some social phenomenon without this project being an instance of SNA. In this section, we illustrate this possibility by contrasting one example of SNA to an example of a historical study that builds a network representation but does not use the tools of SNA. We contrast both cases to better characterize what SNA is and what it can do for the historian of economics. Thereby, our point is not normative: we do not claim that the study not using SNA is defective. In fact, we believe it to be an instance of high-quality historical research. However, this contrast helps us to illustrate the added value of SNA for the historian of economics.

More specifically, the characteristic that we want to highlight is that SNA serves foremost as a *method of discovery and confirmation*, and not primarily as a *method of representation*. The graphical representation of a network is not the core of SNA. Rather, its core is a set of techniques, sometimes computational and statistical, sometimes quite informal, to *search for features* in a network structure. This search can lead to discovering properties of the structure that could have otherwise remained undetected. In this case, SNA serves as a method of discovery in that the researcher explores the network in order to generate new, but fallible knowledge claims, which can then be tested with other methods. The search can also lead to confirming or disconfirming hypotheses already entertained, hypotheses that are perhaps supported by other sources of evidence. In this case, SNA serves as a method of confirmation in that the researcher uses SNA to test a previously formulated hypothesis. In both cases of discovery and confirmation, SNA helps the researcher learn (always fallibly) about the system under study.

The point about the secondary role of graphical representation in SNA merits emphasis because many newcomers to SNA seem to misinterpret it as primarily a method of representation. They consequently produce the now frustratingly common representations of "hairball networks" (see Figure 5.2 for an example). But staring at a hairball typically generates little knowledge. Of course, graphical representations of networks do not always look like hairballs. They can be highly informative. More specifically, they can have at least two functions.[3] First, a researcher can use the network representation as an informal means of discovery or confirmation. If the network has salient properties, representing it graphically can indeed be sufficient to learn much about its structure (this role of representation will be discussed more fully below). For instance, if a network has fully disconnected components (i.e., some groups of nodes share no edge with the rest of the network), a graphical representation using any standard layout algorithms will make this feature salient. The learning toolkit of SNA thus includes the technique of inspecting a graphical representation of the network.[4] But there is no requirement to use this specific tool to be doing SNA. Using the same example, any specialized software can find for us the number of fully disconnected components of a network structure. There is thus a way to learn the same property without going through the process of manually inspecting a graphical representation.

The second function of a network representation is to convey information *to others*. A network representation, provided it is no hairball, can indeed be an efficient way to let others understand some research results. Taking again our network with disconnected components, a researcher who discovered this property by writing the following line of code in R "is_connected(g)" (where g is the network object)[5] might decide to produce a graphical representation for her readers to see the disjoint structures and thus understand almost instantaneously this property. However, what makes this research a case of SNA is not the graphical representation of the network, but rather the technique used for discovery (which is not relying on graphical representation in this case). In reverse, there are research projects that do not use the techniques of SNA for discovery and confirmation but use a network representation to convey the results. This strategy should not be confused with SNA.

Let us illustrate this contrast and the way in which it indicates the usefulness of SNA for the history of economics by comparing two research projects. The first project is from Kevin Hoover in the early 1990s and did *not* rely on SNA. Hoover (1991) wanted to understand the lineages of research in new classical macroeconomics. One of the major results of this research project is the network representation reproduced in Figure 5.1.

The second project is from François Claveau and Yves Gingras (2016). They wanted to study the evolution of specialties in economics from the late 1950s up to today. To do so, they relied extensively on SNA. They did not use the technique of graphically representing the initial networks constructed to perform their analysis because these representations would have led to the infamous hairballs mentioned before – see Figure 5.2 for a graphical representation of the network of articles published between 1991 and 1995 in economics.

The first point of contrast between these two studies is their informational bases from economics. In the case of Hoover, the information that he relied on in the construction of the network is heterogeneous both in source and in format. The researcher knew a lot about new classical macroeconomics from being trained in economics and from participating in debates in macroeconomics (Hoover 1988). This knowledge was coupled with a close reading of published material, especially of who cites whom and for what purposes. In contrast, the main informational basis used by Claveau and Gingras is more homogeneous: the list of references from around 400,000 articles published in economic journals indexed in the Web of Science database. In this database, each article has an identifier and each reference was given another identifier that tracks when a document appears in the bibliographies of two (or more) articles. Figure 5.3 illustrates what this primary informational basis looks like by reporting the first ten lines out of the 10.4 million lines of the table of references they used.

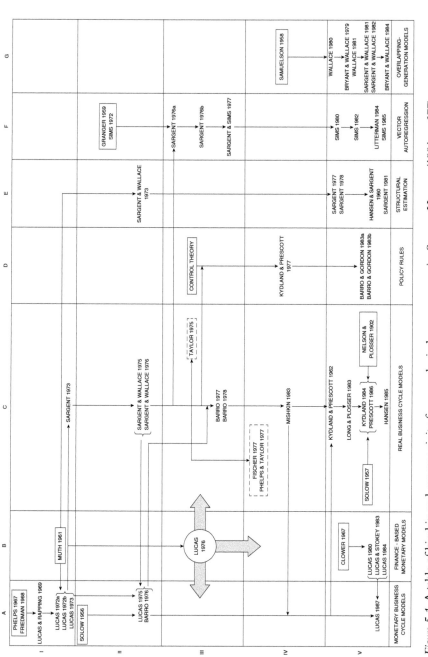

Figure 5.1 A table of kinship and consanguinity for new classical macroeconomics Source: Hoover (1991, p. 377)

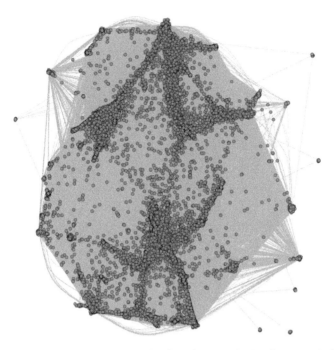

Figure 5.2 "Hairball" network of articles (n = 32,903) for time window 1991–1995 from the project by Claveau and Gingras (2016)

Note: The nodes are the articles published in the time window and the edges are given by the method of bibliographic coupling (described in the main text). The researchers refrained from disseminating such network representations because they are uninformative.

	ID_Art	ID_ref
1	557	3855165
2	557	182313
3	557	133847
4	557	169533
5	557	177021
6	557	176767
7	557	175609
8	558	3663377
9	558	3830394
10	558	182687

Figure 5.3 The first ten lines of the table of 10.4 million references used by Claveau and Gingras (2016) as their main informational basis

Note: "ID_Art" is the identifier of the *citing* article. "ID_ref" is the identifier of the *cited* document. From the extract, we see that the article with id 557 cites seven documents.

This table is the main informational basis of their SNA, but it is not the only information that Claveau and Gingras relied on (see below for the role of historical knowledge in their corpus selection). Yet, the crucial point in contrast to Hoover's project is that they did not build the network to effectively convey knowledge that they already possessed; they built the network to learn about the relational structure.

The second point of contrast between the two studies is the characteristics of the nodes and edges, the two building blocks of networks. Hoover's study allows for quite some *selectivity* and *heterogeneity* in picking out nodes and edges. He tells us that the nodes are "[f]or the most part . . . particular papers that were important in the development of new classical doctrine" (Hoover 1991, p 376). They were selected to be "exemplars of the main lines of new classical thinking" (ibid.). Nodes are also heterogeneous. They are sometimes made of more than one paper or even represent whole fields such as, for example, "control theory"; they are also represented by rectangles if they are "outside the new classical macroeconomics" (Hoover 1991, p. 376).

Selectivity and heterogeneity also hold for directed edges in Hoover's network representation. Hoover did not attempt "to reproduce the full and complex interrelationships between the exemplars listed", for instance omitting links "when it would have overly cluttered the diagram" (ibid., endnote 22). We also have various types of arrows: some point to other nodes, some point to other arrows, and yet others are larger and simply point in a direction (i.e., the ones departing from Lucas 1976, see Figure 5.1).

All these choices can be justified given that the purpose of the network representation is to effectively convey a wealth of information. It is easy to imagine Hoover engaged in a trial-and-error process to find the layout that struck the appropriate balance between being exhaustive and being readable. He already had the knowledge contained in the representation beforehand.

In contrast, Claveau and Gingras produced a network in order to apply computational tools. This purpose constrained their freedom regarding their selectivity and the heterogeneity of nodes and edges. In their network, each node stands for an article in their corpus. The only reason they find to exclude eight articles (out of 400,000) is that these few articles "have vastly more references than the others" (Claveau and Gingras 2016, p. 560). Here, selectivity is only based on technical considerations relative to discovery, such as that they did not want the results "to be driven by these few peculiar papers" (ibid., p. 560). The same properties hold for edges. They were built using the method known as bibliographic coupling: the strength of the edge between two articles is proportional to the extent to which their references overlap. Figure 5.4 illustrates how an edge with a weight of 4/7 between two hypothetical documents is constructed using bibliographic coupling.[6]

Although Hoover also considered citations to identify his relations of kinship, a noteworthy difference with the use of citations in Claveau and Gingras's project is that Hoover's close reading of the documents allowed him to distinguish citations serving different functions – for instance, citations to criticize or to praise some other research. In Claveau and Gingras's project all citations are treated equally. This difference illustrates how SNA, especially when it is used on large corpora, compels researchers to leave out potentially relevant information.

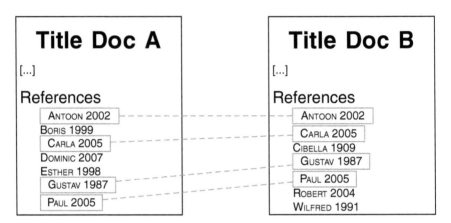

Figure 5.4 Illustration of the method of bibliographic coupling between documents
          A and B

Source: Claveau and Gingras (2016, p. 557)

Note: The figure shows two documents with seven references each. The four references they share are highlighted. The cosine measure that is used to give the weight to the edge between A and B is calculated as 4 divided by the square root of (7 × 7), or 4/7.

A third contrast between the two research projects is in the production of the network. While Hoover has used tacit knowledge to converge on a representation conveying information efficiently, the production of the networks in Claveau and Gingras's project was a matter of instructing the computer to transform the table of references (as in Figure 5.3) into an "edge list" – that is a table with one line per edge – by calculating the strengths of connections using bibliographic coupling. Figure 5.5 gives the first ten lines of their edge list (out of 123 million).

The last point of contrast concerns how the network is used. This is the most important one. Hoover (1991, p. 376) sets out to "investigate systematically the relations of kinship and consanguinity among the concrete exemplars of the new classical economics". His network representation is the main research output of this endeavor. The remaining task for him is to report "[t]he story told by the table" (ibid.), something that he does in less than a page and half.

In contrast, when Claveau and Gingras had produced their network (i.e., their edge list), they had nothing interesting to say yet. They needed to investigate structural properties of this network. Many properties can be studied. Which ones are relevant depends on the question asked. Since they wanted to investigate how economics as a discipline is divided into specialties, Claveau and Gingras opted for what is called "community detection": an automated technique to partition the nodes such that each "community" is made of relatively tightly connected nodes in comparison to the overall degree of connectedness in the network. In other words, the clusters created are made of articles that tend to cite the same documents more than average. When they

	Target	Source	Weight
1	557	768555	0.0714
2	557	43126104	0.0788
3	558	64116	0.0913
4	558	567983	0.1627
5	558	801489	0.2236
6	558	802025	0.1581
7	558	2401596	0.0559
8	686	704	0.1273
9	686	3846	0.0496
10	686	235569	0.0240

Figure 5.5 The first ten lines of the edge list produced by Claveau and Gingras (2016)

Note: The first two columns ("Target" and "Source") give the identifiers of the articles that are connected (the "ID_Art" of Figure 5.3) and the last column gives the strength of the connection (using bibliographic coupling, see Figure 5.4).

had these clusters, they used a text mining technique to find automatically generated keywords that characterize each cluster. They also used other techniques of discovery (see Claveau and Gingras 2016, sections 4–5), but let us limit ourselves to these two. With these techniques they uncovered a structure of specialties that they did not previously know about.

Although they had prior beliefs about some main trends, divisions and schools of thought in economics, what they uncovered is not a map of these beliefs, but some patterns in the data. The specialty structure that they uncovered can be displayed as network representations in a much more informative way than their initial hairball networks. Figure 5.6 represents the uncovered structure for the period from 1991 to 1995 (the same as in Figure 5.2). Each node now represents one cluster (not an article) and each cluster is named with the automatically generated keywords labeling the specialty. The identity and size of a cluster as well as the relationships between clusters inform us about the state of economics in the early 1990s. For instance, we can recognize fields such as development and labor economics, and we see that the smallest community is more tilted toward historical considerations and Keynesianism. Claveau and Gingras also produced another representation of the specialty structure as a timeline over the full period covered by the study, i.e., 1956 to 2014 (see the web application of this project at: www.DigitalHistoryofScience.org/Economics/).

Both studies discussed ended up producing network representations, but the role of the "network" in each was markedly different. Hoover built a graphical representation of a relational structure that illustrates kinship relationships in the new classical macroeconomics. He created this representation from a heterogeneous informational basis. He produced his network representation as a means to effectively convey what he had learned from his study of this school of thought. In contrast, Claveau and Gingras built a network from a standardized source (i.e., indexed references). Their initial network

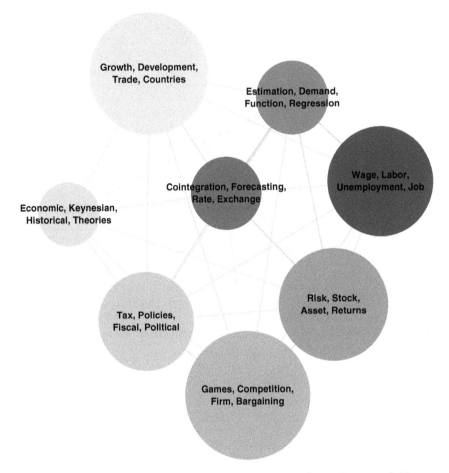

Figure 5.6 Network of economics in window 1991–1995 from Claveau and Gingras (2016)

Note: The size of a node represents the relative share of documents in the time window. The thickness of edges and the distance between nodes give a rough indication of the proximity of clusters in terms of proportion of shared references. Keywords are algorithmically extracted from the data.

was not a graphical representation, but only a list of weighted edges. On this mathematical object, they applied techniques for discovering structural properties from SNA. Ultimately, they produced network representations to convey parts of their results. But what makes their study a case of SNA is the use of methods of discovery on a network structure, rather than the inclusion in their published output of figures like Figure 5.6. Contrasting both projects not only illustrates that they use distinct approaches. It also illustrates how SNA can be a new and highly valuable approach to make new *discoveries* in the history of economics.[7]

Network analysis as a method complementing traditional historiographical methods

In this section, we argue that while SNA can be a useful method for the history of economics, its appropriate use requires more than knowledge of the techniques. Conducting a SNA involves several steps and historical knowledge of economics will be necessary at least at some of these steps. More specifically, we argue that when applied in history, SNA often has to be complemented by traditional historiographical methods in order to generate meaningful results. Traditional methods, such as text analysis, hermeneutic approaches, and source criticism, for example, can be required to generate such historical background knowledge. This point is not new. It relates back to a debate in history and historiography about the usefulness and relevance of quantitative methods, statistical methods in particular, in history that took place in the 1960s and 1970s (see, e.g., Düring and Kerschbaumer 2016; Fogel 1975; Tilly 1973, 2004). This debate – while less forceful in tone today – still influences the current discussion about the usefulness, the purpose, and the limitations of SNA in history more generally (Düring and Kerschbaumer 2016). One argument often raised in this debate is that quantitative methods should be complemented by qualitative historical research rather than replace it. We argue that this also applies to SNA.

What does it concretely mean that SNA should be informed by historical background knowledge generated by applying more traditional methods? We answer this question by tracing the different steps of analysis that are generally involved in an application of SNA in the history of economics. Historical background knowledge is always needed at least at some of these steps and sometimes even at all of them. When needed, it influences the results via the methodological and conceptual choices the researcher has to make. This is one sense, so we argue, in which SNA should be viewed as a method that complements rather than replaces more established approaches in the history of economics.

What are generally the different steps involved in a SNA that get us from the identification of a historical event, object, or process that we want to investigate to the final research results? We can roughly identify the following six steps. The researcher begins by 1) *choosing an object of study*, such as a historical event or process, and *formulating a research question* that allows us to learn something about that event, object, or process. In order to answer the research question, the researcher then has to 2) *select the historical sources* he or she is going to use. Source selection involves an assessment of the quality of the sources that are used in the analysis. It is closely connected to 3) the *specification of the network boundary*. In order to analyze historical sources with quantitative methods, the researcher then has to 4) *process the historical sources* in a particular way. This act of processing can involve transforming historical sources into quantitative data. To analyze the resulting data with tools from SNA, the researcher typically 5) *generates a network representation*. This visualization of the network is a step that is in principle not required when conducting a network analysis but it sometimes allows, among other things, for a fruitful exploration of the data. The researcher subsequently 6) *analyzes the network (i.e., the data)*, oftentimes in an exploratory fashion and in a trial-and-error way. It is here where the role of SNA as a method of discovery and confirmation becomes prevalent. At this step, the results are quantitatively and/or qualitatively presented and they are *interpreted*. The interpretation will usually involve re-contextualizing the obtained results, i.e., interpreting them in light of existing historical narratives and – importantly – in light of the historical sources that grounded the network analysis in the first place.

In the following, we look at each of those steps in turn. Not all steps look alike across the full spectrum of SNA and thus, not every SNA has the same demands with respect to historical knowledge. There are network analyses that involve large bibliometric data sets and are based upon complex computational and statistical analyses, such as Claveau and Gringas (2016) or Herfeld and Doehne (2018). And there are those, which are computationally and statistically less demanding, are grounded upon a small set of relational data, and involve only basic statistical analyses, such as for example Herfeld (ms) and Wright (2016). Both types of analyses are valuable and the difference between them is one of degree, not of kind. Because both ultimately rely upon tools from SNA to analyze quantitative data, they count as methods of discovery and confirmation in the aforementioned sense. But as they differ in the details of the research process, the kind and extent of historical background knowledge needed also differ. We should therefore keep in mind that the following points do not categorically apply in the same way to all network analyses. However, by discussing each of the steps in turn, we see how SNA at several steps is complemented by more traditional methods.[8]

Step 1: The object of study and the formulation of research questions

Serious research starts with selecting a relevant object of study and formulating a sound research question. This is a platitude that is worth repeating in the case of SNA because, much like for other methods, we run the risk that the method takes precedence. As the motto goes: "When you get your first hammer, everything looks like a nail". The methodologically sound recommendation is that the topic and the question must be selected first. Since SNA lends itself to answering some questions but not others, its relevance and usefulness as a method cannot be assumed a priori.

While SNA can be meaningfully applied to study different kinds of relations (e.g., memberships, family relations, exchange relations, competition relationships, relations between research fields), research questions that do not ask for the analysis of relations at all will not be meaningfully answered by SNA. Furthermore, the quantitative empirical tools of SNA require a significant reduction in the complexity of the relations studied and thus in the characterization of a social situation or a historical context. SNA (as probably any other method) cannot capture a social situation in all its complexity (see also Bixler 2016). If a specific object of study should be analyzed in its full "thickness", interpretive methods will be more appropriate than SNA alone. Text analysis or oral history interviews, for example, allow for revealing the nuances and ambiguities of a social relation. Hermeneutic approaches are often justified precisely because they capture ambiguities in the meaning of a text that, for instance, implicitly or explicitly describes a social relation (Düring and Kerschbaumer 2016, 35 ff.). In contrast, abstracting from much detail is an essential part of SNA. In short, a useful SNA takes into account that a network only represents specific aspects of social reality and that it furthermore cannot capture the nuances underlying specific relations.

Both aspects, the danger of applying SNA to everything and its demand for abstraction, ask for particular care when choosing the object of study and formulating research questions. Questions that experienced network analysts pose are often very specific, are adapted to the limited scope of the analysis, and are explicit about what can and cannot be shown (Bixler 2016, p. 104). Researchers often target concrete issues, such as the manifestation of particular social structures, interactions among particular groups of people, the distribution and exchange of specific resources, the identification of roles and positions in a defined social network, social interdependencies among historical actors or within groups, institutional hierarchies, or questions that target the relation between a specific network structure and the level of individual actions (ibid.). Choosing an object of study and formulating a research question also require that the researcher anticipates the set of abstractions made in the process that will imply neglecting certain aspects of the phenomenon in the analysis. Both require a certain level of awareness about, and sensitivity towards, what can and cannot be lost of the "thickness" of the historical context.

To take an example, the research question of Claveau and Gingras (2016, p. 552) is meant to make a contribution to historical knowledge, but at a large scale and not in any detail. They ask "how specialties [in economics] have emerged, grown in relation to each other, and (for some of them) disappeared" from the late 1950s to the early 2010s (ibid., p. 552). They justify their question by noting the recent growth of economics as a discipline and how our "grasp [of] the global structure and morphology" of the discipline is as such limited (ibid., p. 552). To them, the history of recent economics would not cover all the relevant perspectives if historians were solely focused on studying a selective set of social contexts, highly influential economists, approaches, subfields, or economic ideas. They consider discovering and studying properties of the macro-level dynamics of economics as a field to be equally important, but not to be a substitute to more micro-level historical studies. The former suggests a SNA, while the latter would benefit from more detailed and qualitative historical approaches.

This example already indicates that, although it is a case of a SNA extremely reliant on computational methods, prior historical knowledge is necessary at this first step. To argue for the relevance of their research question, Claveau and Gingras needed knowledge about the social structure of economics as a field and how it has changed over time. In general, selecting an object of study and a research question presupposes answering a set of methodological and conceptual questions, such as: 1) What will the network consist of? 2) To what extent do the categories that will be used in the analysis (e.g., categorizing something as a node or as an edge, and determining the properties of an edge) capture the relevant parts of the phenomenon? and 3) Can the research question be adequately addressed with the anticipated categories? (see also Düring, Eumann, Stark, and von Keyserling 2016, p. 173). Answering those questions requires historical knowledge about the object of study to make an informed decision about what can be abstracted from without losing essential historical aspects that are required for the analysis. Furthermore, the researcher has to be clear about the relevant ambiguities that characterize a set of relationships in a particular group and why we can abstract from them. Only then, a SNA can be informative and offer an improved understanding about the subject matter.

Step 2: Selection of sources

The second step in conducting a SNA involves the selection of sources that help answering the question and are appropriate for the analysis. Some SNA use existing bibliometric databases (e.g., Gingras and Claveau 2016). Other research projects have to extract relational data from historical sources, for example written reports, letters, or other kind of archival material that is text-based (e.g., Herfeld ms.; Wright 2016). Historians must select the sources based primarily on relevance, reliability, and ease of access and treatment. Prior historical knowledge or knowledge of other research methods play a role in this assessment.

A major informational basis for SNA in the history of science is bibliometric databases. For example, Claveau and Gingras (2016) use Web of Science and Herfeld and Doehne (2018) use Scopus. The assumption that these sources are acceptable is supported by knowledge about the composition of the databases and by prior knowledge about the aspects of science that the researchers study. For instance, it is well known that Web of Science indexes only what its staff takes to be the "the major academic journals around the world" (Claveau and Gingras 2016, p. 551) and that it is therefore mainly constituted by English publications. If Claveau and Gingras wanted to cover research at the fringe of economics, Web of Science would be a bad choice. In contrast, they want to map mainstream economics and know that researchers based in the United States have dominated the discipline since World War II. Herfeld and Doehne (2018, sect. 5) offer a lengthier justification for drawing on Scopus because they use, perhaps counterintuitively, publications from 1984 to 2014 to study the diffusion of some scientific innovations from 1944 to 1970. On the face of it, this choice seems to be dictated by the poor coverage of Scopus prior to 1984. Yet, they argue that using *published articles* between 1944 and 1970 to study the diffusion process would be inappropriate because knowledge diffusion also "proceeds through working papers and other formats that are not systematically included in citation databases" (Herfeld and Doehne 2018). Again, this claim rests on prior knowledge of the workings of economics in the period of interest.

In contrast to this reliance on already existing databases, some SNA in history rely on relational data that are generated from primary historical sources, which oftentimes comes down to text material of some sort. How to transform this material into a data format appropriate for SNA is not always evident. This is one reason why the researcher will have to decide which sources will do. Some text material contains *explicit* descriptions or other information about interactions or other kinds of relations among entities. This sort of material might appear evidently suitable for SNA. Yet, rarely were the primary sources produced with the goal of performing a SNA; oral history interviews are one example. In consequence, the researcher must assess whether the systematic extraction of relational information from these sources is *useful and feasible*. For example, Herfeld (ms.) studies cross-disciplinary interaction, the spread of methods, and the exchange of information at the Center for Advanced Study in the Behavioral Sciences (CASBS) at Stanford University. She decided to draw upon source material consisting of self-reported scholarly interactions and social exchanges among a cohort of fellows. More specifically, she uses a set of feedback reports of all members of that cohort as sources in which each researcher retrospectively reflected upon their social engagement during their visit. Fellows verbally stated and interpreted their social interactions and relations with other fellows in different ways. To select those reports as suitable for SNA, Herfeld had to interpret the reports, identify the various kinds of relationships those reports contain and decide whether they could be quantified. In short, she needed additional interpretive skills to select those sources as appropriate for the analysis.

Historians also use text material and other historical sources that contain only *implicit* information about relations (for an example of how relational data about illegal helping networks in the German National Socialism are extracted from autobiographical narratives; see Düring 2015). To extract relational information from such historical sources, the demand on interpretive skills is even higher (Stark 2016, p. 155). The historian embarking on such a project must master more traditional (qualitative) methods such as, for instance, textual interpretation and other hermeneutic approaches as well as source handling techniques (e.g., Emmett 2003).[9]

Step 3: Boundary specification

A crucial step in SNA is taking a stance regarding what is called the "boundary specification problem" (Laumann, Marsden, and Prensky 1992; Knoke and Yang 2008, p. 28).[10] Which entities and relations present in the phenomenon of interest should be represented as nodes and edges in our network? When should we stop extending the list of entities and relations? The stakes should be obvious: if entities and nodes are added in a non-systematic way, the resulting network risks being a misleading model of the phenomenon of interest. There is a rich methodological literature offering approaches or strategies to solve the boundary specification problem (see Knoke and Yang 2008, Chapter 2). In what follows, we will only substantiate our claim that solving this problem requires some prior historical knowledge or some knowledge of non-SNA historical methods.

Take the two projects mentioned in the previous step to exemplify research relying on bibliometric databases. After selecting Web of Science or Scopus as the informational source, the next question is what inside these enormous databases should be used to construct the network. Claveau and Gingras (2016, technical appendix, section 1.1) had to use prior knowledge of economics to select only economic journals. More specifically, they started from a classification of journals from the US-based National Science Foundation to construct their economics corpus. Since they knew that this classification is rather restrictive, they added some journals to their corpus that are at the frontier of economics and other fields (e.g., finance) by devising an inclusion procedure using a set of keywords. This procedure could not have been devised without some prior knowledge of the relevant keywords.

Herfeld and Doehne (2018) study the diffusion of rational choice theories across the social and behavioral sciences as a case of the diffusion of a scientific innovation across scientific fields. They sampled Scopus by starting from publications that cite the *Theory of Games and Economic Behavior* by John von Neumann and Oskar Morgenstern in the period between 1984 and 2014. To justify this choice of starting point, they argued that the *Theory of Games* contains the conceptual and theoretical innovations that laid the grounds for rational choice theories in the second half of the 20th century. From the identified publications, they then extracted all references to contributions published in their period of interest, i.e. 1944 to 1970, to finally link publications that were referenced together (i.e., co-cited) at least three times. This allowed them to capture the spread of the innovation. This procedure and its justification required prior knowledge about the history of rational choice theories.

Both of these examples are instances of the "nominalist" strategy to solving the boundary specification problem. Laumann et al. (1992, p. 69) defined this strategy as the self-conscious imposition by the researcher of "a conceptual framework constructed to serve his or her own analytic purposes". This strategy contrasts with the "realist" strategy, where "the network is treated as a social fact only in that it is consciously experienced as such by the actors composing it" (ibid., p. 65). Although the labels used are far from optimal,[11] the underlying distinction is helpful. Indeed, a researcher could decide that two individuals are included as nodes in her network without these individuals being aware of belonging to a specific relational structure.

The point we want to make with this distinction between two strategies is that, to be properly used, the strategies both require knowledge of historical facts or historical methods. Consider the closely connected group of scholars that during the 1940s and 1950s collaborated at institutions such as the RAND Corporation, the Cowles Commission, or the CASBS (e.g., Düppe and Weintraub 2014, Erickson, Klein, Daston, Lemov, Sturm, and Gordin 2013; Herfeld ms.; Klein 2016). Imagine that we want to extract networks based on disciplinary identity among this group of scholars – e.g., having a network of psychologists and a network of economists. Was Patrick Suppes a psychologist albeit working in formal philosophy and statistics? Were Kenneth Arrow and Leonid Hurwicz economists despite working on questions in mathematical statistics and political science? Using a nominalist strategy would require arguing for the relevance of a criterion, perhaps PhD training or rather main publication venues, to distinguish among researchers. The argument for the criterion will need to be based on prior historical knowledge – for instance, about the relative heterogeneity and influence of PhD training at the time. A realist strategy, in contrast, demands to find the disciplinary self-identification of scholars. This task faces the usual pitfalls of self-reported information in history, for instance of written autobiographies, interviews and questionnaires. Indeed, memory loss and other potential biases imply that such information cannot be taken at face value (e.g., Hoddeson 2006; Moggridge 2003, 59f f.; Weintraub 2005; Bernard, Killworth, and Sailer 1982). More importantly, however, no matter which strategy we apply, background knowledge is required to justify one's conceptual and methodological choices.

Step 4: Processing the sources

SNA requires strict data formats. Every network is made of nodes connected by edges. The historical sources do not come in this format. They need to be processed. This processing can sometimes be quite substantial, depending on how far one goes back in time and depending on the kind and quality of the sources. The processing of historical sources might lead to the previously highlighted reduction of complexity and often also to a neglect of ambivalence contained in the historical sources. Furthermore, offering a systematic data set for a clearly defined population frequently necessitates the extensive interpretation of those sources. To do that, the historian has to draw on methods such as textual analysis (if the sources are written texts) and other hermeneutic approaches to text interpretation. He has to be skilled in historical source reading and construction. This, of course, presupposes extensive historical knowledge.

Note, however, that the amount of ingenuity and historical knowledge needed to get the nodes and the edges vary significantly. Consider the network in Herfeld and Doehne (2018). It is built from bibliometric data and constructed to apply computational tools to it.[12] Once they had decided how to set the boundary of their network, its actual construction was primarily a technical endeavor: each node stands for some scholarly contribution (e.g., articles, books, working papers) in their corpus and each edge stands for a co-citation of two articles. Articles are excluded from the analysis on the basis of a set of rules, such as their number of co-citations or their publication date. There was no publication excluded on idiosyncratic grounds. Selectivity is only based on rule-based technical considerations relative to discovery. Edges are similarly homogeneous and not selected. They were built via co-citation in the database.

Yet, as we saw in the previous steps, SNA using bibliometric databases do not exhaust the possibilities of SNA in the history of economics. In analyses using primary sources, there is typically much more work involved in processing the sources. The historian must formulate sharp categories for the entities and their relations although the primary sources are a lot less structured than a bibliometric database. Herfeld (ms.) for example produces nodes and their edges largely by coding the relations she extracts from text material using a pre-determined categorization of relations (e.g., colleague, friend, co-author, etc.). The network thus created can subsequently be analyzed with statistical tools. Here, source processing requires more historical background knowledge than in the previous example. Deciding on a meaningful taxonomy and undertaking this categorization of nodes and edges necessitate – again – a careful interpre-tation of the historical sources as well as drawing adequate inferences about possible hidden relationships.

It can be considerably more difficult to extract data suitable for a SNA from texts that have even less structure than the reports used by Herfeld (ms.); examples would be a prose text containing an autobiographical narrative, diary entries, or personal letters. In these cases, the network analyst must combine specialized interpretive skills with the rigor of formal data analysis to systema-tize text interpretation. In sum, we see that, at the step of processing the his-torical sources, the centrality of prior knowledge of history and of interpretive methods varies significantly across instances of SNA.

Step 5: Generating a network representation

Network analysts often recur to network representations as a first step towards the data analysis. However, as indicated above, an early visualization is not necessary. In the case of Claveau and Gingras (2016), the resulting hairball representations (see Figure 5.2) would not have been particularly insightful. Such network representations are only helpful if they reveal hidden and com-plex patterns of social relations in the data that we could not have easily seen by, for instance, reading the text material alone. Those patterns are often easier to detect via a network representation than when applying more traditional methods to a set of sources. This is simply because the data can be visualized in ways that highlight specific structural characteristics of a network while down-playing others systematically. If we attempt a graphical representation, we have to choose various aspects such as the placement of nodes in space (typically handled by a layout algorithm) and which information to convey through node size, shape, and/or color (as well as edge thickness and color), which set of nodes and edges should be included in the representation, and which of their attributes matter, among other things.

There are at least three goals of visualization (see also Düring and Kerschbaumer 2016). First, it gives the researcher an initial orientation in ana-lyzing relational data. It can point towards interesting properties of the network. For example, exploring their clustered network via visualization, Herfeld and Doehne realized from the graph that not only the clusters but also the connec-tion between clusters were relevant for the spread of rational choice theories. This inspired a typology of roles they introduced to theoretically account for this connection (see Herfeld and Doehne 2018, Table 4).[13] Second, it can help the researcher generate hypotheses that can then be tested by way of a more complex SNA or through other historical methods. For example, in Herfeld and Doehne (2018), the existence of relations between clusters lead to formulating hypotheses about the relationship between different sub-disciplines towards which rational choice theories spread and the conditions in place for such a cross-disciplinary spread to occur. Third, a network representation can establish a basis for assessing the face validity of the network – e.g., whether some major coding errors have been made (Düring and Kerschbaumer 2016, p. 38). With respect to all three goals, a network representation abstracts from a large amount of historical detail. Its function is comparable to that of a map guiding the researcher by reducing details that are not relevant to the research question at hand. However, as with city maps, while they guide you in places that you have never been to, you must still be able to interpret and relate the signs around you to the symbols used in the map to read it and understand where the nearest highway, restaurant, pedestrian walkway, lake, or river is.

Step 6: Network analysis and interpretation of results

As mentioned before, one of the most important steps in a SNA is to analyze the properties of the network. Such analyses can be based on network representations but do not have to. Most of the time, they are executed on the underlying matrix containing the network relations (e.g., Düring and Kerschbaumer 2016, p. 39; Knoke and Yang 2008, p. 45). The choice of techniques for analyzing networks should be motivated by the research question or the hypothesis. Techniques for quantitative analysis include, among others, positional measures (such as different metrics of network centrality as well as similarity and equivalence measures) and clustering algorithms. Choosing among them requires both technical expertise for their application and an understanding of the underlying computation procedures, that is, knowledge about what it is those techniques actually do when applied. However, it also requires an understanding of which of the many techniques available will address the research question at hand. We can ask, for instance, what the hierarchical structure within the Cowles Commission during the 1940s and 1950s was. To find an answer to this question requires the choice of techniques and measures that will help us to discover structural properties in the data that represent this hierarchy.

Once results are produced, they must be interpreted. It is probably the part of the analysis where the need for historical background knowledge is most obvious. The interpretation of the results will often involve re-contextualizing them historically, i.e., interpreting them in light of existing historical narratives and – importantly – in light of the historical sources that grounded the SNA in the first place. In the case of small-sample SNA based upon textual sources, this typically means a return to the primary sources. For example, the network connecting scholars on the basis of their interaction during their year at the CASBS was interpreted by Herfeld (ms.) as a network of information flows and of tools exchange. This required not only to go back to the written reports in which the fellows described the kind of relationship and the kind of information and tools they exchanged during their fellowship year. Additional archival material and other textual evidence about, for example, the specific social context of the CASBS helped to understand characteristics of interactions between scholars at the CASBS. Reconnecting the abstract network analysis with the historical sources might even involve an act of re-interpretation either of the sources or of the network analysis.

What a historical interpretation amounts to is far too complex to be tackled here (see Emmett 2003 for an overview with a focus on the history of economics). But we want to note that historical knowledge is extremely important in the interpretation of results generated by a SNA. Any historical interpretation – and thus also of the results of a SNA – has to be based on considerations about the meaning that gives particular events their historical significance. This is in part a constructive activity. To identify the meaning and thus the significance of a historical event, the historian must decide, among other things, which events – and the results thereof – to focus on and how those events are to be connected. She must decide on categories and concepts that capture this meaning to describe the results of the analysis (e.g., is a series of events best described as a scientific revolution, a methodological turn, or a shift towards new problems?). The implication of all this for SNA in the history of economics is that, at the step of interpreting the results, the researcher must have extensive historical background knowledge and the necessary expertise to use interpretative methods.

Some advantages of network analysis in history of economics

The advantages of using network analysis in history of economics (HET) appear obvious to us.[14] First, network analysis can reveal stable patterns that would be difficult to recognize in a systematic way when studied only by more traditional methods. Exemplary analyses such as by Claveau and Gringas (2016) show how empirical algorithmic procedures can be used to reveal and systematically study non-trivial hidden structures in networks. With the increasing availability of new source materials from personal and institutional archives such as syllabi, personal and professional correspondence, institutional records, etc. (Weintraub 2017, p. 149; Weintraub, Meardon, Gayer, and Banzhaf 1998), SNA can more easily be put to the task of finding and studying these patterns.

Second, SNA offers a distinct perspective in answering the questions of historians of economics. It puts into focus the relational aspect of scientific activity (e.g., Emirbayer 1997). We can liken it to a powerful instrument to study relational structures by allowing "us to draw or to measure, the equivalent of a microscope or periscope" (Lemercier 2015, p. 4). This perspective, the specific data on which it relies, and the results it generates, can be used to assess historical claims arrived at by other methods.

Third, SNA can be used to analyze large data sets. Studying the evolution of economics as composed of multiple specialties (Claveau and Gringas 2016) or the spread of rational choice theories across all the behavioral and social sciences (Herfeld and Doehne 2018) would confront serious challenges when studied only by traditional – qualitative – historical approaches because of the sheer scope of the phenomena. SNA and other bibliometric methods allow the historian of economics to broaden the scope of her research.

Fourth, SNA can mitigate confirmation bias, which is a bias to which historical research is often prone. An appropriate quantitative research design forces the researcher to be explicit about the rule-based assumptions underlying the construction of the network. Furthermore, the actual compilation and analysis of empirical networks is preceded by a systematic process of evidence gathering in the course of which the researcher's attention is turned also to relations that seem improbable at face value. Whenever a constructed network reveals the presence of unexpected relations (or an absence of expected ones), the historian can search for explanations of the result and whether this may have affected the postulated events.

Finally, historians of recent economics should seriously consider using SNA to follow changes in the way economists study the economy. In recent decades, there has been a shift in economics away from great ideas and general theories by important thinkers – e.g., Adam Smith, Karl Marx, John Maynard Keynes – or major schools of thought – e.g., Keynesian macroeconomics and monetarism – towards the development and application of models, of a variety of mathematical, statistical and empirical tools, and the pursuit of different scientific and policy-oriented practices (e.g., Fontaine 2016; Schabas 1992; Weintraub 1999, 2017). This shift led historians of economics to complement the history of ideas with a concentration also on contextualized histories of those methods, tools, and practices within their respective social, economic, cultural, or political contexts. Applying SNA allows us to take a relational perspective on this period to reveal how the development and application of those methods, tools, and practices have been crucially influenced by contextual factors.

Despite its usefulness, SNA – as we have argued – is not a substitute for other historical methods. Used alone, it makes for terse histories. The example on the specialty structure of economics is a case in point: this primarily algorithmic work only becomes insightful when its results are combined with narrative accounts of the recent history of economics or when it identifies "intriguing patterns that invite more in-depth, qualitative research" (Claveau and Gingras 2016, p. 552). SNA can also be implemented in unreasonable ways, especially when the desire to use the method takes precedence over the soundness of the research strategy. Indeed, SNA does not apply to all questions. Even questions that ask for an analysis of relations might not best be answered by SNA. This is because some questions can only be answered adequately by an approach that allows for a thick history and not by an analysis that demands – at least in a first step – a simplification of those relationships. SNA is thus a complement to other methods, bringing its specific strengths to the systematic study of relational structures in the history of economics.

Applying SNA in history of economics requires not only mastering the traditional set of methods that historians of economics have been using all along. It also requires of the historian of economics to acquaint himself or herself with a set of computational tools and computer programs to analyze relational data. We want to conclude by noting that while this might sound challenging, many tools are user friendly. Among the multitude of computer programs that have emerged in the last decades to conduct SNA, only some are useful to the historian (of economics). There are packages for beginners, packages for network representation, and a set of general-purpose programs. Two websites to find further information should be mentioned here. *Programming Historian* offers tutorials and instructions for some of the relevant software packages (see https://programminghistorian.org). *Historical Network Analysis* (see http://historicalnetworkresearch.org) provides a wide array of sources, such as an extensive bibliography on the use of SNA in history, links to software tools, tutorials, a list of events for historians applying SNA, among many other resources.

Conclusion

In this chapter, we discussed the usefulness and limitations of SNA as a method for the historian of economics. Our main argument was two-fold. First, we showed how SNA could serve not only as a tool for representation but foremost as a tool for discovery and confirmation. Second, the application of SNA requires historical knowledge at various steps in the analysis. At least in that sense, its meaningful application has to be complemented by more traditional approaches. We hope to have shown why historians of economics have reasons to add SNA to their toolbox. Being a method that helps us to discover hidden patterns in historical data, SNA can complement more traditional methods of the historian of economics.

Notes

1 Authors are in alphabetical order; they contributed equally to this chapter.
2 For detailed introductions to SNA and its techniques, see Wassermann and Faust (1994) and Scott (2000). See Claveau and Herfeld (2018) for a short overview of the use of SNA in the history of economics.
3 For a discussion of other goals of network representations when it is used at the start of the phase of data analysis (e.g., finding coding errors), see step 5 in the second section of this chapter.
4 This technique has recently been used in the history of economics by Claire Wright (2016), see her Figure 1.
5 This function is part of the igraph package in R (Csardi and Nepusz 2006).
6 Networks can have weighted edges, which capture the intensity or tightness of a relation, and not only the fact that a relation exists.
7 A similar point could have been made about SNA as a method of confirmation (rather than discovery) if, instead of using a primarily inductive approach as Claveau and Gingras do, one of the few existing SNA in the history of economics would have started with a hypothesis to be tested.

8 Note that those six steps do not necessarily occur in a perfect sequence when conducting the analysis – they can overlap.
9 For a discussion about applying hermeneutic methods in the history of economics, see Emmett (2003).
10 This step can be analytically distinguished from the previous step of source selection, but the temporal order of these two steps is rarely neat.
11 Indeed, Laumann et al. (1992, 66fn) state in the footnote right after introducing their distinction that what they call "nominalist" is called "realist" by another scholar.
12 In these respects, it is similar to the SNA of Claveau and Gingras (2016) extensively discussed earlier in this chapter.
13 This is not to say that in their analysis, Herfeld and Doehne would not have detected those connections and their relevance without the representation but it certainly helped.
14 For a further elaboration of some of those arguments, see also Doehne and Herfeld (ms.).

References

Bixler, Matthias (2016). "Die Wurzeln der Historischen Netzwerkforschung." In Düring, Marten et al. (eds.), *Handbuch Historische Netzwerkforschung: Grundlagen und Anwendung*, Münster, Hamburg, Berlin, Wien, London, LIT Verlag: 45–61.
Bernard, H. Russell, Killworth, Peter D., and Sailer, Lee (1982). "Informant Accuracy in Social-Network Data V. An Experimental Attempt to Predict Actual Communication from Recall Data." *Social Science Research* 11: 33–66.
Borgatti, Stephen P., Mehra, Ajay, Brass, Daniel J., and Labianca, Giuseppe (2009). "Network Analysis in the Social Sciences." *Science* 323: 892–895.
Claveau, François, and Gingras, Yves (2016). "Macrodynamics of Economics: A Bibliometric History." *History of Political Economy* 48(4): 551–592.
Claveau, François, and Herfeld, Catherine (2018). "Network Analysis in the History of Economics." *History of Political Economy* 50(3).
Csardi, Gabor, and Nepusz, Tamas (2006). "The Igraph Software Package for Complex Network Research." *InterJournal Complex Systems*, 1695, available at: www.inter journal.org/manuscript_abstract.php?361100992
Doehne, Malte, and Herfeld, Catherine (ms.). "Five Reasons for the Use of Network Analysis in the History of Economics." Unpublished manuscript.
Düppe, Till, and Weintraub, E. Roy (2014). "Siting the New Economic Science: The Cowles Commission's Activity Analysis Conference of June 1949." *Science in Context* 27(3): 453–483.
Düring, Marten, Eumann, Ulrich, Stark, Martin, and von Keyserlingk, Linda (eds) (2016). *Handbuch Historische Netzwerkforschung: Grundlagen und Anwendung*, Münster, Hamburg, Berlin, Wien, London, LIT Verlag.
Düring, Marten, and Kerschbaumer, Florian (2016). "Quantifizierung und Visualisierung. Anknüpfungspunkte in den Geschichtswissenschaften." In Düring, Marten et al. (eds), *Handbuch Historische Netzwerkforschung: Grundlagen und Anwendung*, Münster, Hamburg, Berlin, Wien, London, LIT Verlag: 31–43.
Düring, Marten (2015). Verdeckte Soziale Netzwerke im Nationalsozialismus. Berliner Hilfsnetzwerke Für Verfolgte Juden. Berlin, De Gruyter.
Düring, Marten, and von Keyserlingk, Linda (2015). "Netzwerkanalyse in den Geschichtswissenschaften. Historische Netzwerkanalyse als Methode für die

Erforschung von historischen Prozessen." In Schützeichel, Rainer, and Jordan, Stefan (eds), *Prozesse*. Wiesbaden, Springer: 337–350.

Emirbayer, Mustafa (1997). "Manifesto for a Relational Sociology." *American Journal of Sociology* 103(2): 281–317.

Emmett, Ross (2003). "Exegesis, Hermeneutics, and Interpretation." In Samuels, Warren J., Biddle, Jeff E., and Davis, John B. (eds), *A Companion to the History of Economic Thought*. Oxford, Blackwell Publishing: 523–537.

Erickson, Paul, Klein, Judy L., Daston, Lorraine, Lemov, Rebecca M., Sturm, Thomas, and Gordin, Michael D. (2013). *How Reason Almost Lost Its Mind: The Strange Career of Cold War Rationality*. Chicago, London, The University of Chicago Press.

Fogel, Robert (1975). "Limits of Quantitative Methods in History." *American Historical Review* 80(1): 329–350.

Fontaine, Philippe (2016). "Other Histories of Recent Economics: A Survey." *History of Political Economy* 48(3): 373–421.

Herfeld, Catherine (ms.). "Not More than Exchanging Tools: Early Encounters Between Mathematical Economists and the Behavioral Sciences Movement, 1950–56." Unpublished manuscript.

Herfeld, Catherine, and Doehne, Malte (2018). "The Diffusion of Scientific Innovations: A Role Typology." *Studies in History and Philosophy of Science: Part A* (forthcoming).

Hoddeson, Lillian. (2006). "The Conflict of Memories and Documents: Dilemmas and Pragmatics of Oral History." In Doel, R. E. and Söderqvist, T. (eds), *The Historiography of Contemporary Science, Technology, and Medicine: Writing Recent Science*. London, Routledge: 187–200.

Hoover, Kevin D. (1988). *The New Classical Macroeconomics: A Sceptical Inquiry*. Oxford, Basil Blackwell.

Hoover, Kevin D. (1991). "Scientific Research Program or Tribe? A Joint Appraisal of Lakatos and the New Classical Macroeconomics." In De Marchi, Neil, and Blaug, Mark (eds), *Appraising Modern Economics: Studies in the Methodology of Scientific Research Programs*. Aldershot, Edward Elgar: 364–394.

Klein, Judy (2016). "Implementation Rationality: The Nexus of Psychology and Economics at the RAND Logistics Systems Laboratory, 1956–1966." *History of Political Economy* 48(1): 198–225.

Laumann, Edward O., Marsden, Peter V., and Prensky, David (1992). "The Boundary Specification Problem in Network Analysis." In Freeman, Linton C., White, Douglas R., Romney, and Antone Kimball (eds), *Research Methods in Social Network Analysis*. New Brunswick, Transaction Publishers: 61–79.

Lemercier, Claire (2015). "Formal Network Methods in History: Why and How?. Social Networks, Political Institutions, and Rural Societies." In Fertig, Georg (ed.), *Brepols*: 281–310.

Lucas, Robert E., Jr. (1976). "Econometric Policy Evaluation: A Critique." *Carnegie-Rochester Conference Series on Public Policy* 1(1): 19–46.

Knoke, David, and Yang, Song (2008). *Social Network Analysis*, 2nd ed. Los Angeles, London, New Delhi, Singapore, SAGE Publications.

Moggridge, Donald E. (2003). "Biography and the History of Economics." In Samuels, Warren J., Biddle, Jeff E., and Davis, John B. (eds), *A Companion to the History of Economic Thought*, Oxford, Blackwell Publishing: 588–605.

Newman, M. E. J. (2010) *Networks: An Introduction*. Oxford, Oxford University Press.

Schabas, Margaret (1992). "Breaking Away: History of Economics as History of Science." *History of Political Economy* 24(1): 187–203.

Scott, John (2000). *Social Network Analysis: A Handbook*, 2nd ed. London, Sage Publications.

Stark, Martin (2016). "Netzwerkberechnung. Anmerkungen zur Verwendung formaler Methoden." In Düring, Marten et al. (eds), *Handbuch Historische Netzwerkforschung: Grundlagen und Anwendung*. Münster, Hamburg, Berlin, Wien, London, LIT Verlag: 155–171.

Tilly, Charles (1973). "Computers in Historical Analysis." *Computers and the Humanities* 7(6): 323–335.

Tilly, Charles (2004). "Observations of Social Processes and Their Formal Representations." *Sociological Theory* 22(4): 595–602

Wassermann, Stanley, and Faust, Katherine (1994). *Social Network Analysis*. Cambridge, Cambridge University Press.

Weintraub, E. Roy (1999). "How Should We Write the History of Twentieth-Century Economics?" *Oxford Review of Economic Policy* 15(4): 139–152.

Weintraub, E. Roy (2005). "2004 HES Presidential Address: Autobiographical Memory and the Historiography of Economics." *Journal of the History of Economic Thought* 27(1): 1–11.

Weintraub, E. Roy (2017). "Game Theory and Cold War Rationality: A Review Essay." *Journal of Economic Literature* 55(1): 148–161.

Weintraub, E. Roy, Meardon, Stephen J., Gayer, Ted, and Banzhaf, H. Spencer (1998). "Archiving the History of Economics." *Journal of Economic Literature* XXXV: 1496–1501.

Whetherell, Charles (1998). "Historical Network Analysis." *International Review of Social History* 43 (Supplement): 125–144.

Wright, Claire (2016). "The 1920s Viennese Intellectual Community as a Center for Ideas Exchange: A Network Analysis." *History of Political Economy* 48(4): 593–623.

6 Prosopography

The missing link in the history
of economics

Andrej Svorenčík[1]

Introduction

Prosopography, or less accurately collective biography, is an established historiographical method with a long history and development (Keats-Rohan 2007a; Verboven, Carlier, and Dumolyn 2007). Although it lacks a universally agreed definition, let me define it for the purposes of this chapter as a historiographical method that that collects and analyzes shared biographical features of a group of people from a specific, well-defined historical or social contexts.[2] Prosopography is both the collection as well as the analysis of such biographical data. It goes beyond a mere systematic compilation of biographical data about people of interest according to some pre-determined criteria. It is the study of biographical details of individuals in aggregate, not a biography of groups. Therefore the alternative, more appealing term collective biography is somewhat misleading (Keats-Rohan 2007b). The result of a prosopographic research is a statistically based group biography, not "a group portrait pieced together from a series of case studies" (Stone 1971, p. 51).

Prosopography is a term familiar to historians, but is almost unknown amongst economists and historians of economics.[3] One of the oldest prosopographic projects is the Prosopographia Imperii Romani. It covers notable, high-profile people who lived in the Roman Empire from 31 BC until AD 261, the high-period of the Empire. It first appeared in the late 19th century and was then followed by an extended second edition published over the years 1933–2015.[4] It has not only become the ultimate biographical reference book for scholars working on that period, it also allowed identifying various patterns linking different groups within the Roman aristocracy, how they dominated the political scene across generations, and protected their own interest (Syme 1939, 1989; Barnes 2007). Similarly 41 volumes have been published so far in the History of Parliament Project that canvasses the members of the House of Commons since 1386 with some gaps until 1832. Additional periods are still being added, but currently 21,426 biographies of members of Parliament (MPs) on more than 20,000 pages have been published since the 1960s.[5] Earlier prosopographic studies of MPs in the Elizabethan era by the historian John E. Neale in the 1950s showed for instance that most of the seats in the Commons, which were reserved for townsmen, were, in fact, occupied by the gentry who gained them through a system of "clientage" (Neale 1949, 1953–7).

Both are examples of the elitist approach to prosopography. The other type is mass prosopography which studies a wider target population. Lawrence Stone in his classic treatment of prosopography argued that it is more statistically oriented and more sociological in its analysis (Stone 1971). Both approaches analyze phenomena that are supra-individual. Put differently, prosopography analyzes "the shared conditions and experiences of a group of individuals via the examination of their (collective) lives" (Stuckey 2007, p. 499).[6]

Steven Shapin and Arnold Thackray advocated already in the early 1970s that prosopographic research could reform the key notions of "the scientist" and "the scientific community" (Shapin and Thackray 1974). But historians of science had been interested in prosopography since the inception of the field by George Sarton and prosopographic research has pertained to history of science topics even prior to that (Merton 1979). Lewis Pyenson argued that "of all the techniques used in the history of science, collective biography has produced some of the most suggestive analyses" and that "prosopography is a particularly appropriate technique for examining the ordinary scientist" (Pyenson 1977, p. 157, 179). Some of the many applications of prosopography to history of science include the analysis of attendees of immunology conferences in the 1950s and 1960s, and a study of over 160 subscribers of De Moivres' 1730 mathematics book *Miscellanea Analytica* (Söderqvist and Silverstein 1994; Bellhouse, Renouf, Raut, and Bauer 2009).[7]

However, the most typical prosopographic research related to history and sociology of science are studies of medieval universities which typically provide a comprehensive social analysis of individual universities with emphasis on social stratification and mobility, geographical origin, and academic peregrination of their students and faculty. Collating multiple such university studies has allowed examining "personal, institutional and ideological links between individual universities" and in regards to medieval society as a whole career trajectories of graduates, "their relation to political and social elites, gradual promotion of education as a qualification pre-requisite for certain vocations" have been investigated (Neškudla 2007, p. 253 and references therein).

Prosopography is particularly well suited for identifying hidden hierarchies or relationships that remain elusive when the focus is on the most prominent members of a group. The prosopographic method provides an interpretative framework for understanding academic communities that is novel to the history of economics and this paper show where its potential lies (Svorenčík 2014). Nevertheless prosopography "does not have all the answers, but it is ideally fitted to reveal the web of sociopsychological ties that bind a group together" (Stone 1971, p. 66). Ultimately, in connection with other historiographic methods, prosopography could lead to richer, more complete historical narratives about communities that are better empirically grounded. The rest of the chapter provides some of the possible avenues for achieving that in history of economics.

The rising number of economists – a case for prosopography

Economics evolved over the centuries emerging from moral philosophy at first as political or national economy and only towards the end of the 19th century the current name was adopted. However, that did not imply that educational standards required for being an (academic) economist were the same as was demonstrated by Marion Fourcade (2009). Only in the postwar period homogenization of the discipline took place, with American economics academe becoming the paragon to be emulated across the globe while various local and national traditions gradually faded into the past. The normalization process is nowadays essentially complete. Without a PhD in economics one cannot become an academic economist anymore.[8] In other words, PhDs in economics are the building blocks of any academic economics community. And to understand such communities, the processes in which these blocks are built must be understood.

In American economics academe, certainly in the economics postwar period, career promotion is regulated through a tenure track system and each step of the ladder – starting with the job market, promotion reviews, and, to a lesser extent, attribution of scientific credit – heavily relies on advisers' letters of recommendation. Advisers and their PhD students are key parts of academic production and reproduction cycle and thus can be viewed as basic units of a prosopographic study in the history of economics. This implies that the advisor-advisee relation is a key relationship to be understood and investigated.

Just take a look at the numbers of PhD degrees in economics awarded in the USA in the period 1950–2013. There were 43,693 degrees granted in total, as reported by the National Center for Education Statistics (Figure 6.1). The number of all economists produced in the 1950s is nowadays produced within two years alone. In contrast, by 2017 there have been 79 (with 59 American) economics Nobel winners worldwide since 1969 and just 39 John Bates Clark medalists since 1947 (Cherrier and Svorenčík 2017). They are the prime candidates of the traditional approach that depicts history of economics as a series of great minds and their path-breaking ideas. Yet, they represent only a small fraction of the tens of thousands of American economists of the postwar period. A similar growth can be observed in the number of economics departments with a doctoral program (Figure 6.2). There have been over 100 such programs since 1970.

To understand postwar history of economics one needs to deal with the staggering rise in size and specialization of the economics discipline. Prosopography with its focus on the aggregate, the forest rather than individual trees, might be particularly useful in shedding light on this problem.

More than half of PhDs in the period 1904–1939 graduated from just four universities: Harvard, Columbia, Wisconsin, Chicago (Spellman and Gabriel 1978, p. 183). The growth of economics PhD programs has lowered this production concentration. Yet, it remains highly unequal as depicted

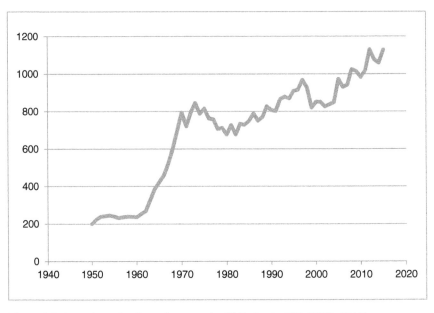

Figure 6.1 Annual production of economics PhDs in the US (1950–2015).

Source: Data from the Digest of Education Statistics (2015), National Center for Education Statistics.

Note: Data for the 1950s are reported every other year. The graph interpolates the missing values.

in Table 6.1. Furthermore, analyzing the background of faculty members with a doctoral program in 1992, almost 45 percent graduated from just ten departments (Pieper and Willis 1999). Taken together this suggests that the concentration in the output of economics PhDs translates into a similar concentration of supervising faculty and vice versa.

Table 6.2 further zooms onto the replication mechanism by summarizing the educational background of 30 most productive advisers at three most iconic American economics departments: Harvard, Chicago, and MIT. Almost two-thirds, 56 out of 90, of these prolific advisers graduated from one of those institutions.[9]

The PhD program at MIT was established more than half a century after Harvard's or Chicago's (Weintraub 2014). This may explain why MIT has a much lower number – 9 instead of 15 – of their own most productive advisers. However, MIT's youth did not impede its meteoric rise as indicated by its early 1990s ranking, share of faculty, and share of graduates in Table 6.1 as well as in Svorenčík (2014). Moreover, around two-thirds of all PhDs of these three departments – either since the inception of the programs or since 1944 when MIT produced its first PhD – can trace their academic lineage to these advisers.

One can construct academic family trees with generations of economists being connected via the advisor-advisee relation. For MIT, a relatively young program, I was able to connect up to three generations of MIT educated

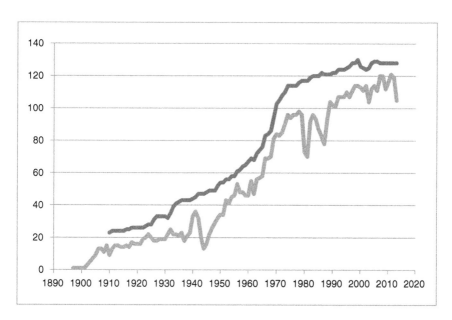

Figure 6.2 Number of economics departments in the US based on the Annual Lists of Doctoral Dissertations in Economics conferred at North American institutions published by the AEA from 1905 until 2014

Note: The lower line indicates the number of departments which have reported at least one PhD in a given year. The upper line estimates the number of economics departments with an active doctoral program (i.e. at least one graduate within a five year window). Given the low quality of reports prior to 1910, the upper line starts only then. Reporting by departments is voluntary which may explain some of the blue line drops in the post-war period.

Table 6.1 Summary statistics of leading US economics departments

Economics department at	Number of graduates 1904–2013	Number of graduates 1950–1991	Share of US economics faculty in 1992 who graduated from the department	Number of US economics faculty in 1992 and the (rank) of the department
Harvard University	2,872	1,463	7.1%	233 (1)
Columbia University	2,379	871	3.0%	100 (10)
University of Wisconsin, Madison	2,226	1,043	4.0%	130 (7)
University of Chicago	2,097	817	5.6%	184 (3)
UC Berkeley	2,038	1,214	5.3%	174 (4)
University of Minnesota	1,295	689	3.5%	115(8)
University of Pennsylvania	1,293	609	2.8%	93 (11)

(continued)

Table 6.1 (continued)

Economics department at	Number of graduates 1904–2013	Number of graduates 1950–1991	Share of US economics faculty in 1992 who graduated from the department	Number of US economics faculty in 1992 and the (rank) of the department
University of Michigan	1,284	755	2.3%	77 (13)
MIT	1,263	684	6.5%	213 (2)
Stanford University	1,233	635	4.6%	150 (5)
TOTAL	**17,980**	**8780**	**44.7%**	**1,495**(-)

Source: Data in the second and third columns are calculations by the author from the Annual Lists of Doctoral Dissertations in Economics for the years 1904–2013. Data in the fourth and fifth columns are from Pieper and Willis (1999).

Table 6.2 PhD background of 30 most productive advisers in the period since the inception of each program until 2013 at three leading economics departments

30 most Productive Advisers active at Department:	Share of Graduates Since Inception	Share of Graduates Since 1944	Adviser Graduated From		
			Harvard	Chicago	MIT
Harvard	55.5%	61.0%	12	2	2
Chicago	72.3%	74.5%	3	15	1
MIT	70.0%	70.0%	10	2	9

Source: Data from author's unpublished prosopographic research.

Note: Only the third column refers to the period post-1944. The share of MIT graduates refers to the intensive supervision measure (Svorenčík 2014). Chicago's 30th most productive adviser Lloyd Mints is the only adviser that does not have a PhD degree, although he did some graduate work at Chicago. He is not included in Chicago's count of 15 Chicago-graduating faculty.

advisers and four complete generations of advisers working at MIT (Svorenčík 2014, pp. 122–123). A similar pattern emerges for the other two departments. Given how often the most productive advisers are graduates of these departments, the elite of the economics profession – defined by their membership to these three departments – is very much interconnected. What does it imply about the structure and operation of the economics discipline? What about the rest of the economics academe that is outside this triad?

The prosopographic method is underutilized in the history of economics. To my best knowledge, my work on the MIT economics department is the very first research that explicitly refers to and applies prosopography.[10] I showed that by 2011 there were 1,449 members of the departmental population: 1,316 MIT PhD holders and 133 supervising faculty without a PhD from MIT. There were 31 additional advisers who received their doctorates from MIT. These second-generation advisers together with their advisers form a group of 49 faculty, or 30 percent of all faculty, and they effectively supervised around 65 percent of all graduates.

A similar picture emerges for Chicago and Harvard: a small circle of advisers who have supervised a disproportionally large portion of students, and such supervisors very likely graduated from the same department. My work on other US economics departments indicates that this might be a universally shared feature across American economics academe.

How to apply prosopography in history of economics and elsewhere

Economics departments with their networks of PhD graduates linked to supervising faculty are not the only playground for prosopography in the history of economics. Prosopography can be applied to a variety of topics including but not limited to entire subfields within economics or schools of thought, academic societies such as the American Economic Association (AEA) (Hoover and Svorenčík 2018), scientific awards such as the John Bates Clark Medal (Cherrier and Svorenčík 2017), conference and summer school participants, epistolary networks, women in economics (Johnson 2017), and funding agencies. The author of this chapter dreams of eventually applying prosopography to the entire economics discipline. Such a massive prosopography could produce a unifying framework for understanding major changes economics underwent in the 20th century – economics becoming a mathematical discipline that started using models, econometrics, and eventually experiments; a discipline that shifted its center of gravity from Europe to the US as well as changed from being pluralistic to mostly homogenous (Weintraub 2002; Düppe and Weintraub 2014; Morgan 1990, 2012; Svorenčík 2015, 2016, 2017; Svorenčík and Maas 2016; Morgan and Rutherford 1998; Backhouse and Cherrier 2017).

Typically prosopographic analysis begins with the delineation of a target population and relational structures of interest. Then it continues with the collation and assembly of relevant biographical data which result in a core biographical directory or database. Subsequently, a set of questions about factors related to relational structures – such as educational background, adviser name, and career trajectory – are uniformly applied to everyone in the population. The answers to such questions are then examined for patterns and variations within the target population, and analyzed with more advanced tools. The objective of prosopography is "to unveil otherwise concealed influences within political or social structures and organizations, influences which may not be apparent from analyses of overt political statements or institutional arrangements" (Stuckey 2007, p. 499). These steps are explained in more detail in the following two sections.

Target population and its relations

Each prosopographic project starts with the identification of a target population, its members' biographical characteristics and relational structures. In general, the population might be limited by a thematic, chronological, and geographic scope.

Such limits and boundaries can already be a representation of various relational structures. In most cases, members of the population are not entirely known prior to the beginning of the project. They need to be identified and for each of them data about pre-selected characteristics and relations collected.

My joint work with Beatrice Cherrier on the history of the John Bates Clark Medal had at first a clearly defined target population – all the 39 winners since the Medal's inception in 1947 (Cherrier and Svorenčík 2017). We wanted to know: 1) where these Medalists got their education – both undergraduate and graduate; 2) where they worked since graduation and in particular at the time of receiving the Medal; and 3) did they go on to win a Nobel Prize in Economics Sciences. The relational structure was as simple as it gets – which economist is a Medalist and which Medalist is also a Nobel laureate. This is an example of the elitist approach to prosopography. Soon we realized that we needed also to collect information on who supervised the Medalists and who was a member of the AEA Committee on Honors and Awards which selects a Medalist from a pool of eligible distinguished American economists under the age of 40. Members of this expanded target population with their new relations to the Medalists could potentially produce additional insights into the relation that drew our research – who is a Medalist. Are there any Medalists who have supervised some Medalists? Are there any links between the Medalists and those who select them? These questions were in part motivated by other, mostly ongoing prosopographic projects and in part by historical research on prizes in other sciences that typically argue that besides scientific merit being the right person at the right place and time is another important factor of success.

A far more ambitious inroad into the operations of the AEA and its leadership is my joint research with Kevin Hoover (Hoover and Svorenčík 2018). Our target population includes all members of the electoral pool of the AEA for the period 1950–2018. The electoral pool consists of: 1) annually elected members of the AEA Executive Committee (president, two vice-presidents, two ordinary members of the Executive Committee); 2) members of the AEA Nominating Committee, which is appointed by the president-elect and recommends to the Executive Committee a slate of candidates for next elections; and 3) losing candidates (two losing vice-presidents and two losing ordinary members of the Executive Committee). These target population subsets represent some of the relational structures that we are interested in. Other structures included biographical, educational, and job-related (permanent positions) histories as well as information on significant awards such as elected Fellowship of the Econometric Society.

Overall there were 1,037 positions identified including 65 presidents, 130 vice-presidents, 130 ordinary elected members of Executive Committee, 65 chairs of Nomination Committee, 387 members of Nominating Committee, 130 losing vice-presidential candidates, and 130 losing ordinary-member candidates. However only 537 distinct individuals occupied all these positions, filling on average 1.93 positions per person. These individuals became the core biographical directory of this prosopographic study. They graduated from only

43 different universities and worked for 140 different employers. Information was collected using official published records of the AEA including its membership lists, various editions of *Who's Who in Economics* (Blaug 1986), online CVs, and, infrequently, direct email inquiries.

The historian's input in creating this dataset was actually in disentangling the intricate details of how AEA's leadership reproduces and how changes in bylaws affect this process. Especially the link between the Executive Committee and the Nominating Committee was crucial as it provides another connection and reinforcement between the successive generations of the AEA's leadership. Another input came in making sure that the data are consistent across all people in our target population. Entries in CVs varied a lot in the description of degrees and names of schools. In rare instances, almost exclusively only in the 1950s, there were members of the electoral pool who studied in Europe and had not earned a PhD. Therefore the variable highest degree had to be introduced to account for these exceptions.

In the MIT Economics Department case mentioned earlier, the pre-selected characteristics included the full name of the student, names of their advisers including their roles – adviser, co-adviser, chair, committee member – when available, year of graduation, and the title of the dissertation (which was actually not analyzed) (Svorenčík 2014). The key relational structures were who advises whom, who is a student, who is a faculty member. Almost all required data were easily obtained from MIT library records. Information on just 1 percent of PhDs was obtained through an inquiry with the MIT Archives. The former took no longer than an hour, the latter several weeks. Unfortunately, this was a rare instance of low-hanging fruit and such a quick data collection cannot be replicated with other economics departments. Instead, based on my experience of collecting such data for various departments, a variety of strategies need to be pursued. Let me briefly list some of the effective ones, starting with the easiest.[11]

There are available, though incomplete, lists of graduates reported annually by the AEA. Often library records can be used to identify not only PhD students, but also their advisers. Dissertation databases with scanned dissertations are quite helpful for the period after 1990. Rarely, such as in the case of Wisconsin (Lampman 1993), there are already published department histories that can contain valuable registers. University-wide graduation lists can identify omitted PhDs and faculty members.

Contacting the target department can be quite helpful, especially if you know the chair or someone who can vouch for you. In my experience, it is quite usual that there is no response. If there is one, then often there are no data to be shared, or alleged privacy reasons prevent the department from doing so. But even if the department is willing to share its data, they are typically incomplete and often ridden with errors such as inconsistent reporting of roles. Departmental, graduate office, or student records might yield further evidence, though such files are typically restricted as they contain sensitive private information such as grades and social security numbers.

When all these attempts are unsuccessful or yield little, the best recourse is to directly consult the doctoral dissertations. Typically they contain an inserted or pasted leaf with the name of the student, dissertation title, year of the defense, and advisers or committee members. This can be quite a laborious task, especially if hundreds or thousands of dissertations need to be checked. It took me over two years to do that for the Harvard PhDs. For instance, well into the late 1950s Harvard committee members only signed the acceptance sheet in the dissertations and their names were not typed. Even more importantly, information on the various roles adviser, co-adviser, chair, and committee member might be missing or incomplete. Then historian's input becomes crucial. If the inserted leaves follow the same pattern such as that the chair is always listed first, one can infer this important role without clear textual evidence.

The construction of a dataset thus requires collating various sources, merging records, transcribing contemporary hands, understanding the rules behind the order of names (various types of positions) and general cleaning of raw data. While this type of research has a technical element to it, a historian's hand is essential.

From analysis to interpretation

Once data about the target population are collected, analysis can proceed. Though the reality is less clear-cut. Often preliminary analysis is conducted to quench curiosity while data are still being collected and this leads towards unexpected questions that require additional data or new relational structures to be added to the existing dataset. Those include but are not limited to information about career trajectories, undergraduate education details, leadership positions, membership in influential bodies, distinctions, awards, prizes, editorial positions, publication and citation records.

The most basic analytical tools for prosopography are simple descriptive statistics such as averages of relevant variables, frequency counts (e.g. Table 6.1) and contingency tables (e.g. Table 6.2). Take for instance the following distribution of educational and work locations for John Bates Clark Medalists (JBCM) observed by Cherrier and me (Table 6.3). On its own, the table contains a subset of all departments; namely the most frequent education and job locations of the Medalists. These frequency counts are accompanied by a count of distinct locations for each category which actually drives the interpretation of the data.

Based on Table 6.3 we observe an increasing concentration of locations or, put differently, their decreasing diversity – from undergraduate, then graduate education, first employment, and to employment at the time of the JBCM. Medalists between 1947 and 2017 earned their undergraduate degree from 23 different institutions. Of these institutions, however, 18 educated only one medalist each – though this cannot be seen from the Table 6.3. Medalists graduated from just 12 different institutions, approximately just half the number of distinct undergraduate degree institutions. Harvard and

Table 6.3 Increasing concentration of locations where JBC Medalists studied and worked

Location	Under-graduate degree	PhD or highest degree	First employment	All jobs prior to JBCM	Employment at the time of JBCM
MIT	1	10	4	4	8
Harvard University	9	9	9	9	9
University of Chicago	2	4	5	8	7
Stanford University	1	3	5	9	4
Oxford University	3	3		2	
Princeton University	2	2	5	5	4
Columbia University	0	2	2	2	1
University of Minnesota	1	1		1	
UC Berkeley	2	0	3	3	3
University of Michigan	0	0	2	2	1
University of Pennsylvania	0	0	1	2	1
Yale University	1	0	1	2	1
Pittsburgh	0	0	1	1	
Number of distinct locations	**23**	**12**	**11**	**13**	**10**

Note: The fifth column provides a cumulative count of all jobs for all 39 Medalists—some worked at multiple institutions before becoming a medalist (Cherrier and Svorenčík 2017).

MIT together account for half of the Medalists. Both departments educated at least twice as many graduates than the third most-frequent institution, Chicago with four Medalists. When we move from education to employment locations, we see another increase in concentration. The number of distinct locations where Medalists were first employed and where they were active at the time of the award is even smaller than the number of graduate degree institution. Clark Medalists belonged to only ten different universities at the time of the award. Harvard leads the list with nine Medalists, MIT has eight, and Chicago seven. The increasing concentration of locations follows the same pattern that is observed among the AEA leadership documented by Hoover and Svorenčík (2018).

While the Table 6.3 clearly shows that Harvard and MIT outperform other departments in the number of PhD with a JBCM, it does not reveal much about the historical dynamics that can be teased out from the dataset when the temporal and departmental dimensions are superimposed. Figure 6.3 depicts how the cumulative count of the number of Medalists graduating from three selected departments evolved in time. It shows that from early on Harvard dominated all other departments and was an incubator for JBCMs. However, from the late-1990s MIT experienced a rapid surge from just three Medalists to ten and in 2010 it overtook Harvard. Between 1999 and 2012 seven out of the nine newly minted Medalists were MIT graduates. Until the mid-1990s MIT competed with Chicago for the second place.

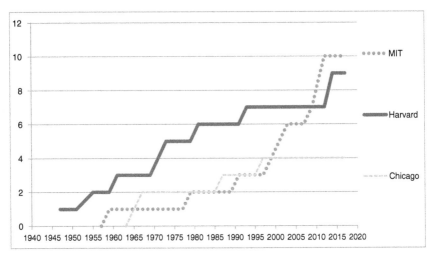

Figure 6.3 Cumulative view of three selected PhD Institutions and the number of
their graduates who received the Clark Medal

Note: Harvard's longstanding dominance and MIT's surge in the 1990s and 2000s is the most
salient feature.

MIT's dominance among JBCMs can be also demonstrated through a contingency table that contains all Medalists who either graduated from MIT,
were faculty members at the time of winning, or at least at some point during
their career were MIT faculty. Table 6.4 show that 17 out of 39 Medalists had
some sort of affiliation with MIT and just two of them were neither graduates
nor faculty at the time of award.[12]

Table 6.4 MIT-affiliated Clark JBC Medalists

		MIT Faculty at the time of award of the Clark Medal		*Sum*
		Yes	*No*	
PhD from MIT	Yes	3 Krugman 1991, Duflo 2010, Finkelstein 2012	7 Klein 1959, Stieglitz 1979, Shleifer 1999, Rabin 2001, Levitt 2003, Saez 2009, Levin 2011	10
	No	5 Samuelson 1947, Solow 1961, Fisher 1973, Hausman 1985, Acemoglu 2005	2 Summers 1993, Athey 2007	7
Sum		8	9	17

Source: Based on Svorenčík (2014, p. 124)

My last example deals with the issue how to assess multiple advisers in case of departmental prosopographies. When information on their role is available, then focusing on chairs and co-chairs and not on other committee members makes sense. In all other cases one can choose shared supervision is divided in equal parts (Svorenčík 2014). For instance, Susan Athey, the 2007 Clark Medalist and MIT faculty member from 1995 to 2001, was involved in supervising four graduate students at MIT, and her total supervision share was 1.83 students – the result of three half supervisions and a one-third supervision. In my interpretation, Athey influenced four MIT doctorates, but the actual strength of her influence was 1.83 students. I refer to these measures as *extensive* and *intensive supervision measures*. I give preference to the intensive supervision measure, as I implicitly assume that the each co-supervisor has an equal impact on a student. The available data for MIT do not allow establishing who had the decisive influence on a student.

Prosopographic analysis has benefited from the closeness to a number of disciplines such as genealogy, biography, onomastics, and sociography (Keats-Rohan 2007a, pp. 15–18). That is due for historical reasons how it emerged as a historiographic method. Another reason is the nature of data that prosopographic studies collected, especially in the early days. Often they dealt with sparse data that were dispersed across a large number of fragmentary sources, leading often at best to structured qualitative data about the target population.[13] Hence many projects devoted significant effort just to create an authoritative core biographical directory, that its full publication with comprehensive descriptive statistics in a book form was a major achievement in its own right. However, once we move to historical periods with abundant data – as is the case of 20th century economics – and make use of the advances in computing power, prosopographic research provides also the necessary data for more advanced approaches such as (social) network analysis and bibliometrics.

The techniques of network analysis such as centrality measures of entities in a group or cluster analysis and tools such as directed and undirected graphs, and graphs allow studying the intensity and closeness of relations as well as the temporal changes of those relations. There is a number of prosopographic studies that utilize social network analysis to gain insights into the social and political dynamics of a specific society such as 6th century configuration of Byzantine-Egyptian society, 18th century judges in Portugal, and the pillarization of the Belgian society in the belle époque (Comarinhas 2007; Verbruggen 2007; Graham and Ruffini 2007).

Many research questions in history of economics outlined in this chapter are also suitable for social network analysis. There are however biographical features that might not be fully susceptible to social network analysis, but are of substantial historical interest such as patterns of supervision and common features of PhD students of particular faculty (e.g. Solow or Fisher at MIT), interactions of lower and upper-tier departments in terms of sending their undergraduate students to graduate programs and back as faculty, and the decision-making of the AEA.

The crucial different that makes prosopography distinct from social network analysis is the necessary input of the historian in building up the dataset from raw historical data into clean data susceptible to statistical analysis. Prosopographers have been typically extensively involved in building their dataset, to a far greater degree than social network analysists. To exemplify that one can take the main example of Claveau and Herfeld's chapter on social network analysis in this volume, built on the work of Claveau and Gingras (2016). They used a list of references from around 400,000 articles published in economic journals that were obtained from a proprietary Web of Science database in order to perform a dynamic network analysis that allowed them to identify a changing specialty structure in economics from the late 1950s to 2014. True, the level of sophistication of their analysis is far above the average level of history of economics and they are well informed about the nature and limitations of their initial dataset (Lange, Schumacher, and Svorenčík 2017). Yet, they capitalize on an existing dataset. Such resources are not yet available for historians of economics who would like to skip the data collection part of prosopographic research.

Prosopography is coming!

Prosopography is a historiographical method that identifies and unearths shared biographical features between various people within a specific, well-defined historical or social context by collecting and analyzing shared biographical data. With a focus on individuals in aggregate, it provides an interpretative framework for understanding communities including academic ones. Prosopography is both the collection as well as the analysis of biographical data. In the course of this chapter, I have described various steps in constructing a core biographical directory of a target population with its various relations. The various examples of prosopographic analysis and interpretation highlight the importance and necessity of a historian's input in the whole endeavor.

Although prosopography is a well-established historiographic method, it is novel to the history of economics. I argued in this chapter that prosopography allows pursuing an alternative view of the history of economics, namely that it is largely a history of communities of economists, not a progression of singular minds. For instance, since the late 19th century American economics academe has been marked by its adoption of the PhD degree as the universal pre-condition of being an economist. This model has spread all over the world and has become the dominant one. With the rapid growth of the number of economists in the post-war period, with over 1000 new PhDs minted annually in recent years in the US alone, prosopography as an approach to the history of economics that considers the entire population instead of a select notable few is sorely needed.

Notes

1 Andrej Svorenčík, Department of Economics, University of Mannheim, L7 3–5, 68159 Mannheim, Germany. Email: svorencik@uni-mannheim.de Acknowledgment: I would like to express my gratitude to the participants of this book project, especially E. Roy Weintraub for early encouragement, and the attendees of the HES 2017

conference in Toronto. An abridged version of this paper appeared in a special issue of the journal *History of Political Economy*.

2 The classic treatment of prosopography was delivered by Lawrence (Stone 1971, 1987). In Stone's words, "prosopography is the investigation of the common background characteristics of a group of actors in history by means of a collective study of their lives" (1971, p. 46).

3 A notable exception are economics historians. They have studied business leaders networks along the elitist approach to prosopography at least since the 1930s, although they did not use the term prosopography initially (Cassis 1984; Mills 1945; Miller 1949). Prosopography has gained on prominence in economic history recently (Fellman 2014; Kansikas 2015).

4 Prosopography of the Later Roman Empire covering the subsequent period until AD641 was published in the years 1971–1992. The ongoing Prosopography of the Byzantine World is supposed to expand the coverage until 1265. See also (Cameron and British Academy 2003).

5 For more details see www.historyofparliamentonline.org/about (accessed on February 1, 2018).

6 Prosopography has evolved with the changing interests of historians. For an overview of the history of prosopography see (Keats-Rohan 2007a; Merton 1979, pp. 27–36).

7 Book subscribers are people those who financially supported the printing of a book and in the past were often listed in the book itself.

8 The process of curricular homogenization and career path pattern (tenure track) is still ongoing.

9 Furthermore while the ties between Harvard and Chicago are marked by equal standing, those between Harvard and MIT show Harvard's dominance in sending more advisers to MIT than it receives. However, the interaction between the two Charles River departments is more nuanced.

10 The work of Harald Hagemann on the interwar emigration of European, particularly Jewish economists, contains elements of prosopographic research; see for instance (Hagemann 2011).

11 Those include for instance Chicago, Harvard, Stanford, Berkeley, Columbia, Princeton, Yale, Northwestern, Wisconsin, Texas A&M, Caltech, Duke, UCLA, and many more.

12 This implies that the two Medalists were faculty either before or after being awarded the JBCM.

13 Some of the sources have included papyri, brick stamps, and tombstones.

References

Backhouse, Roger E., and Beatrice Cherrier (2017). "The Age of the Applied Economist: the Transformation of Economics since 1970." *History of Political Economy* 49(5).

Barnes, T. D. (2007). "Prosopography and Roman History." In Katharine Stephanie Benedicta Keats-Rohan (eds), *Prosopography Approaches and Applications: a Handbook*. Oxford, Unit for Prosopographical Research, Linacre College, University of Oxford: 83–93.

Bellhouse, D. R., E. M. Renouf, R. Raut, and M. A. Bauer (2009). "De Moivre's Knowledge Community: An Analysis of The Subscription List to the Miscellanea Analytica." *Notes and Records of the Royal Society of London* 63(2): 137–162.

Blaug, Mark (1986). Who's Who in Economics: A Biographical Dictionary of Major Economists, 1700–1986. Cambridge, MIT Press.

Cameron, Averil, and British Academy (2003). *Fifty Years of Prosopography: The Later Roman Empire, Byzantium and Beyond*. Oxford, New York, published for the British Academy by Oxford University Press.

Cassis, Youssef (1984). *City Bankers, 1890–1914*. Cambridge, Cambridge University Press.

Cherrier, Beatrice, and Andrej Svorenčík (2017). "Defining Excellence: Seventy Years of John Bates Clark Medals." Available online: https://papers.ssrn.com/sol3/papers.cfm?abstract_id=3004944. Accessed February 27, 2018.

Claveau, François, and Yves Gingras 2016). "Macrodynamics of Economics: A Bibliometric History." *History of Polical Economy* 48 (4): 551–592.

Comarinhas, Nuno (2007). "The Crown's Judges – the Judicial Profession in Ancien Regime Portugal, 1700–1709." In Katharine Stephanie Benedicta Keats-Rohan (eds), *Prosopography Approaches and Applications: A Handbook*. Oxford, Unit for Prosopographical Research, Linacre College, University of Oxford: 541–554.

Düppe, Till , and E. Roy Weintraub (2014). *Finding Equilibrium: Arrow, Debreu, McKenzie and the Problem of Scientific Credit*. Princeton, Princeton University Press.

Fellman, Susanna (2014). "Prosopographic studies of business leaders for understanding industrial and corporate change." *Business History* 56(1): 5–21.

Fourcade, Marion (2009). Economists and Societies : Discipline and Profession in the United States, Britain, and France, 1890s to 1990s. Princeton, Princeton University Press.

Graham, Shawn, and Giovanni Ruffini (2007). "Network Analysis and Greco-Roman Prosopography." In Katharine Stephanie Benedicta Keats-Rohan (eds), *Prosopography Approaches and Applications: A Handbook*. Oxford, Unit for Prosopographical Research, Linacre College, University of Oxford: 325–336.

Hagemann, Harald (2011). "European Émigrés and the Americanization of economics." *The European Journal of the History of Economic Thought* 18(5): 643–671.

Hoover, Kevin D., and Andrej Svorenčík (2018). "Who Runs the AEA? A Preliminary Analysis." Presentation at American Economics Association conference.

Johnson, Marianne (2017). "Daughters of Commons: Wisconsin Women and Institutionalism." Available online https://papers.ssrn.com/sol3/papers.cfm?abstract_id=2908348. Accessed February 27, 2018.

Kansikas, Juha (2015). "The Business Elite in Finland: A Prosopographical Study of Family Firm Executives 1762–2010." *Business History* 57(7): 1112–1132.

Keats-Rohan, Katharine Stephanie Benedicta (2007a). "Chameleon or Chimera? Understanding Prosopography." In Katharine Stephanie Benedicta Keats-Rohan (eds), *Prosopography Approaches and Applications: A Handbook*. Oxford, Unit for Prosopographical Research, Linacre College, University of Oxford: 1–32.

Keats-Rohan, Katharine Stephanie Benedicta (2007b). *Prosopography Approaches and Applications: A Handbook*. Oxford, Unit for Prosopographical Research, Linacre College, University of Oxford.

Lampman, Robert James (1993). *Economists at Wisconsin: 1892–1992*. Madison, Board of Regents of the University of Wisconsin System.

Lange, Jérôme, Reinhard Schumacher, and Andrej Svorenčík (2017). "From Antiquity to Modern Macro: An Overview of Contemporary Scholarship in the History of Economic Thought Journals, 2015–2016." *History of Economic Ideas* 25(2): 172–207.

Merton, Robert King (1979). *The Sociology of Science: An Episodic Memoir*. Carbondale: Southern Illinois University Press.

Miller, William (1949). "American Historians and the Business Elite." *The Journal of Economic History* 9(2): 184–208.

Mills, C. Wright (1945). "The American Business Elite: A Collective Portrait." *The Journal of Economic History* 5: 20–44.

Morgan, Mary S. (1990). *The History of Econometric Ideas*. Cambridge,New York, Cambridge University Press.

Morgan, Mary S. (2012). *The World in the Model: How Economists Work and Think*. Cambridge, New York, Cambridge University Press.

Morgan, Mary S., and Malcolm Rutherford (1998). *From Interwar Pluralism to Postwar Neoclassicism*. Durham, Duke University Press.

Neale, John Ernest (1949). *The Elizabethan House of Commons*. London, Cape.

Neale, John Ernest (1953–7). *Elizabeth I and her Parliaments*. 2 vols. London, Cape.

Neškudla, Bořek (2007) "The Prosopography of the Prague University of Laws, 1372–1419." In Katharine Stephanie Benedicta Keats-Rohan (eds), *Prosopography Approaches and Applications: A Handbook*. Oxford, Unit for Prosopographical Research, Linacre College, University of Oxford: 253–274.

Pieper, Paul J., and Rachel A. Willis (1999). "The Doctoral Origins of Economics Faculty and the Education of New Economics Doctorates." *The Journal of Economic Education* 30(01): 80–88.

Pyenson, Lewis (1977). "'Who the Guys Were': Prosopography in the History of Science." *History of Science* 15: 155–188.

Shapin, Steven, and Arnold Thackray (1974). "Prosopography as a Research Tool in History of Science: The British Scientific Community 1700–1900." *History of Science* 12: 1–28.

Söderqvist, Thomas, and Arthur M. Silverstein (1994). "Participation in Scientific Meetings: A New Prosopographical Approach to the Disciplinary History of Science: The Case of Immunology, 1951–72." *Social Studies of Science* 24: 513–548.

Spellman, William E., and D. Bruce Gabriel (1978). "Graduate Students in Economics, 1940–74." *American Economic Review* 68(1): 182–187.

Stone, Lawrence (1971). "Prosopography." *Daedalus* 100(1): 46–79.

Stone, Lawrence (1987). *The Past and the Present Revisited*. London, New York, Routledge & Kegan Paul.

Stuckey, Michael (2007). "'Enjoyed by the Laws of this Assembly': The Elizabethan Society of Antiquaries and the Prosopographical Approach." In Katharine Stephanie Benedicta Keats-Rohan (eds), *Prosopography Approaches and Applications: A Handbook*. Oxford, Unit for Prosopographical Research, Linacre College, University of Oxford: 499–525.

Svorenčík, Andrej (2014). "MIT's Rise to Prominence: Outline of a Collective Biography." *History of Political Economy* 46(5): 109–133.

Svorenčík, Andrej (2015). "The Experimental Turn: A History of Experimental Economics." PhD thesis. University of Utrecht.

Svorenčík, Andrej (2016). "The Sidney Siegel Tradition: The Divergence of Behavioral and Experimental Economics at the End of the 1980s." *History of Political Economy* 48 (suppl 1): 270–294.

Svorenčík, Andrej (2017). "Allocating Airport Slots – The History of Early Applied Experimental Research." *History of Political Economy* 49 (suppl 1): 240–263.

Svorenčík, Andrej, and Harro Maas (2016). The Making of Experimental Economics: Witness Seminar on the Emergence of a Field. Dordrecht, Springer.

Syme, Ronald (1939). *The Roman Revolution*. Oxford, Clarendon Press.

Syme, Ronald (1989). *The Augustan Aristocracy*. Oxford, Clarendon.

Verboven, Koenraad, Myriam Carlier, and Jan Dumolyn (2007). "A Short Manual to the Art of Prosopography." In Katharine Stephanie Benedicta Keats-Rohan (eds), *Prosopography Approaches and Applications: A Handbook*. Oxford, Unit for Prosopographical Research, Linacre College, University of Oxford: 35–70.

Verbruggen, Chrostophe (2007). "Literary Strategy during Flanders' Golden Decades (1880–1914): Combining Social Network Analysis and Prosopography." In Katharine Stephanie Benedicta Keats-Rohan (eds), *Prosopography Approaches and Applications: A Handbook*. Oxford, Unit for Prosopographical Research, Linacre College, University of Oxford: 579–601.

Weintraub, E. Roy (2002). *How Economics Became a Mathematical Science*. Durham, London, Duke University Press.

Weintraub, E. Roy (ed.) (2014). *MIT and the Transformation of American Economics*. Durham, Duke University Press.

Part III

Histories of the teaching of economics

7 Syllabi and examinations

Irwin L. Collier

Introduction

When it comes to economists, those contemporary or the academic scribblers of only a few years back, there can be no nature vs. nurture debate. Economists are simply not born, they are made, and they are made in graduate schools. It is there that they acquire the original kit that distinguishes them from other social scientists and policy analysts. Some go on to have brilliant careers refining the tools and contributing to the stock of knowledge that get passed on to subsequent generations. Most find a full life in applications of what had been learned in graduate school and in the delight of discovering for themselves what it was that they were once taught but only later comprehended.

Prospective historians of economics interested in the last 130 years of the discipline are well advised to pay attention to the evolution of the undergraduate and graduate programs within which successive generations of economists have been trained.[1] Anyone who has gone through the mill of a modern graduate education in economics should need little convincing that the graduate school experience was a major, if not *the* major, factor in establishing one's own scientific identity regarding the "interesting" questions of economics and those core methodologies and materials used to seek answers. Anyone who has an interest in the history of ideas sufficiently strong to survive the grind of that mill of graduate economics will not be surprised to hear that undergraduate and graduate economics programs today differ in both scope and method even from those of a generation ago, i.e., what was taught *then* to students who have just *now* crossed the retirement threshold.

Variation in economics education is not merely observed along a historical dimension. There have been enormous national differences in the economic canons taught to successive generations of students as well as program or institutional differences as well. One might argue that an indicator of the maturity of a discipline is the softening of these international/institutional accents. Historical questions concern the speed of convergence and the dynamic forces behind that convergence to something that arguably constitutes the canon of modern economics.

As we move back through history to the generation that taught the baby-boomers, the ranks of living witnesses to that history become thinner, a problem compounded by the natural decay of memory. We can be grateful for the earlier published autobiographical memoirs and transcribed oral histories that have provided us filtered glimpses of scientific experience. Nonetheless, undergraduate and graduate education has always been but an early slice of an economist's life well-lived, and only sometimes worthy of an early chapter in these memoirs. Sooner rather than later, the historian of economics even of the mid-20th century must lean more heavily on the documentary record, those conventional publications and other written artifacts found in libraries and archives, to track the contents of the analytical toolboxes passed across overlapping generations of economists.[2]

In comparison, historians of recent economics are facing information-engineering challenges of learning to harness the power from the enormous current of weblog postings, tweets, working papers, media transcripts and exploding databases to study the processes of scientific innovation and diffusion in the economics of this age. The pedagogy of walk-talk-and-chalk is almost relegated to the stuff of legend, and successive waves of duplication technologies have been forced to yield to the pdf-ing of lecture notes, syllabi, spreadsheets, and problem sets. The accumulation of video and audio recordings of lectures, panel discussions, and interviews contribute as well to a curse of dimensionality faced by historians of recent economics.

Now somewhere I imagine must be an invisible divide in our informational past that marks the frontier between the methodological problems that come from the relative scarcity of artifacts relevant for the study of the earlier evolution of the education and training of economists and the current problems of judiciously sampling from an ever-expanding Big Data universe. But whether as historians we are working one side of this frontier or the other, it makes great sense to embed our specific empirical concerns within a common framework. I am presuming that there is a great arc of continuity (I am not presuming smooth!) that connects the 1880s with, say, the 1980s with respect to the scope and methods of economics. Without a common framework, our respective narratives would resemble tunnel building from opposite sides of a mountain with the most likely result being two non-communicating parallel tunnels in the end. Does anyone really think there is a parallel Harvard, Chicago, Columbia, Wisconsin, Michigan universe? We really did get here from there.

I approach my task (working on the relatively deprived side of the digital frontier) in the spirit of Jacob Viner, whose own contributions to the history of economics were exemplary. In 1950 in a famous address he dared make the case for greater emphasis to be given to *scholarship* in the training regime of university education:

> My proposal is both sincere and modest. I give also only an old-fashioned and modest meaning to the term "scholarship". I mean by it nothing more than the pursuit of broad and exact knowledge of the history of the

working of the human mind as revealed in written records. I exclude from it, as belonging to a higher order of human endeavor, the creative arts, and scientific discovery.[3]

Now of course many, if not most, historians of economics believe themselves to be doing precisely that when not reaching for the high-hanging fruit of "scientific discovery". One presumes it takes little encouragement to continue reading old books and articles – that part of Vinerian scholarship is taken for granted here, as is to cultivate a working knowledge of economic history (especially the history of economic policy). The common purpose of the papers of this volume is to provide suggestions, conditional on a scholar's choice to contribute to the history of economics, about how to go about it. My recommendation is to allocate significant research time to mining, à la Viner, the written records that litter university and historical archives *plus* – a contemporary twist – to transcribing some of what has been mined into the *digital record* shared by the history of economics research community of the present and future.

This digital extension to Viner's advice brings in one of the pioneers of systems thinking and management science, Russell L. Ackoff, author of the seminal article, "From Data to Wisdom" (1989).[4] In its canonical form Ackoff's idea is referred to as the DIKW-pyramid that conjures up an image of a broad foundation of Data upon which layers of Information, Knowledge, and Wisdom are successively added. The data to be discussed below include the raw historical record of syllabi/reading lists and examination questions that are found in the archived papers of individual economists and in the records of their departments and universities. The job of a Viner-Ackoff-inspired historian of economics is to transform such data into information useful for expanding our knowledge with regard to the development of economics. For now we can postpone a trek to the summit of Mt Ackoff, where knowledge gets transformed into wisdom (making graduate school great again?) in order to get into the business of mining data and processing it into potentially useful information.[5]

Before starting an econometric project, several generations of empirical researchers have been taught to first imagine what questions could be asked if *all* the relevant statistical information were easily available. Analogously, before descending into the archives, I think it is useful to look across that imaginary digital divide and consider what a complete data set for a project on the history of economics education might look like. One could imagine having MOOC-style lecture videos together with complete batteries of ancillaries combined with all the presentations, handouts, problem sets, and exams (with answers!) for each course. Further these course data would span the entire teaching careers of all professors across all universities and colleges and all that information would be easily summoned from the Cloud – in short, one imagines the mother of all panel data sets to provide us the complete variation of content across time, space, course subject, and instructor. Indeed it would be as though one had a time-machine that allowed the historian of economics to visit any particular lecture in a course or even attend the entire course, in any department at anytime as taught by any particular instructor. I suppose to be consistent with Ackoff, we should call this a full panel *information* set.

OK, now it's time to wake up and smell some coffee. At least for the 19th and a qualified majority of the 20th centuries our (very) incomplete data are filed away in folders of written records within archival box upon box, imperfectly catalogued and dispersed across our finite universe of archives. With such a hypothetical full panel information set in mind, I next provide an overview of the kinds of material that I have come across over the past six years since beginning my project "Origins of the Graduate Economics Canon in the United States".[6] Space constraints make it necessary to strictly limit most exemplary name-dropping to endnotes.

Existing published material

Before delving into the archives proper, we must first pay respects to the extensive and increased publication of *textbooks* that offer the most easily accessible entry point for viewing the evolution of economic education. Sometimes it even seems that everyone who has ever taught the introductory course of economics has published a textbook. But as in so much of economic activity, the division of labor has been limited by the extent of the market here – the textbook offerings are seen to dwindle rapidly as one moves into the realm of graduate studies and/or narrower fields of specialization. It is a relatively modern development that instructors and students face a broad range of textbooks written for intermediate and advanced courses, in the theoretical and empirical core, as well as for the standard fields (labor, money and banking, industrial organization).

An honorable shout-out needs to go to publications such as the legendary Edward Tower compilations of "economics reading lists, course outlines, exams, puzzles & problems" that roughly cover the two decades running from the late-1970s and early-1990s.[7] Once copyright on these valuable volumes can be transferred to a Creative Commons license, all of that material will become available to be read at the HathiTrust digital library. While the Tower volumes are important for the last third of the 20th century, valuable transcriptions of archival material (especially course lecture notes but also reading lists and other material) for the first half of the 20th century have been published in the B and C volumes in the series *Research in the History of Economic Thought and Methodology*.[8] Random privately printed or official university published course syllabi and examinations can sometimes found in university libraries and up through the early 1920s and are available for reading or even downloading at web archives such as hathitrust.org or archive.org.[9] Occasionally we are even fortunate to have a Joseph Dorfman or a Douglas Irwin and Stephen Medema come along who then get published copies of semi-stenographic student course notes that have long circulated privately.[10]

Mining archival records

At this point the overview segues to the yet unpublished records, archival artifacts of earlier economic education. I think it is useful first to order these kinds of records according to the granularity of course content provided. The question I then pose concerns the adequacy of the relatively abundant course outlines and examination questions for providing a reasonable basis for reconstructing course content. If this is the case, there is then hope for our much reduced information sets to allow us to identify differences/changes in content across time, place, and individual by fields.

At the top of the list of course material are *professors' own course lecture notes*. This turns out sometimes to be a case of "too much information" compounded by handwriting noise (in the case of Joseph Schumpeter this means indecipherable notes for all but those who are willing to master an old Austrian system of shorthand). It is not uncommon for some course notes to have been modified and/or transferred to other semesters and courses. But it is my experience that when any course notes have survived to the file-in-a-box stage, there will be rich enough content for a persistent scholar to be able to reassemble the notes into some semblance of order.[11]

With greater frequency and almost with the same granularity of the lecture notes of professors, we have the *course notes taken by students*. It is not surprising that typically those economists with the most complete files of their own teaching have also kept the most course notes from their own student days. The fact that the courses are generally only taken once means that there is less likelihood of contamination of later with earlier versions of course notes. Two of my favorite examples display the use of note cards for note-taking (who would have expected?). The carefully ordered index note cards for most, if not all, courses taken by Milton Friedman (at Chicago and Columbia) and Frank Knight (at Cornell), respectively, can be found in the Hoover and University of Chicago archives. Especially during the first 50 years of graduate education in economics, reproduction of course material was rather limited and instead course reading assignments would simply be written on the blackboard for students to write into their notes so that student notes are often the only record of what parts of standard works had been assigned for reading and then discussed in class.[12]

There are at least two ways that a professor's own notes or those taken by the students in the course can prove useful in the quest of building an imperfect information set. The first way is to distill the implicit course syllabus and reading assignments from the notes, something the historian naturally does – taking notes on notes. The second way to exploit full course notes when found is to use them to gauge the degree to which other course material, e.g. the syllabus and examination questions, accurately reflect course content.

A major reduction in granularity occurs once we begin to consult the *course syllabi and reading lists*. It is a bit like only having an abstract and a bibliography instead of an article. In the earliest days the outlines and syllabi were often quite detailed, not a textbook by any means, but they resembled a complete local train schedule providing times and full identifications of the stops along the way.[13] Most of the syllabi I have found are scattered across the papers of individual economists, mostly for their own courses (taught or taken earlier as students) but also on occasion for courses of colleagues near and far. The largest single collection I have found is contained in the ten boxes of the Harvard Archives *Syllabi, Course Outlines and Reading Lists in Economics, 1895–2003.* Judging from handwritten comments, these syllabi were copies sent to the library in order to reserve course readings for the term. More often than one would want, course outlines are found lacking such metadata as course title, instructor's name, and date. Generating course lists from announcements and departmental records of actual course staffing is particularly important in filling in such blanks.

Continuing to proceed along the granularity spectrum we next come to *examination papers* that range from particular course exams through advanced field exams up through comprehensive/general exams. Often the final examination questions for a course or questions in a field examination are all that appear to have survived in written form. Fortunately most courses are repeated with reasonable regularity and, as in the previous case of course syllabi and bibliographies, professors turn out to be fairly reliable custodians of these written records.[14] Yet even for the career of a single professor over time, it is unusual for the files to be complete, with Frank Taussig's personal scrapbook of *all* of his Harvard course examinations being a notable exception.[15] Sometimes the departments themselves or the greater university maintain more systematic collections of the examinations.[16]

In official university/division/department *announcements and catalogues,* besides the standard information of course number, course name, instructor name(s), times, and rooms, we frequently come across brief (one or even two paragraph) course descriptions. The brief course descriptions are usually only marginally more valuable than the course titles alone, but changes in content or emphasis can be reflected in changes in the descriptions. The value of having the official "order of battle" for a department has been mentioned earlier for completing the identification of other course materials. However due to the fact of being published in advance of academic years, these announcements are sometimes incomplete ("N.N." listed as instructor) or even incorrect as *ad hoc* staffing adjustments were required by unanticipated contingencies. Convenient collections of actual *ex post* course staffing are regrettably rare in my experience.[17]

This overview shows that there is no general shortage of course-related data in the archives that are of interest for a historian of the economics education in the United States. Nonetheless it is fairly clear that we will fall short of obtaining anything resembling a full panel information set.

While we should probably consider ourselves lucky when we at least have syllabi, reading assignments, and examinations in the absence of a full set of course notes, we still have a duty to consider the adequacy of having only some these data to work with. It is an important exercise, one calling for multiple replications, to compare the relatively scarce existing course notes with the other course material at our disposal. I close with an illustrative report on one such test run.

Elizabeth (Bess) Ringo's notes to courses taught by Paul Samuelson at MIT (1943)

Elizabeth Ringo was a Swarthmore College graduate and, as it turned out, future wife of James Tobin (a relevant fact because it is probably decisive for why *her* notes survived at all). She was an honors economics major and went on to do graduate work at MIT because one of her Swarthmore professors, Wolfgang Stolper, had been able to tap his graduate school network of Harvard classmates and friends to serve as distinguished external examiners for the honors economics examinations at his college. Paul Samuelson served as examiner at the end of January 1943 when he recruited Elizabeth Ringo for the MIT graduate economics program.[18] I stumbled across Ringo's student notes to four courses that she took with Samuelson in James Tobin's papers.[19]

We have in these notes, at least as far as I am aware, our closest observational report of the initial Big Bang of the Samuelson era at the MIT Department of Economics. For the first of a two-term economic theory sequence (Economics 17) attended by Elizabeth Ringo,[20] the Appendix to this chapter provides an illustrative display of increasingly granular course-related materials: the official catalogue course description, three mimeographed course reading lists (with hand-written additions of reading assignments or suggestions), final examination questions for the course (found in Paul Samuelson's papers for an earlier and later version of the course), and finally my own summary outline of topics covered in the course following Ringo's notes.[21]

The question I wish to consider here – I invite the reader to draw one's own conclusions after examining the Appendix materials as well – is how much information would we lose for this course, were we restricted only to a combination of mimeographed reading lists and carbon-copies of exam questions?

First the good news. When I look at the sequence of topics that provides the implicit course outline (a definite improvement compared to the meager published course description) and then compare that sequence to the assigned/ suggested course readings, I would be hard-pressed to say the reading lists offer a distorted picture of the course content. Call this not rejecting an unbiasedness hypothesis. I did not claim this is great news.

The bad news is that unzipping these reading lists into a detailed syllabus matching the Ringo notes is simply infeasible just as a Gini-index and an average income number are not enough to distinguish between an infinity of interestingly different income distributions. Limiting ourselves to the reading lists when we have these reasonably complete notes would mean neglecting what Elizabeth Ringo recorded in those Samuelson lectures. So it looks like it could be difficult to distinguish course content in say a pairwise comparison across space or time when we find ourselves constrained to two reading lists of a core theory course – except for extremes of distance between competing "schools" or for timeframes beyond a half-generation. Could it be that expanding the sample across departments and time will permit us to get a tighter bead on differences due to instructor cohorts or to the school where graduate training took place? Let me reiterate what I said earlier, my archival research to date has had it greatest "successes" in the collection of course specific reading lists and examination questions. Perhaps like the some tools in prehistoric times, they simply possess the physical properties for survival that spoken words in seminar rooms or chalk on blackboards clearly lack.[22]

The present as past and preparing for the future

Let me return to the image of historians of economics on separate sides of the digital information divide digging tunnels that may or may not meet. With respect to the specific topic of the training of economists I propose one hypothesis as a possible orientation for the borings of the two teams. Suppose there is indeed such a process that has taken place more-or-less continuously across that great hypothetical digital divide.

The distillation of the canon hypothesis. As economics departments emerged from the pools of relatively undifferentiated social sciences in their evolution going into the early 20th century, one observes how different departments or schools have successively branched off over time. This can be seen very early in the rise of independent schools of social service that took with them those economists particularly interested in the delivery or administration of social services and research on crime, race, urban housing, etc. Business schools became a magnet for those economists focused on business and finance. Departments of sociology often grew out of (escaped?) the economics department (e.g. Harvard, though independent at Chicago from the very beginning). The same pattern can be seen for home economics, agricultural economics, and schools of public policy, industrial relations, and international affairs. The academic market for PhD economists grew while the core of theory *cum* statistics à la Cowles came to increasingly characterize the kit new PhDs were outfitted with. The replacement of economic history with a new-tools-for-old-data approach has made it easier to find economic historians in a history department or area studies program than as a constituent member of an economics faculty.

While I firmly believe the first order of business of historians of economics is to find more space in the curriculum for future economists that will expose students to earlier (indeed competing) economics, it is not entirely premature to think of what could constitute a sort of Viner-meets-Ackoff project of scholarship. Analogous to the practice of having students attempt to duplicate the empirical results of some recently published paper, why not have in a graduate history of economics class a requirement to transcribe and edit an old course syllabus and examination or even course notes to contribute to the stock of material in a global (Wiki-) History of Economics? The scholarly marginal value of a digitally accessible artifact from archival material on the old side the divide is high for the obvious reason of relative scarcity but its value is further enhanced by providing material to fit into possible research designs for the historians of future economics in what we know will be an increasingly data-rich environment.

Appendix: Information regarding course content of Graduate Economic Theory (Ec 17) taught by Paul A. Samuelson during the MIT summer term of 1943

The following items provide a typical illustration of different levels of granularity found in archival/library material with which a historian of economics can use to establish a working record of the development of the curriculum of graduate economics.

Course Description:[23]
Ec17, Ec18. Economic Analysis (A). A review of the interdependent growth of theory and fact, followed by a study of the general theory of equilibrium under competition and monopoly. Findings will be revalued under conditions which more closely approach reality.

READING LIST FOR ECONOMIC THEORY 1941–42
1943[24]

[mimeographed]

A. Internal theory of the firm: revenue and cost analysis

Assigned reading

  1. Joan Robinson, Economics of Imperfect Competition
     Chapters 1, 2, 3, 4, 5, 15, 18

  2. Alfred Marshall, Principles of Economics (4th edition or later)
     Book III, Chapters 3, 4, 6; Book V, Chapters 4, 7, 8, 9, 14;
     Mathematical Appendix, Notes 3, 4, 22, 23

  3. Cournot, Researches into the Mathematical Principles of the Theory
     of Wealth
     Chapter 4

  4. R. Triffin, Monopolistic Competition and General Equilibrium Theory
     Pages 3–6

  5. H. Schultz, The Theory and Measurement of Demand
     Pages 5–13

  6. R. G. D. Allen, Mathematical Analysis for Economists
     Pages 107–121, 152–157, 254–260

7. J. Viner, "Cost Curves and Supply Curves," Zeitschrift fur National-economie
[sic, für Nationalökonomie]

8. E. H. Chamberlin, Theory of Monopolistic Competition
Chapter II (omit note), Pages 71–81, 130–149

9. R. L. Hall & C. J. Hitch, "Price Theory and Business Behavior," Oxford Economic Papers, May 1939. Pages 12–45

10. U. S. Steel T. N. E. C. Papers
Vol. I, Pages 305–323

11. George J. Stigler, The Theory of Competitive Price
Part I. [this reference typed onto the mimeograph]

Reading List Ec 17²⁵ 1942–1943
[mimeographed]

The Economic Theory of the Firm: Production and Cost

1. At least one of the following:

   S. Carlson, Theory of Production, Ch II
   R. G. D. Allen, Mathematical Analysis ......, pp. 284–288

2. F. H. Clark Knight, Risk, Uncertainty & Profit, Ch. IV

3. J. B. Clark, The Distribution of Wealth, Chs. VII, VIII, XII

4. Joan Robinson, Economics of Imperfect Competition, pp. 235–306

5. J. R. Hicks, Value & Capital, Ch. VI

6. E. H. Chamberlin, Theory of Monopolistic Competition, 3rd edition, Ch. 8, also
   F. W. Taussig, Explorations in Economics, pp. 237–249

7. Paul H. Douglas, Theory of Wages, Ch. II
8. J. R. Hicks, Theory of Wages, Ch. I, II, III, IV, pp. 181–183

Additional Optional Reading

on Marshall [handwritten note, apparently referring to Stigler]
G. Stigler, Theories of Production & Distribution [sic](all or any part)

J. M. Cassels, "On the Law of Variable Proportions," in the F. W. Taussig, Festschrift, Explorations in Economics, pp. 223–236.

J. R. Hicks, Value & Capital, Ch. VII.

G. Stigler, The Theory of Competitive Price, Part II

Reading List Economics 17[26]
[mimeographed, no date, probably 1943]

Theory of Consumer's Behavior

1. Marshall, Principles, Chapters of Book III not previously assigned.

2. Meyers, Elements of Modern Economics (2nd edition)

3. J. R. Hicks, Value and Capital, Part I.

4. K. Wicksell, Lectures on Economic Theory, Vol. I, Part I.

5. R. G. D. Allen, Mathematical Analysis, pp. 124–126.

6. H. Schultz, Theory and Measurement of Demand, pp. 12–58.

7. H. Mendershausen, "The Relationship Between Income and Savings of American Metropolitan Families," American Economic Review, Vol. 29 (1939), pp. 520–537. [sic, *521–537*]

(Do not worry if you can understand only a little of what you read. Do not spend time rereading.)

Ec17[27]
Final Examination
Wednesday, January 20, 1943

1. You run a firm producing one commodity from many productive factors. In order to make correct decisions you would require certain information from your sales' experts and engineers. Describe this information and show in detail how you would use it. Give the correct conditions of equilibrium in each sphere of action, indicating the assumptions upon which each is based. Integrate the various decisions showing their relationships to each other. (Do not waste words.)

2. Describe briefly the problems involved in one of the following:

   (a) Definition of complementarity
   (b) Consumer's surplus
   (c) Inferior goods and Giffen's Paradox
   (d) Measurement of utility

Ec 17 ECONOMIC THEORY[28]
Final Examination
1–2 hours
June 17, 1944

A firm produces one commodity utilizing two or more productive factors. Discuss fully its conditions of internal equilibrium as far as production, cost, revenue, price and profit are concerned, in the long-run and in the short-run. Specify the technological and market data needed by the firm in making its various decisions.

Course Outline as Reconstructed from Elizabeth Ringo's Notes[29]
Ec 17
Summer Term 1943

I. The economic theory of the firm
    12. (32 lectures. July 6, 1943 to September 10, 1943)
    A. Revenue and cost analysis
        1. Price elasticity of demand
            Property of points on a demand curve, to compare two demand curves you must specify which points are being compared. Special case of constant elasticity demand curve.
        2. Cost curve as function of quantity
            Conditions of profit maximizing equilibrium
            a. Marginal cost equal to marginal revenue
            b. Cost function cuts revenue function from below
            c. Revenue equals or exceeds variable costs (otherwise shut down).
    B. Production and cost
        1. Vinerian cost curve analysis
        2. Perfect competition's supply curve as the rising marginal cost curve as long as it exceeds average variable costs
        3. Since price is constant, marginal revenue equals average revenue
        4. Under imperfect competition there is no supply curve independent of the demand curve.
    C. Shifts of demand curve
        1. Case of perfect competition, cost curves unshifting.
        2. Case of monopolist, cost curves unshifting.
        3. Relations between short-run and long run cost curves
        4. Intuition behind empirical fact of U-shaped average cost curves
        5. Envelope relationship: First explicit mention of Viner in Ringo notes.
    D. Advertising and product differentiation
        1. Product differentiation

   a.   Multiproduct firm iso-profit (concentric circles in quantity place)
   b.   One product, two markets (discriminating monopoly)
   c.   Allocation of output between two plants, analogous to allocating given output between two markets.
   d.   Multiproduct firm iso-profit (concentric circles in quantity space)
   2.   Advertising costs
   a.   Determining optimum advertising
   b.   Impact of advertising on price, output
   3.   Product differentiation, again.
   a.   Goods and advertising as a joint product
   b.   Joint cost problem and allocation of costs.
E.   The production function
   1.   Historical survey
   2.   False problem of imputation (Austrians assumed supplies of all factors were inelastic, hence price of factors determined by demand)
   3.   Relative shares and elasticity of substitution
   4.   General equilibrium including factor markets
F.   Firm's cost curve
   1.   Minimize cost of attaining a given isoquant, given factor price. Tangency of iso-cost to iso-quant
   2.   Expansion path for increasing iso-quants provide the relation between quantity produced and costs, given prices.
G.   Relation of factor prices to marginal revenue products
   1.   Complication when production function has corners.
   2.   Kinks in demand curve (Sweezy model of oligopoly)
H.   Exhaustion of product issue. Linear homogeneity is neither necessary nor sufficient. Entry, exit (the behavior of other firms leading to shifts in revenue and cost schedules lead to the exhaustion of product)
I.   Monopsony and labor supply curve
   1.   Labor Supply curve (Hicksian possibility of "backward rising" labor supply curve due to income effect exceeding substitution effect)
   2.   First-order conditions for monosonist confronted with supply curve of labor. Use Robinson method of drawing marginal curve to supply of labor.

II.   The theory of consumer's behavior (7 lectures of notes. begins 9. 15.43, ends 9.30.43)
   A.   Jevons/Walras/Menger resolve the water/diamonds paradox,
   B.   Edgeworth, Pareto using ordinal utility introduced indifference curves: (mention of integrability problem for more than two goods)
   C.   Linear budget constraint tangent to highest feasible indifference curve where relative price equals the marginal rate of substitution. Enables us

to find restrictions on demand functions "Gives meaningful (refutable) hypotheses"

D.   Income expansion path, price-consumption curve (Giffen's paradox of inferior good accounting for a large fraction of spending)

E.   Compensated demand curve response to price change à la Hicks. Also used as a measure of complementarity.

Notes

1   As is so often the case, Robert Solow manages to pose the essential question with deceptive simplicity "nowadays economists arrive at their conclusions by using an evolving collection of analytical techniques, most of them non-intuitive, the sort that have to be learned laboriously...The interesting question is why economics stopped being clubbable and became technical sometime in the 1940s and 1950s, and why model-building took over as the standard intellectual exercise." Robert M. Solow. "How did economics get that way & what way did it get?" *Daedalus*, Vol. 126, No. 1 (Winter, 1997), pp. 39–58.

2   As a working illustration of what I have in mind here, the reader is without apology referred to the growing collection of archival artifacts bearing on the evolution of economics education that have been transcribed and are curated at my weblog, *Economics in the Rear-View Mirror* (www.irwincollier.com).

3   Jacob Viner, "A modest proposal for some stress on scholarship in graduate training." Address before the Graduate Convocation, Brown University, June 3, 1950. *Brown University Papers* XXIV, Providence Rhode Island: Brown University, p. 1.

4   Russell L. Ackoff, "From data to wisdom," *Journal of Applied Systems Analysis* 16 (1989), pp. 3–9.

5   I am mildly embarrassed to admit that I had never heard of the DIKW-pyramid until the early summer of 2017 when the chief economist of Google, Hal Varian, spoke in Berlin about the information engineering behind a self-driving automobile. Varian organized his remarks using Ackoff's framework. Since the folks at Google have clearly demonstrated genius in the art of processing data into information, I hope to be excused in grafting Ackoff to Viner here.

6   This is an appropriate moment to gratefully acknowledge the inaugural research grant from the Institute for New Economic Thinking that allowed me to begin my archival work seven years ago.

7   E.g. 25 volumes providing "teaching materials . . . from both undergraduate and graduate programs at 105 major colleges and universities" in the series *Economics Reading Lists, Course Outlines, Exams, Puzzles & Problems* compiled by Edward Tower were published in September 1995 (Chapel Hill: Eno River Press).

8   For example: "Economic Theory by Taussig, Young, and Carver at Harvard" edited by Marianne Johnson and Warren J. Samuels in *Research in the History of Economic Thought and Methodology*, Volume 28-C (Bingley: Emerald Group Ltd, 2010), pp. 11–190. These were the typewritten, bound notes of the Harvard student Maurice Beck Hexter from 1921–22.

9   Published copies of the final examinations in economics at Harvard from 1913–15 found in the University of Wisconsin library can be read at hathitrust.org. One outstanding example that may be downloaded from archive.org is the *Outline of Lectures upon Political Economy* by Henry Carter Adams (76 page 1st edition (Baltimore, 1881), 83 page 2nd edition (Ann Arbor, 1886).

10   *Types of Economic Theory*, 2 vols, by Wesley Clair Mitchell and edited by Joseph Dorfman (August M. Kelley, 1967/1969) and *Jacob Viner: Lectures in Economics 301*, Douglas A. Irwin and Steven G. Medema, editors (London: Routledge, 2017).

11 For the year of economic theory (Economics 205–206) at Columbia taught by John Bates Clark (e.g. 1907–08) Columbia University Rare Book and Manuscript Library. John Bates Clark Papers (MS#1419), Series II:.1 Box 4, Folder 1 "Economic Theory 1907–08". For the semester course "Introduction to the Mathematical Treatment of Economics" (Economics 8a) in Harvard University Archives, *Wassily Leontief Papers* (HUG 4517.30) *Manuscripts and Research Notes 1930–1970*, Box 5, Folder "Introduction to Mathematical Economics (notes)".

12 The gold-standard of student notes was set by James Tobin's neatly handwritten and bound student notes from his Harvard coursework (1936–41) found in the James Tobin Papers (MS 1746), Boxes 6 and 7 at the Yale University Archives. For Chicago economics courses one excellent source is the notes taken by Don Patinkin located in his papers at the Economists' Papers Archives, Duke University. Thanks to the keen eye of his Rochester colleague, Stanley Engerman, Norman Kaplan's Chicago course notes were identified as valuable archival material during the examination of Kaplan's papers upon his death. Kaplan's notes can be consulted at the University of Chicago archives.

13 A nice example is the detailed printed outline by topics with reading assignments for ca. 1926–27 by Edwin Seligman found in the papers of his successor Robert M. Haig in the Columbia Archives (Box 16).

14 I can't emphasize enough that Duke University's Economists' Papers Archive at the David M. Rubenstein Rare Book & Manuscript Library provides the best first-stop archive for those looking for course materials kept by individual economists.

15 Harvard University Archives. *Examination Papers in Economics, Prof. Taussig, Scrapbook* (HUC 7882).

16 Johns Hopkins University [1903–65, incomplete] Department of Political Economy: Series 6, Boxes 1–3 in The Ferdinand Hamburger, Jr. Archives. University of Chicago, *Department of Economics Records 1912–1961*: Qualifying Examinations 1947–52 (Boxes 38–39), Comprehensive Examinations 1934–47 (Boxes 39–40); Harvard University Archives *Harvard University Final Examinations 1853–2001* (HUC 7000.28): 284 boxes for all subjects! [incomplete coverage, 1900–15 missing].

17 Two *ex post* reports of staffing that I have found particularly useful: the annual reports of the President of Harvard College Harvard University [available at the website: *Harvard-Radcliffe Online Historical Reference Shelf*, http://guides.library.harvard.edu/c.php?g=638791&p=4471938]; MIT (1953–79, incomplete). MIT, Institute Archives and Special Collections. *Department of Economics Records* (AC 394), Box 3, two folders "Teaching Responsibilities".

18 "My booty from the countryside was Ringo's promise to come to MIT's new graduate program in economics, which was starved for draft-proof students." Letter to James and Elizabeth Tobin (August 1, 1992). Duke University, Rubenstein Library. Papers of Paul A. Samuelson, Box 73, Folder "Tobin, James". Out of fear that some young researcher might consult an Internet urban dictionary, I hasten to add that "booty" is meant here in the sense of pirate's plunder (cf. the corresponding German word *Beute*). Ringo wasted no time and enrolled in courses the following month (February 1943).

19 Actually, *none* of the mimeographed materials in the file refer either to the school or the instructor, and the first two explicit mentions of Samuelson (and then only by initials) in the course notes are found one month into the course, namely, for August 4 ("PAS: Tends to raise price – probably decrease quantity throughout industry") and August 17 ("PAS: this is false. You'd never find this situation. General equilibrium approach more fruitful"). Consulting the MIT course catalogues from that year confirmed that this was indeed Samuelson's course. Later Elizabeth Ringo

begins to refer to PAS more playfully, e.g. September 2 "Remind Sammie to talk about monopsony".

20 In point of fact Elizabeth Ringo actually took these two courses in reverse order, the two courses covered different clusters of theoretical topics, i.e. she first took Ec 18 and then Ec 17.

21 When I presented an early draft of this chapter at a workshop for contributors to this volume held at the Centre Walras Pareto of the University of Lausanne in mid-October 2017, I was moderately surprised at much of the concern expressed about the potential for senseless destruction of innocent detail by my summary outline. What is important to me here is less extracting Samuelson's signal from Ringo's reception than is having a richer description of course content than the typical artifacts of reading lists and examination questions at our disposal. Given that my own MIT training followed that of Ringo's by only about 32 years and that Samuelson himself was still part and parcel of the required sequence of economic theory courses in my training, I ask the reader to trust me on this point – at least until the time when I am able to publish a full version of the Ringo notes.

22 Adam Smith himself would have preferred to use long historical time series for wages to deflate nominal prices but was able to convince himself that the reports of market prices of grain were more reliable and would serve as an adequate proxy for nominal wages.

23 *Massachusetts Institute of Technology Bulletin*, Vol. 78, No. 4. Catalogue Issue (July 1943), p. 107.

24 Yale University Library Manuscript Collections, *James Tobin Papers*, Accession 2003-M-005, Group No. 1746, Box No. 18, Folder "Ec 17 Ringo".

25 Ibid.

26 Ibid.

27 Duke University. David M. Rubenstein Rare Book & Manuscript Library. Economists' Papers Archive. *Paul Samuelson Papers*, Box 33, Folder "Miscellaneous Teaching Materials".

28 Ibid. It appears that a separate question for consumer theory might have been put on another slip of paper that did not survive together with this single question.

29 The typed transcription I have made of Ringo's notes for Ec 17 runs to about 80 pages so that for the purpose of this paper it is sufficient to limit ourselves to a "constructed" course outline derived from a careful reading of the Ringo notes.

8 Textbooks in the historiography of recent economics

Yann Giraud

Introduction

Economics textbooks can be encountered on the most unlikely of occasions. In an episode of the TV crime series *Cold Case*, the police detectives who try to solve an old murder case that happened in the early 1950s interrogate a now 80-year-old woman, who once knew the victim. In her 20s at the time when the murder happened, she was a submissive housewife, married to an abusive and unfaithful husband and looking for a freer, more independent life. That sense of freedom is exemplified in a flashback sequence in which she is seen reading the university book she is studying, A. Smith Pond's *Elementary Economics*. This was one of those textbooks that notoriously copied Samuelson's leading text *Economics: An Introductory Analysis* in appearance but was simplified for a mathematically untrained audience, for instance housewives such as the one we see in the episode, who might take evening classes at a women's college nearby. At the end of the episode, the textbook makes another appearance: now that the murderer has been caught, we see the old woman, relieved that the case has been solved, who decides to remember the past by skimming through that same Pond's text she has kept at home for years as a representation of that life she was longing for but never managed to build for herself.[1] *Cold Case*'s screenwriters may not be perfect historians. They use a textbook first published in 1954 in a sequence that is supposed to occur in 1953. Yet, like good historians of economics – and of science – should do, they seem to have understood something about textbooks: that they are not just repositories of past knowledge, that they are used in certain contexts and sometimes hold a cultural significance that can exceed their sole academic value.

In this chapter, I do not argue that all contributions to – or using – economics textbooks should be as thick in their outlook as to encompass all of these cultural and societal aspects altogether. In fact, as we will see further, few if any existing contributions do – and this applies to my own work on this topic. Yet, what I want to stress is that a general lack of reflection on the role of textbooks in the discipline can lead to exceedingly thin accounts that consider this literature as a shortcut to study the state of economic doctrine at some point in time. This "reductionist approach" to textbooks, as I call it, cannot be fully rewarding, as the idea of studying a whole field of knowledge through the choices made by some particular sub-group of authors and editors seems flawed from the start. In addition, the reductionist approach to textbooks seems to overlook the very reason why textbooks are used in the first place: as teaching aids, located in specific pedagogical and institutional environments – although, as I will detail later on, some textbooks have also been used for other purposes. Therefore, it can be said that economics textbooks have been simultaneously overused and neglected as tools to study the history of economics.

Yet, my purpose here is not to lament over the current situation and what I want to suggest, by surveying the existing historical literature, is that there are many possibilities and untouched areas that future researchers may be interested in exploring by regarding textbooks as major elements in the material culture of past and present economists. In the next section, I will turn to the larger history of science by looking at how textbooks have been studied there. Although a few scholars have thought deeply about historiographical issues regarding textbooks, it is clear that, on the whole, textbooks still have low status in the field. In a second section, reviewing the history of economics literature, I will point to a number of historiographical issues and stress the similarities and divergences with what has been observed in the history of science. Finally, in the concluding section, I will try to outline a program for future research on economics textbooks. In the following, while I am mostly interested in the historiography of postwar economics, I will occasionally mention works that have addressed pre-World War II textbooks as a way to emphasize what is specific to the more recent period. Also, I must recognize that this chapter is mostly concerned with introductory and undergraduate texts: this is because the existing literature mostly focuses on those, something that future research will hopefully counterbalance in favor of the more technically sophisticated books used in graduate education.

Textbooks in the larger history of science

Historians of science have not necessarily reflected more on textbooks than historians of economics, as two recent historiographical essays (Vicedo 2012; Simon 2016) show. In his account, Josep Simon (2016, p. 401) writes: "historians of science have shown a longstanding interest in textbooks, but it has not resulted in more and better studies displaying significant historiographical and methodological discussions". He observes that most existing contributions still focus on textbooks written by major scientists, therefore ignoring the vast majority of textbooks written by lesser authors, particularly those who have helped develop scientific disciplines outside of Europe or the United States. Simon's main claim is that a better understanding of textbooks should contribute to highlight the truly international dimension of science and help reverse a number of national hierarchies commonly taken as granted by historians of science. Marga Vicedo's (2012) contribution expresses similar dissatisfaction with the existing historiography of scientific textbooks, arguing that most of the time historians have simply followed scientists' own lack of interest in them, as they consider them as "mere repositories for scientific knowledge". She attributes this ignorance to the "received view" of science diffusion, which considers science education – along with popular accounts and applications – as hierarchically inferior to knowledge creation, and takes Thomas Kuhn to task for treating textbooks as collections of exemplars whose sole role was to indoctrinate students into the dominant paradigm.[2] Besides, sociologically inflected historians and philosophers of science who have dismantled the "received view" of knowledge production over the past two decades have focused more on laboratories and field research than on science education and textbooks, leaving this topic relatively untouched.[3]

However, both Vicedo and Simon show that the situation has been partially reversed in recent years, thanks to the emerging subfield of science education history. This literature has shown that textbooks are entrenched in pedagogical practices and that in order to understand how knowledge becomes standardized, it can be useful to start with classroom notes to unveil a number of features that are hidden in printed texts. Looking at the pedagogical uses of textbooks also helps understand what differentiates "textbooks" from "treatises" or "elements". Patiniotis (2006) asserts that while the English word "textbook" dates from 1730, its current meaning – i.e. "a book containing a systematic presentation of the principles of a subject or a collection of writings dealing with a specific subject" – coincides with the development of systematic scientific education in the 19th century. Therefore, a book is not a textbook by nature: influential treatises can become required readings in the classroom and acquire the status of textbooks even though they were not intended as such in the first place. The transformation of books into textbooks, Simon argues, is generally a circular process: the authority of textbooks comes from their use in the classroom and, reciprocally, some books become used in the classroom because of their authority, which comes from a great number of factors: the scientific credentials of the author, the efforts of the publishers or some external pedagogical authority for instance. More generally, Vicedo (2012, p. 85) identifies a number of threads that the historical study of textbooks has helped explore in recent years and should help explore further in the future: the use of textbooks in pedagogical and training practices; their role in shaping new disciplines and/or subfields of science; the development of ideas throughout time and space; the changing epistemological concerns in a field; the study of priority disputes; the study of external influences on science (religion, politics, and business). That list is of course not meant to be exhaustive.

In practice, though, few historical contributions on textbooks deal with postwar social science, as most studies focus on a period ranging from the French Revolution to the beginning of the 20th century and on the natural sciences, chemistry being the only field that has been extensively analyzed following more than a decade of research (e.g. Lundgren and Bensaude-Vincent 2000; Bensaude-Vincent, Garcia-Belmar, and Bertomeu-Sanchez 2003; Rocke 2010). They point to the mid-19th century as the period of emergence of the textbook genre in these fields, following the development of national systems of secondary education and the appearance of a publishing industry to supply that market. Rocke's work on the role of visualization in the development of chemistry highlights the importance of August Kékulé's textbook *Lehrbuch der organischen Chemie* (1859–66) in the dissemination of the author's own representation of molecular structure – known as "sausage formulas" – and of his valence theory. Kékulé's fascicles emanated from his seminars and his graphic formulas adopted the same shape as the physical, wooden, molecular models he used there. Kékulé's text was immediately considered a success by his peers because of its author's high credentials as a scientist and due to the structure of Germany's higher education system. Most early reviewers of the texts had witnessed his teaching first hand because teaching took place in small laboratories, as higher education was still intended for an elite audience, so that teachers and students were on an almost equal footing.

One of the rare extensive investigations of textbooks in postwar science is that provided by Kaiser (2005) as part of his larger study of Feynman diagrams in physics. Kaiser's book is a rather extreme plea for the materialistic turn in the history of science; he argues that there is no such thing as "theoretical physics", and that in fact, even the most abstract developments in this field are rather the result of countless hours of dull calculation, allowed in part by the use of different instantiations of the Feynman diagram, a visual technique that permits the simplification of enormous systems of simultaneous equations. After narrating the first appearance of the diagram at a 1948 physics conference, Kaiser devotes most of his book to the subsequent dissemination and transformation of this diagram, looking at a wide array of teaching materials and textbooks. Kaiser shows that the early postwar period witnessed the rise of a "textbook age" in physics, mostly as a consequence of the G.I. Bill of Rights, which sparked an unprecedented rise in enrollments in science departments. As a result, science publishers were open to new materials, encouraging younger researchers to publish their course notes as soon as possible. Because all of these researchers were using different forms of Feynman diagrams and were all involved in frontier research, the resulting textbooks were far from standardized and, contrary to Kuhn's claim, did not look like repositories of "finished achievements". Feynman diagrams there had various shapes and were used in a variety of ways, most of that initially intended by their creator. Yet, Kaiser's analysis also yields some negative results: Feynman diagrams are not as disseminated in textbooks as in class notes and unpublished drafts and therefore textbooks do not fully reflect the upsurge in creativity generated by their appearance at the time. The reason is not just related to the high costs of introducing visuals into textbooks. It is just that when it comes to the new techniques, direct teaching proved more efficient than the use of printed materials. Graduate students had quickly become so used to the diagram that they could use them in their mind's eye, without having to resort to paper tools (Kaiser 2005, p. 279). A subsequent paper (Kaiser 2012) dealing with two specific physics textbooks, *Gravitation* (1973) and *The Tao of Physics* (1975), serves as an illustration that lines are blurry between textbooks and books, as a mix of authorial intent, publishing strategies, readers' response, and critical reaction transform them into highly successful essays. Although Kaiser details the numerous factors behind this transformation, he clearly regards these two books as "outliers", therefore undermining the significance of his own monograph to the larger history of postwar physics textbooks.

All in all, whereas recent works in the history of science have helped renew interest in textbooks and begun to ask interesting questions about them, existing contributions are still very fragmentary. Whereas it is obvious from the preceding paragraphs that a transdisciplinary study of science textbooks would be highly beneficial, most of the existing work has been done within discipline histories of science with little regard to what has been done in neighboring fields. Though specific, history of economics is no exception.

The current historiography of economics textbooks

As many commenters have noted (see for instance Fontaine 2016 and Weintraub 2016b), disciplinary history of economics differs from the larger history of science in that it is still vastly subjugated to the economics discipline as a whole, trying to look at past theories in order to settle current debates within the field. When it comes to textbooks, this subjugation translates into one specific genre of historical narratives that considers textbooks critically, looking at their apparent standardization in order to point to possible biases against innovative – often non-orthodox – ways of thinking in economics. However, this is only one among several ways historians of economics have used textbooks. In this section, I am depicting three other genres of narratives: the second uses a selection of textbooks as a way to reflect on the dissemination of ideas in the postwar period; the third studies some particular textbooks as part of larger biographical accounts; finally, the fourth points to the more active role that textbooks play in the shaping of economics departments.

The over-representation of Samuelson's Economics

Before I begin to detail these four narrative genres, however, I need to stress how over-represented Paul Samuelson's undergraduate textbook *Economics* is in all of these studies.[4] In fact, with the exception of one paper on Joan Robinson's *An Introduction to Modern Economics*, which I will detail later in this section, Samuelson's textbook is the only postwar text having been the object of monographs.[5] In addition, it is present in many contributions that use textbooks as data for the dissemination of ideas. The reasons why *Economics* is so ubiquitous in these endeavors are quite obvious. First, the fact it was revised many times over the period makes it the perfect item for those who want to trace the development of a concept or tool over the second half of the 20th century. Samuelson himself encouraged that kind of practice, writing in the 14th edition:

A historian of mainstream-economic doctrines, like a paleontologist who studies the bones and fossils in different layers of earth, could date the ebb and flow of ideas by analyzing how Edition 1 was revised to Edition 2 and, eventually, to Edition 14.

(cited by Skousen 1997, p. 138)

The second reason is the author's undisputable stature and influence over economics research in the postwar period. Historians of economics, who are still interested, in spite of some recent historiographical trends, in the study of "great figures", would be inclined to follow his incantation.

To say that *Economics* is over-represented in the existing historical accounts is not to deny its impact. Described retrospectively by the author as part of "the revolutions that hit economic introductory textbooks half a century ago" (Samuelson 1997, p. 153), it is said to have "dominated the college classrooms for two generations" (Skousen 1997, p. 137). Kenneth Elzinga (1992) brings quantitative evidence to that claim, showing that *Economics* outsold all other competitors until the mid-1960s. However, the textbook's impact is not only quantitative: past contributions have also emphasized Samuelson's role in disseminating "the textbook Keynesian model" and the consolidation of the "neoclassical synthesis", a term Samuelson coined in the third edition (Pearce and Hoover 1995). Subsequent textbooks did not just borrow the theoretical content of *Economics*, but its pedagogical approach and mode of presentation. David Colander (2012) even calls the current textbook age in economics "the Samuelsonian era", claiming that it "became the template for almost all key books after that up until 2010" (Colander 2012, p. 324). According to him, the subsequent decline in sales did not undermine its influence on today's leading textbooks, which, he argues, are still following its path "even though economics has changed considerably in the interim" (p. 337). The result in his view is a widening gap between what economists do and what they teach.

Textbooks as proxies for the economics discipline's prejudices

Even though Colander's piece is not downright critical of mainstream economics, his remark on the textbooks lagging behind research is indicative of the normative attitude a number of contributors have when they study textbooks, with these being used as proxies for the many biases of mainstream economics and its tardiness to reform itself. Although historically informed, these contributions are most often authored by practitioners who have a strong interest in economics education or are members of communities that defend traditions alternative to the dominant neoclassical framework. This is the case of Colander who, in addition to his historical work, is also the author of several introductory textbooks whose approaches are overtly critical of the standard literature. What is not clear, however, in these accounts, is whether textbooks are inherently conservative because of their passive character or if textbook authors and other forces such as the publishing market or larger education policies have been active in maintaining the status quo. In another contribution, Colander and two co-authors (Colander, Holt, and Rosser Jr 2004) make it more explicit that their views on textbooks are borrowed from Kuhn, therefore ranging with the "passive" camp. Their piece argues that mainstream economics is no longer the unified framework most people believe it is but that its evolution into a more pluralistic endeavor, which is already effective "at the edge" of the discipline, is slowed down by textbooks. Here, the authors write:

> The process from conception of an idea to its appearance in graduate textbooks can take up to ten years. Intermediate and upper level undergraduate textbooks usually take another five to ten years to include these ideas . . . Principles books take another five to ten years to actually incorporate the idea as a central element, although, like their undergraduate upper level counterparts, they may add them as addenda so that they look modern . . . Consequently, textbooks, especially lower level texts, often do not reflect the diversity of views acceptable to the mainstream, but instead reflect an older orthodox position.
>
> (Colander et al. 2004, pp. 494–495)

This account, however, would require further investigation into the editorial process and the market for economics education to be completely convincing.

Other similarly critical contributions, however, seem to assume authorial intent, implying that some textbook authors have been active in trying to slow down progress in economics. Two examples of this historiographical genre are particularly striking. Nelson (2001), which places itself in Deirdre McCloskey's rhetorical approach, argues that mainstream economics, as exemplified among other works in Samuelson's *Economics*, acts more like religion than science, having "faith" in the market mechanism and "preaching" scientific management of the economy. Nelson claims, not erroneously so, that Samuelson is as much an heir of late 19th century American progressives, who were deep into the social Gospel of their time, than of Keynes. Nelson makes this claim by looking at the wording used in the textbook. He writes:

> From time to time, Samuelson drops his posture of scientific neutrality and adopts an explicitly moralistic tone that more accurately conveys his fundamental values. At one point in *Economics*, for example, he says that the current unequal distribution of income in the United States is "improper" and in fact an outright "evil" . . . Monopolistic practices by which the powerful exploit the weak are another "evil." Indeed, the use of the term evil occurs with surprising frequently throughout the pages of *Economics*.
>
> (Nelson 2001, p. 54)

Another instance is Levy and Peart (2009), which uses different textbooks – by Samuelson, Campbell McConnell, Leland Bach, Lorie Tarshis, and Robert Heilbronner – to study how they treat the issue of Soviet growth through several editions. They show that all textbooks overestimated Soviet growth, claiming that its gross national product could catch up with that of the United States. Levy and Peart argue that this manipulation betrays, not the authors' ideological prejudices, but their methodological ones, namely their overconfidence in models of prediction relying on the production possibilities frontier. These contributions, too, have underlying methodological premises, sometimes quite unthinkingly. First, they assume that because textbooks are more likely made of verbal assertions as opposed to the mathematical research dominating in the discipline, looking at them could help identify beliefs that are usually obscured by the technique. Second, they often focus on textbooks written by relatively well-known figures because they believe that their views and biases are symptomatic of the views and biases of some subset of the economics profession. In the end, there is something relatively paradoxical about this genre of analysis, which simultaneously expects textbooks to cope with recent research – as passive recording devices do – and, nonetheless, pays attention to an author's idiosyncrasies, adopting therefore a more active view of textbooks. These accounts would be more convincing if they included a deeper enquiry on the textbook authors' motivations and their limitation in view of all the other factors that influence textbook making.

Textbooks in studies of dissemination

In his historiographical account, Simon (2016) argues that studies in dissemination – i.e. studies that retrace the development of a concept through successive editions of a sample of textbooks throughout over a given period – often dominate disciplinary histories of scientific textbooks and it is true that there is a fair number of those in our field, even these are more easily found in student's essays or master theses than in articles published in peer-reviewed journals. Indeed, studies in dissemination are rather unlikely to fully convince referees because most of the times they are subject to too much questioning. How are we sure that the sample of textbooks that has been surveyed is sufficiently representative of the profession? Why did the author ignore the context of publication of such or such textbook? Are the results observed explained by changes in the profession or are they more affected by publishing market issues? Most of the time, the essay will conclude that there is a "time lag" between research and teaching, therefore falling into the "diffusion model" that historians of science are so eager to get rid of. Yet, studies in dissemination through textbooks can be satisfying on certain occasions, for instance when textbook authors were themselves involved in the development of the concepts they help disperse through textbooks. James Forder's recent study of the Phillips curve – the statistical curve showing a decreasing relationship between wage increase and unemployment that turned into a theoretical relationship between them – in introductory textbooks (Forder 2015) indeed involves Samuelson and Lipsey, two major players both in textbook writing and in the development of the curve itself – both gave the curve its standard interpretation in two separate contributions published in 1960. In addition, Samuelson's *Economics* and Lipsey's *An Introduction to Positive Economics* had several editions over the period under scrutiny, which allows for comparisons between editions. Forder's main use of the textbook literature is to show that the view that the Phillips curve was used as a plea for inflationary economic policies, spread in recent textbooks, is a distortion of what was actually published in older texts. Yet, Forder makes it clear that he does not consider his paper as a contribution to textbook history, whose specific role in constructing "the Phillips curve myth" he does not discuss. Textbooks, therefore, do not appear as different as other sorts of treatises and the only reason why they are informative in this case is because their authors are of a sufficient stature that we can assume authorial intent.

The work recently undertaken by Steven Medema on the dissemination of the Coase theorem through textbooks is another instance of a compelling dissemination study. Medema had already used textbooks in the study he wrote with Roger Backhouse on the evolving definition of economics (Backhouse and Medema 2009) and, unlike most historians of economics, he is familiar with the current historiography of scientific textbooks, on which he reflected in a previous contribution (Medema 2012). In this piece, which is a transcript of his 2011 Blanqui lecture, Medema argues that using "textbooks as data" does not necessarily mean that they should be considered as passive recording devices of past economics. Citing Bensaude-Vincent et al.'s works on the history of chemistry textbooks, Medema stresses that textbooks play a crucial role in the making of normal science, the latter being no less worthy of attention than its revolutionary counterpart and warns fellow historians against the temptation to treat textbooks in a critical, retrospective way, even arguing that as increasingly standardized items, they tend to be the best proxies of the assimilation of one specific idea or technique. He adds that textbooks can be used in order to tell stories of science education and mass communication. As the lecture turns more specifically to the issue of how the Coase theorem was incorporated into the textbook literature, Medema claims that misinterpretations of Coase's original intent do not matter from a historical point of view. What matters, however, is why such deviations from the original "theorem" occur. Medema, therefore, lists several reasons: some that are related to pedagogical concerns and some which he relates to the author's stances, either personal or reflecting his affiliation. Because of its quite general scope, the lecture does not really detail the textbook literature. That is done in a subsequent working paper (Medema 2014) devoted to the dissemination of the theorem in intermediate microeconomics textbooks. Here, the author studies in detail 48 textbooks published between 1960 – the year of publication of Coase's "The Problem of Social Cost" – and 1979. Using a relatively exhaustive number of US texts means that textbooks written by relatively authoritative figures such as George Stigler are treated along with lesser-known authors. Just like Kaiser's study of the dispersion of Feynman diagrams, Medema's textbook analysis shows many different variants of the Coase theorem. Medema's main finding is that while Coase's use of the theorem was mostly theoretical, it is presented in these textbooks in ways that makes it more suited to the treatment of environmental issues. His interpretation is that textbooks are more interested in practical applications of the theorem because their authors want to keep the students interested. The paper, therefore, argues that textbooks have played a role in making the Coase theorem a staple of environmental economics.

Textbooks within an economist's life

Another way in which textbooks are introduced in the history of recent economics is in monographs and biographical accounts. There are generally thick histories – relying on archival materials – even though their main intent was not necessarily to reflect on textbooks per se. Here, again, studies on Samuelson's textbook clearly prevail. The MIT economist himself wrote an autobiographical piece on the textbook (Samuelson 1997) in response to one of his critics (Skouzen 1997) using anecdotes to do so – Samuelson's own historiographical approach when dealing with contemporary economics (see Weintraub 2016a). Following the arrival of Samuelson's personal papers at Duke in 2011, narratives about the birth and development of the textbook, which are not weighed down by its author's attempts to protect his legacy, have been written. Backhouse's (2017a) biography of Samuelson, which ends with the publication of the first edition of *Economics*, clearly points to the textbook, along with the theoretical contribution *Foundations of Economic Analysis* published a year before, as the touchstone of modern economics. But claiming this would not differ from Samuelson's own claim if it was not accompanied by another claim: that the textbook also played a more intimate role in Samuelson's life career, namely to allow him to "become Samuelson". The textbook presented a public face of the author that was not contained in his academic papers, that of an "applied macroeconomist", following his participation in the National Resources Planning Board during World War II and his writing articles on policy in the *New Republic*. *Economics*' allegedly Keynesian bent was influenced by these war and postwar experiences, as well as by the proximity to Harvard Professor Alvin Hansen, more so than by an allegiance to Keynes' own writing. When the textbook was received with controversies, mostly coming from the anti-Roosevelt, right-wing industrial milieu, Samuelson sought to deter criticisms by softening the textbook's relatively political overtone and by pretending that he had never been a true Keynesian, thus constructing a somewhat ambiguous middle-of-the-road position (see also Giraud 2014). Looking at the textbook through the influence of Hansen, Backhouse shows that the textbook was not solely intended as a principles text. Although it served specific purposes at MIT – training future engineers with little interest in economics – it was also conceived as an intellectual contribution to public finance, while Hansen and other so-called Keynesians were doing the same in more conventional treatise form.

Moving away from the first edition also brings useful information to understand the textbook. In a recent paper, Backhouse (2017b) reasserts that the textbook is not just a pedagogical device but also Samuelson's main contribution to policy issues, even more so than his pieces in newspapers and magazines. Samuelson even used materials prepared for the fifth edition of his textbook to advise the Senator John Kennedy. Not unlike the story told in Kaiser (2012) for postwar physics textbooks, this story illustrates how fluid is the textbook status and how a piece conceived for the classroom can also serve other purposes. Similarly, Giraud (2017) explores the role of *Economics* in the late 1960s and early 1970s, showing how the textbook was revised in order to respond to attacks from younger radical economists. The story told is not just one involving ideological divergences in the economics profession, but also sheds light on how an increasingly competitive textbook market influenced the textbook in its period of maturity. Facing criticisms but also the emergence of a new generation of textbooks, such as McConnell or Richard Lipsey, Samuelson is forced to introduce numerous changes in-between editions and is helped for this purpose by his editorial team at McGraw-Hill. The book that bears his name is still pretty much his own but following the authors' unwillingness to do these revisions from the late 1970s onward, it slowly transforms into a franchise. The standardization of postwar textbooks, therefore, is not just the story of all of the textbooks resembling more to Samuelson's but one of mutual stabilization. Thicker accounts of textbooks, therefore, are an invitation to reconsider the line between authorial intent and external constraints.

J.E. King and Alex Millmow's (2003) account of Joan Robinson and John Eatwell's *An Introduction to Modern Economics*, the only monographic contribution to textbooks not dealing with Samuelson's, constitutes a welcome counterpoint, and not just because Robinson was known as one of mainstream economics' most ardent critics. Robinson's textbook was indeed intended as an alternative to Samuelson and to other leading American texts of the time – interestingly, it was also published by McGraw-Hill – but the authors' depiction of its stinging failure to do so tells us something about how textbooks work. While both Giraud (2010, 2014) and Backhouse (2017a) emphasize that *Economics* arose from pedagogical issues, namely the necessity to teach engineering undergrads at MIT, King and Millnow observe that neither Robinson nor Eatwell had taught an introductory class. As a result, the textbook structure and content were solely driven by its authors' theoretical bent when those of *Economics* reflected both theoretical positions and educational concerns. Whereas Samuelson accepted to revise his manuscript in order to deter early criticisms, and would go on doing so edition after edition, Robinson's stubbornness generated numerous tensions with the team of students and staff who were supposed to advise her on and whose ideas she most often rejected. McGraw-Hill eventually refused to release the book in the United States as it was deemed unsuitable for American undergraduate students. As King and Millnow observe at some point in their narrative, Robinson and Eatwell's book simply lacked the "feel" of an actual textbook. The paper convincingly conveys that textbooks can only work within certain pedagogical practices. It is not so much the dissenting character of Robinson and Eatwell's text that explains its lack of success but the fact that they tried to write a textbook without much introductory teaching experience, as opposed to Samuelson's ability, not just to convey the Keynesian revolution, but also to address students' concerns.

Textbooks and departments

The recent shift in the focus of historians of economics from the study of individuals to that of creative communities (Forget and Goodwin 2011) has produced a few enlightening accounts of economics departments in the postwar period, some of which show that textbooks have played a role in creating a sense of community inside these institutions or an image towards outsiders. Two departments in particular have been studied: MIT and the Chicago School.

As it is well known, there was not anything like an identifiable economics department at MIT before the arrival of Paul Samuelson whose textbook *Economics* served first and foremost as a tool to teach economics principles and policies to future engineers but soon contributed to promoting MIT economics as whole. As Harro Maas (2014) argued, what made the textbook so controversial in its first years was how it was expected to present an image of MIT to a broader audience. Conservative critics often claimed that Samuelson's alleged left-wing bent would be detrimental to the Institute's notoriety as a serious, apolitical, engineering school. In response to these attacks, Samuelson carefully constructed a middle-of-the-road position through the textbook and promoted it in various leaflets and press interviews that helped strengthen the reputation of the department as a purveyor of balanced, technical economics expertise. Expanding the study beyond Samuelson's case, Pedro Teixeira (2014) shows that MIT economists have had "significant involvement with the production of textbooks". He identifies 72 textbooks written by 39 economists who have studied or taught at MIT in the postwar period, contributing to teaching and research at the undergraduate and graduate levels. These textbooks did not only reflect MIT's focus on teaching – which was important in the first decades following World War II – but its commitment to technicality and generality – MIT economists wrote few specialized graduate texts and rather focused on microeconomics, macroeconomics, and mathematical and quantitative methods.

Textbooks played a role at the University of Chicago as well. Although written when George Stigler was at Columbia, his graduate text *The Theory of Competitive Price* (1942), later republished with additional materials as *The Theory of Price* (1946), along with other practices such as the Chicago workshop, was essential in disseminating the "Chicago Price Theory Tradition" (Medema 2011). Using an alteration of Robbins' definition of economics as "the allocation of scarce means among competing ends", Stigler paved the way for the kind of economic analysis of non-economic problems the Chicago School became famous for – for instance, Becker's economic approach to or Posner's economic analysis of law. Jean-Baptiste Fleury (2012) explores a different kind of textbook literature, one that stands at the crossroads between academic writing and popular economics, the "economics-made-fun movement", represented today by Chicago economist Steven Levitt's best seller *Freakonomics*. Fleury shows that Levitt's highly popular book is only the latest instantiation of a sort of text that applied economic analysis to a range of everyday problems. One of its predecessors was Richard McKenzie and Gordon Tullock's *The New World of Economics* – Tullock was a former student at the University of Chicago – which resembled Levitt's, although its targeted audience were undergraduate and graduate students, rather than the public at large. These textbooks arose from pedagogical debates happening in the 1960s, when economics education suffered a crisis of "relevance" and principles text like Samuelson's were deemed unsuitable for the issues of the day. Like Kaiser's piece on physics textbooks, Fleury's article is a good example of how flexible the frontier between academic texts and popular books can be (see Chapter 10 by Mata in this volume).

The existing literature on this topic is still fragmentary but more should be expected when historians of economics expand their studies to other economics departments or to the study of economics taught in social science departments or engineering schools.

Towards better and thicker histories of economics textbooks

As the above sections hopefully conveyed, there is much more to historical studies of economics textbooks than depictions of how textbooks lag behind the latest advances in economics research or studies in the dissemination of economics concepts. Yet even the latter, if done properly, can yield important results, showing how textbooks do not just disseminate knowledge, but by altering it, contribute to create new meanings and uses of preexisting economics ideas. An accurate account of how textbooks disperse and affect knowledge requires a lot of research in order to build a good database of textbooks to analyze. When Steven Medema began his research on this subject, he did not have much accumulated knowledge to rely on.[6] There is still some progress to be made on this side of economics textbook research. While individual authors like Medema have been able to assemble large personal collections of textbooks in order to substantiate their accounts, there has been, to the best of my knowledge, no attempt at building a list of the most popular undergraduate and graduate textbooks over time. To build such a list would require to cross-check a great number of reading lists in departmental archives. This can be helped by the use of some publishers' reports, containing detailed studies of available textbooks at a certain point in time. Some of McGraw-Hill reports are found in the Samuelson archives at Duke University. They contain some sales figures as well as a list of institutions using such or such textbook. These documents are necessarily fragmentary and are rarely available over the long period, yet even a fragmentary or incomplete list would help. Besides, the kind of digital collection Irwin L. Collier has assembled for economics departments' curriculums would be equally useful for textbooks.[7] There are of course a number of factors limiting such endeavors. Copyright is one of them: whereas some prewar textbooks are easily findable on websites such as archive.org, postwar texts still fall, for the most, under copyright laws. Another limitation is that building a textbook collection, while useful for further research, is rarely seen as well-spent research time. When many members of the community still see textbooks as low-status items, as opposed to research articles one can now easily find on databases such as JStor or EconLit with Full Text, it is not easy to convince funding agencies that such undertaking is vital to the understanding of how economics works. However, we can hope that in the near future, a more systematic recourse to blogs and social networks could help gather more information on textbooks.

Beyond studies in dissemination, there is a vast horizon for future research. What we need are studies that look further than Samuelson's *Economics* and focus on lesser-known authors such as McConnell, Bach, or Heilbronner for instance. The economic journalist and textbook author Leonard Silk, whose archives are also located in the Economists' Papers collection, could be an interesting case study. A closer look at the story behind the making of Lipsey's *An Introduction to Positive Economics* and its North-American counterpart Lipsey and Peter Steiner's *Economics* could offer an interesting view in the changing textbook cultures on each part of the Atlantic. Moreover, echoing Simon's (2016) concerns with the overrepresentation of American and European science in existing historical accounts, future studies should also focus more on textbooks published in other parts of the world and in texts not initially published in English. This could help enlighten the role of scientific education and reveal specific scientific policies concerns in developing and peripheral countries, for instance. Studies of translations of American texts would also offer interesting cases of dispersion, offering more accurate studies of standardization – or lack thereof – in postwar economics. They would certainly highlight the role of figures that were neglected in the current historiography, not only textbook authors but also translators of British and North-American texts.

One importance deficiency of the existing literature, which we already spotted earlier in this chapter, is the lack of studies focusing on graduate textbooks. It is now well established that a number of economic traditions in the postwar period have been associated with the creation of successful graduate programs. François Claveau and Yves Gingras' (2016) recent bibliometric analysis of the formation of economic specialties in the recent period points to graduate texts such as Jean Tirole's *The Theory of Industrial Organization* (1988) or Olivier Blanchard and Stanley Fischer's *Lectures on Macroeconomics* (1989) as some of the most cited references in fields their authors often contributed to create or develop. The genesis of these texts, their uses in their respective specialties for teaching and research purposes need to be better studied. Granted, this would require from the historian's side more openness to the sophistication of recent economics, while studies of undergraduate texts do not require much mathematical proficiency.

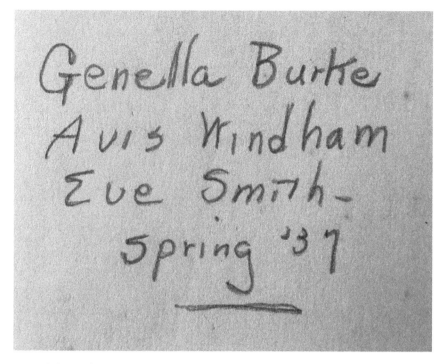

Figure 8.1 Handwritten note on the free front page of Garver and Hansen's *Principles of Economics* (author's copy)

On a final note, I would like to tell a personal anecdote about textbooks that reminds me of the *Cold Case* story. The first textbook I bought for historical purposes was Frederic Garver and Alvin Hansen's *Principles of Economics* (1928). My interest in this was that it seemed to have been one of the most popular textbooks when Samuelson was a student. As it is often the case with used copies of textbooks, mine came with a number of notations in pencil and underlining to the text. On the fore edge, it had "AGE" written with a pen, an acronym for Avis, Genella, and Eve, as a handwritten note on the free front page made clear.

Who were Genella Burke, Avis Windham, and Eve Smith, who bought this book in the spring of 1937? Were they pursuing a degree in economics or were they studying economics as part of a more general curriculum? They may have attended a women's college but they may as well have bought it for the sake of intellectual curiosity. I will probably never clear that out. I have tried to look for more elements but they are few and quite uncertain to start with. Having bought this through an online seller and having no clue about the location of the used books store does not make it easy. There is an obituary record for a Genella Burke, who died at the age of 87 in 2005 in Birmingham, Alabama, and a few Avis Windham who could match the note – Eve Smith, by contrast, may be too generic a name to find, but all of this proved to be much too meager to be followed seriously. Yet, that handwritten note on an old textbook helps envision a different kind of economics textbook history, one that is written, not from the point of view of their authors, but from that of the "ordinary" people for whom economics education was intended in the first place. Other historiographical techniques depicted in this volume can help write such histories and, hopefully, more "cold cases" will soon be solved.

Notes

1 "Devil Music", *Cold Case*, Season 5, Episode 4 (2007). This textbook sequence was first brought to my attention by Loïc Charles' (2008) blog post, although at the time he misidentified the textbook as Samuelson's *Economics*. I subsequently wrote a blog post myself in response (Giraud 2011).
2 See Kuhn's negative comments on textbooks in his 1959 lecture at the University of Utah (in Kuhn 1977 [1959], pp. 228–229): "Except in their occasional introduction, science textbooks do not describe the sorts of problems that the professional may be asked to solve and the variety of techniques available for their solution. Rather these books exhibit concrete problem solutions that the profession has come to accept as paradigms ... Nothing could be better calculated to produce 'mental sets' or *Einstellungen*".
3 Vicedo is referring to the "diffusion model" described and criticized in Latour (1987).
4 Now discontinued after 19 editions, Samuelson's textbook was first published under the title *Economics: An Introductory Analysis* in 1948 before being shortened to *Economics* for its 8th edition (1970). The 10th edition (1976) was written with the help of MIT economic historian Peter Temin, who took care of the empirics. From the 12th edition onward, William Nordhaus stepped in as Samuelson's co-author.
5 Here, as the author of two published papers and one draft paper on the subject, I clearly must assume my part of the blame for this situation.
6 A query he posted on our profession's main mailing list to look for the most popular textbooks of the 1970s and 1980s yielded little useful information. See "SHOE: QUERY – The Relative Popularity of Economics Textbooks in the 1970s and 1980s" and responses, Archives of SHOE@YORKU.CA Societies for the History of Economics, available at https://listserv.yorku.ca/archives/shoe.html (last accessed October 10, 2017).
7 Economics from the rear-view mirror: archival artifacts from the history of economics, www.irwincollier.com/ (last accessed October 6, 2017). See his chapter in the volume as well.

References

Augello, Massimo M., and Marco E. L. Guidi (eds) (2012). *The Economic Reader: Textbooks, Manuals and the Dissemination of the Economic Sciences during the 19th and Early 20th Centuries.* London, Routledge.
Backhouse, Roger E. (2017a). *Founder of Modern Economics: Paul A. Samuelson. Volume 1: Becoming Samuelson, 1915–1948.* Oxford, Oxford University Press.
Backhouse, Roger E. (2017b). "Samuelson and Kennedy: Textbook author as policy adviser." Working Paper (Preliminary draft, March 2017).
Backhouse, Roger and Steven G. Medema (2009). "On the Definition of Economics." *Journal of Economic Perspectives* 23(1): 221–233.

Bensaude-Vincent, Bernadette, Antonio Garcia-Belmar, and José R. Bertomeu-Sanchez (2003). *La naissance d'une science des manuels (1789–1852)*. Paris, Edition des Archives Contemporaines.

Charles, Loïc (2008). "The Icon." Blog entry. https://historyofeconomics.wordpress.com/2008/09/26/the-icon/ (last accessed, February 9, 2018).

Claveau, François and Yves Gingras (2016). "Macrodynamics of Economics: A Bibliometric History." *History of Political Economy*, 48(4): 551–592.

Colander, David (2012). "The Evolution of US Economics textbooks." In M. Augello and M. Guidi (eds) *The Economic Reader*. London, Routledge: 324–339.

Colander, David, Richard Holt B., and Barkley Rosser Jr (2004). "The Changing Face of Mainstream Economics." *Review of Political Economy* 16(4): 485–499.

Elzinga, Kenneth G. (1992). "Eleven Principles of Economics." *Southern Economic Journal* 58(4): 861–879.

Fleury, Jean-Baptiste (2012). "The Evolving Notion of Relevance: An Historical Perspective to the 'Economics Made Fun' Movement." *Journal of Economic Methodology* 19(3): 303–316.

Fontaine, Philippe (2016). "Other Histories of Recent Economics: A Survey." *History of Political Economy* 48(3): 373–421.

Forder, James (2015). "Textbooks on the Phillips Curve." *History of Political Economy* 47(2): 207–224.

Forget, Evelyn L. and Craufurd D. Goodwin (2011). "Intellectual Communities in the History of Economics." *History of Political Economy* 43(1): 1–23.

Giraud, Yann (2010). "The Changing Place of Visual Representation in Economics: Paul Samuelson between Principle and Strategy, 1941–1955." *Journal of the History of Economic Thought* 32(2): 175–197.

Giraud, Yann (2011). "A Cold Case." Blog entry. https://www.ineteconomics.org/perspectives/blog/a-cold-case (last accessed February 9, 2018).

Giraud, Yann (2014). "Negotiating the 'Middle-of-the-Road' Position: Paul Samuelson, MIT and the Politics of Textbook Writing, 1945–55." *History of Political Economy* 46 (Supplement): 134–152.

Giraud, Yann (2017). "The Contestable Marketplace of Ideas: Paul Samuelson's Defense of Mainstream Economics Through Textbook Making, 1967–1976". Working paper, https://papers.ssrn.com/sol3/papers.cfm?abstract_id=3009252 (last accessed July 26, 2017).

Kaiser, David (2005). *Drawing Theories Apart: The Dispersion of Feynman Diagrams in Postwar Physics*. Chicago, University of Chicago Press.

Kaiser, David (2012). "A Tale of Two Textbooks: Experiments in Genre." *Isis* 103(1): 126–138.

King, J. E. and Alex Millmow (2003). "Death of a Revolutionary Textbook." *History of Political Economy* 35(1): 105–134.

Kuhn, Thomas (1977 [1959]). "The Essential Tension: Tradition and Innovation in Scientific Research." In T. Kuhn (ed.), *The Essential Tension: Selected Studies in Scientific Tradition and Change*. Chicago, University of Chicago Press: 225–239.

Latour, Bruno (1987). *Science in Action*. Cambridge, Harvard University Press.

Levy, David M. and Sandra J. Peart (2009). "Soviet Growth and American Textbooks." Working paper, http://ssrn.com/abstract=1517983 (last accessed June 29, 2017).

Lundgren, Anders and Bernadette Bensaude-Vincent (eds) (2000). *Communicating Chemistry: Textbooks and Their Audiences, 1789–1939*. Canton, Science History Publications.

Maas, Harro (2014). "Making Things Technical: Samuelson at MIT." *History of Political Economy* 46 (Supplement): 272–294.

Medema, Steven G. (2011). "Chicago Price Theory and Chicago Law and Economics: a Tale of Two Transitions." In Robert van Horn, Philip Mirowski and Thomas Stapleford (eds), *Building Chicago Economics: New Perspectives on the History of America's Most Powerful Economics Program*. Cambridge, Cambridge University Press: 151–179

Medema, Steven G. (2012). "Textbooks as Data for the Study of the History of Economics: Lowly Beast or Fruitful Vineyard?" *History of Economic Thought and Policy* 2: 193–207.

Medema, Steven G. (2014). "How Textbooks Create Knowledge and Meaning: The Case of the Coase Theorem in Intermediate Microeconomics." Working paper, https://papers.ssrn.com/sol3/papers.cfm?abstract_id=2479732 (last accessed June 29, 2017).

Nelson, Robert H. (2001). *Economics as Religion: From Samuelson to Chicago and Beyond*. University Park, Pennsylvania State University Press.

Patiniotis, Manolis (2006). "Textbooks at the Crossroads: Scientific and Philosophical Textbooks in 18th Century Greek Education." *Science and Education 15*: 801–822.

Pearce, Kerry A. and Kevin D. Hoover (1995). "After the Revolution: Paul Samuelson and the Textbook Keynesian Model." *History of Political Economy 27*(Supplement): 183–216.

Rocke, Alan J. (2010). *Image and Reality: Kekilé, Kopp and the Scientific Imagination*. Chicago, University of Chicago Press.

Samuelson, Paul A. (1997). "Credo of a Lucky Textbook Author." *Journal of Economic Perspectives 11*(2): 153–160.

Simon, Josep (2016). "Textbooks." In Bernard Lightman (ed.) *A Companion to the History of Science*. Chichester, John Willey and Sons: 400–413.

Skousen, Mark (1997). "The Perseverance of Paul Samuelson's Economics." *Journal of Economic Perspectives 11*(2): 137–152.

Teixeira, Pedro (2014). "Serving the Institute and the Discipline: The Changing Profile of Economics at MIT as Viewed from Textbooks." *History of Political Economy 46* (Supplement): 153–174.

Vicedo, Marga (2012). "Introduction: The Secret Lives of Textbooks". *Isis 103*(1): 83–87.

Weintraub, E. Roy (2016a). "Paul Samuelson's Historiography: More Wag than Whig." *History of Political Economy 48*(2): 349–363.

Weintraub, E. Roy (2016b). "Game Theory and Cold War Rationality: A Review Essay." Economic Research Initiatives at Duke (ERID) Working Paper No. 208, https://ssrn.com/abstract=2737005 (last accessed October 4, 2017).

Part IV

Material histories of economics

9 Artifacts in the contemporary history of economics

Verena Halsmayer[1]

Introduction

An artifact is an object made by a human being. As economists do or make economics, they employ artifacts. Historians of science have turned their attention to the practices of scientists, their actual "doing" and have often turned away from viewing science as a sequence of ideas and theories. As economists make economics with models (Morgan 2012; Boumans 2005; Maas 2014), in an earlier paper (Halsmayer 2018) I explored a historiographical perspective that follows models as artifacts. This means 1) to follow the shifts and changes in their form and meaning, 2) to follow the ideas, theories, fictions, and imaginary worlds they provoke, and 3) to investigate the ways in which some of them stabilize and remain as infrastructures of economic reasoning in mundane, academic, and policy realms, as well as the ways in which some of them either do not circulate at all or simply get lost.

Such perspectives regarding the complexity and dynamics of knowledge creation lead us out of the narrower history of disciplinary knowledge and, moreover, direct our attention to different temporal scales. Seeing artifacts as relational and sometimes ephemeral leads to further reflections on the character of the artifacts that are involved in creating, saving, and mediating economic knowledge.[2] What kinds of questions emerge from following these artifacts? If the historian follows their changes and shifts, in what ways might this help in investigating not only what is seen as "the economy" and as "economic" at certain times and places, but the material effects of economic knowledge? The following essay will approach these questions through looking more closely at the notion of "artifacts", and through exemplifying this notion by way of the various artifacts involved in the making of input–output knowledge, at the Harvard Economic Research Project. But first, what is it to historicize "the economy"?

The economy as artifact

One of the themes related to the history of economics that has received increased attention over the past few years, primarily from scholars outside the community of historians of economics, has been the "making of the economy". This interest in the emergence of the economy as a self-contained social whole with its own laws has a long history that appears to have peaked in the 1990s. In a seminal paper from 1995, Susan Buck-Morss situated the object of the economy as an invention of Enlightenment Europe, necessitated by the idea that the exchange of goods was the basis of collective life (1995, p. 439). Displayed as a self-regulatory system from its very beginnings, the economy was based on metaphors of flows and cycles, in which goods, capital, work, and money circulated (Vogl 2014). Whether in encyclopedic, organic, mechanic, hydraulic, or bookkeeping form, this object and the various concepts associated with it were not separable from the artifacts which made this economy visible. New images brought about new visibilities, and motivated actions and interventions.

The prime example of an image of the economic whole is François Quesnay's Tableau Èconomique (Charles 2003). As an artifact, the tableau presented a display of the body politic, and a model which could be manipulated and experimented with (Morgan 2012, pp. 3–5). Arranging a balanced whole, the tableau not only laid the visual foundation for technologies of governance but also provided an instrument for organizing empirical material for the systematic measurement of this economy. Since existing statistics did not conform to the tableau's theoretical categories, the physiocratic project investigated various possibilities to create suitable empirical material, seeking to provide numbers for economic governance—some of which were successful, and some of which failed (Charles and Théré 2012). The tableau did not only make the economy intellectually manageable through providing an overview from above but nurtured actions to order the economic-empirical reality it suggested.

Irrespective of earlier usages of the term, Timothy Mitchell noted that the economy, as compared to the "nation" or the "state", was a rather young concept. He argued that it was only from the 1930s on that the economic whole became an aggregate of national production, consumption, and distribution, separate from other spheres of social life (Mitchell 1998, p. 84 and 91).[3] Just a year later, the philosopher of science Ian Hacking used the economy as a formidable example in explicating constructionist approaches.

> Every day we read that the economy is up or down, and we are supposed to be moved to fear or elation. Yet this splendid icon, the economy, was hard to find on the front pages of newspapers even forty years ago. Why are we so unquestioning about this very idea, "the economy"?
>
> (Hacking 1999, p. 13)

His point was to lay out the complex ways in which ideas are entrenched in matrices – assemblages of institutions, material infrastructures, etc. – and thereby co-create realities. Since then, several contributions investigated the creation of the economy (for instance, Desrosières 2003; Breslau 2003; Mitchell 2005, 2014; Düppe 2011; Speich Chassé 2013; Dommann, Speich Chassé, and

Suter 2014).[4] Whether from the perspective of social theory, phenomenology, science studies, global history, or economic sociology, at the center of most of these works is a focus on the vast ensemble of statistical entities and mathematical techniques that gave new form to older visions of the economy, and imprinted the new entity and associated notions like "growth" or "global inequality" in governmental procedures, business routines, and everyday practices. Institutions were established that assembled and distributed new knowledge about the economy and created experts who, with their apparati at their sides, were deemed capable of investigating this entity, finding out about its workings, and making it an object of governance.

When thinking of the economy, artifacts have at least a dual role to play: on the one hand, they are a historiographical resource, a heuristic tool for the historian to think about the epistemic practices of making economic knowledge and its effects on "doing the economy". On the other, they are also a way of addressing and questioning issues of "economization" without presupposing a category of the economy but rather asking for the changing qualities of what is related to as "economic", and what is seen as "non-economic". In this sense, it is not merely the tools and techniques, the aesthetics, and pragmatics of creating economic knowledge that is at issue, but rather, as sociologist Ute Tellmann emphasizes, "a historical ontology of an attribute" (2014, 169). There are several examples from the study of material culture (predominantly paying attention to the semantic and symbolic dimensions of things) that can easily be related to histories of economic knowledge. These examples blur the subdisciplinary boundaries between economic, social, and cultural history, and deal with business ephemera such as the stock ticker, the spread sheet, and the office memo (for instance, Yates 1989; Guillory 2004; Lipartito 2016 provides an overview). In one of the texts that have recently pushed for new histories of capitalism, historian Seth Rockman (2017) denotes such artifacts as "paper technologies of capitalism", which were essential for the success of capitalist business practices. Looking at the character and workings of paper technologies, he argues, sheds light on "capitalist ways of seeing", and gives life to the social history of production, consumption, and distribution organized in the form of books, documents, and paper. These forms, the kinds of communication and cooperation they afford, and the formatting of information they present, so the literature suggests, might be more important than their content. It is argued, for example, that early modern integration is crucially prefigured by price currents, i.e., printed sheets of exchange rates of commodity prices at specific markets, which were shipped from one place to the other and thereby formed a new web of exchange. These technologies and the related practices of record keeping not only made markets visible and made you see arbitrage right in front of you but formatted new personae and framed specific ways of seeing.

The attention to artifacts, the related practices to collect, organize, save, and process knowledge and their interaction with texts, theories, ways of seeing, and possibilities of reasoning have been at the center of the history of science and science and technology studies under the labels of the "circulation" or "transfer" of knowledge, or as "biographies" of knowledge objects.[5] Looking for the ways in which locally situated practices relate to global formations of knowledge, these literatures have developed their own pool of concepts enhancing the status of artifacts that create scientific objects and make phenomena visible (images, models, photographs, tables, statistics, etc.). Concepts such as "boundary object", "immutable mobile", "inscription device", and "infrastructure" focus on the study of the practices and processes, the intermediate steps, and also the unsuccessful aspects in the making of knowledge, and ask whether these are not much more important for its understanding than its finished products.

Artifacts as boundary objects

Artifacts are relational objects, which means that they are artifacts not because of some specific inherent characteristic, some essential attribute such as a particular kind of materiality, but rather because they are treated as such (Riles 2006, pp. 16–17). Artifacts can be concrete, physical objects (such as books, survey forms, tables, or computers) or more abstract objects (such as lists of factors, equations, shared ideas, or systems of proposition and proof). One feature of artifacts is their interpretive flexibility while keeping a certain coherence in all their different manifestations and variations so that it is – roughly – the same artifact. This feature has been emphasized by science studies scholars Susan Leigh Star and James R. Griesemer (1989) in their concept of "boundary objects". They investigate how different actors worked together in projects of Berkeley's Museum of Vertebrate Zoology (one of the museums created since the 19th century and that constituted a crucial step in the professionalization of natural history).[6] Despite having different interests, aims, and goals, the actors ("the first director of the museum, university administrators, professors, research scientists, curators, amateur collectors, private sponsors and patrons, occasional field hands, government officials and members of scientific clubs" (Star and Griesemer 1989, p. 392)) were brought together both through the standardization of methods, and through boundary objects. A set of standardized methods was put in place to make the information collected by laypeople accessible to professional analysis; however, the control of methods was not enough to enable the project of the museum. Overly disciplinary action would have stoked resistance and decreased willingness to cooperate, which is why Star and Griesemer emphasize the role of boundary objects: they live in different social worlds at the same time. These worlds provided radically disparate meanings to the objects of common interest to the actors, and thereby promoted collaboration.

Cooperation in this sense does not hinge on a consensus theory or world view but rather on the flexibility and robustness of a shared object. Such boundary objects can be all kinds of artifacts. Star and Griesemer (1989, pp. 409–411) catalogue four of many possible types, for which several exemplary artifacts in the making of economic knowledge come to mind:

1) repositories, piling and indexing heterogenous objects in a standardized way, such as libraries or archives, which bring together different kinds of books, archival sources, etc. so that people from different social worlds – empirical researchers, economic journalists, or business historians – can access them without having to care about their differences; 2) ideal types such as diagrams or models, which are vague enough to serve as a common object for various heterogenous aims and purposes. Seen as historical documents, Debreu's axiomatic systems, for instance, were ambivalent in their economic meaning (Düppe 2017), but this very ambivalence – perhaps irritating to the author himself – provided the necessary openness in interpretation to circulate widely; 3) "coincident boundaries", which describe the common contours of an object with different contents. An example is when data for the same categories of economic measurement are aggregated by different means, or the creation of a physical artifact like the Phillips-Newlyn machine, which was compatible with heterogenous theories but constituted a common object of the macroeconomy for all of them (Morgan and Boumans 2004); 4) standardized forms such as standardized indexes or labels, which ensure that the information collected is homogenized. As bureaucratic media they work like Bruno Latour's "immutable mobiles", as artifacts, which can be transferred over long distances, eradicating local uncertainties (1990).

In all these examples, artifacts stand out through their interpretative flexibility, which brings us back to the following of artifacts as relational objects:

> Boundary objects are objects which are both plastic enough to adapt to local needs and the constraints of the several parties employing them, yet robust enough to maintain a common identity across sites . . . They have different meanings in different social worlds but their structure is common enough to more than one world to make them recognizable, a means of translation.
>
> (Star and Griesemer 1989, p. 393)

Star and Griesemer focus on a specific feature of artifacts, namely their social acceptance and usage, rather than on their materiality, stubbornness, and recalcitrance – which take center stage when looking at the practices of modeling or experimenting. They urge us to look more closely at the relation between actors' day-to-day work, and the resulting tools and applications. This does not mean that the materiality and thingness of boundary objects is neglected. Rather, it shifts the focus to their embedding into irreducible practices of scientific work, which hinge on a certain degree of cooperation, with or without a consensus on what the work is all about (cf. Gießmann 2015).

With these boundary-characteristics of artifacts in mind, what historiographical (rather than ethnographical) perspectives can be gained with regard to the contemporary history of economics? While commonly referring to a material thing, here an "artifact" is simply "something people . . . act toward and with. Its materiality derives from action, not from a sense of prefabricated stuff or 'thing'-ness (Star 2010, p. 603). Artifacts, in this sense, essentially structure economic research work: they organize various practices engaged in the making of economic knowledge, enable the cooperation of different actors, they shape the results of research, are crucial in transferring these results into different realms, and – not least – they frame the very objects that qualify as "economic".

Following artifacts at the Harvard Economic Research Project

One of the essential components of the ensemble of artifacts that brought about the notion of "the economy" between the 1930s and 1950s, and contributed to breaking down and thereby stabilizing this opaque entity, was input–output tables. As a distinctive empirical approach that developed around the same period as national income accounting and (macro)econometric modeling, input–output analysis made the economy visible in more detail than did existing displays and showed it as a system of "production flows". The relevant standards and techniques were developed at the end of the 1940s in one of the first large-scale data creation and processing projects of the immediate postwar era in the US.

At the time, common research work of economists consisted of writing narratives and developing numerical examples; research instruments were pencils and paper, probably slip boxes to capture excerpts from the many books that populated economists' libraries. When Leontief – four years after emigrating from the Soviet Union and with working experience at the National Bureau of Economic Research (NBER) – asked for a humble grant ($ 1,500) that exceeded what the "solitary thinker"-economist required, "the senior faculty", as Anne P. Carter (2012, p. 54), herself a long-time Harvard Economic Research Project (HERP) researcher recalls in her retroactive account on the role of "physical capital" in the Project's work, was "puzzled and skeptical". Eventually, the Harvard University Committee on Research in the Social Sciences approved the funding and the first input–output table of the US industry was finished by 1935. Yet this kind of research remained dubious in the eyes of the department (Dorfman 1995, p. 307). It took ten years, up to 1942 with the United States' entry into the war, for Leontief's research to become one of the many federal statistical services financed on the basis of a governmental effort to measure economic activity for wartime planning purposes. As a consultant at the US Office of Strategic Services and for the Department of Labor, Leontief supervised the compilation of a 92-sector table for the organization of the war economy at the US Bureau of Labor Statistics (BLS). With the help of a four-year grant from the Rockefeller Foundation, the collaboration led to the establishment of the HERP in 1947 at Harvard University (Kohli 2001, p. 191). Only the establishment of an institution like the HERP, backed by strong public funding and having early access to computing machines, afforded the large-scale creation of data, the computation of input–output coefficients, and the creation of input–output tables as tools of economic governance. A big part of the HERP's research that would lead to its major publication *Studies in the Structure of the American Economy* (Leontief and members of the Harvard Economic Research Project 1953), was financed by a contract with the US Air Force.[7] Intimately tied to the new techniques of linear programming and activity analysis, the HERP was organized as an *empirical* research institute.[8]

The many assistants of the HERP – as was usual for statistical workers and computing personnel at the time, they were mostly female – aimed at compiling "direct observations" of the material realities of production, which should then be filled into the tables.[9] Integrated in systems of simultaneous equations, the resulting coefficients demonstrated what would happen to the system in case of changes from the outside, and informed governmental action to counteract such effects. Looking at the HERP's research through the lens of artifacts enables several historiographical narratives. Portraying input–output tables as artifacts in the making rather than as ready-made knowledge allows us to study the intricate and manifold interrelations among research practices, various kinds of artifacts, new visibilities, objects, concepts, and knowledge for intervention.[10]

The work of researchers, following Star and Griesemer (1989, p. 393 and 406), consists in "translation", that is in creating abstract objects from concrete ones. The HERP embarked on the project of presenting "the economy as a whole" in this sense, as an abstract object that brought together several formal, empirical, and political endeavors at the time on a new scale by providing more comprehensive and more detailed empirical knowledge on production than any other contemporary statistical compilation. To this end, a whole variety of concrete and abstract artifacts, mathematical, statistical, technical, and verbal sediments of earlier research were engaged in creating the tables: from theoretical concepts such as the circular flow to the old economic metaphor of the "flow"; from the numbers given in engineering handbooks, corporation reports, and balance sheets to attempts to "direct empirical information" by interviews with production engineers; from accounting rules and balancing requirements to the affordability and restrictions that came with the new computing machines.

Creating empirical material

The historian interested in following the artifacts of the HERP's research is dependent on the material available in the archives. The Project's publications, as is common in economics, neither mentioned the work that was necessary to create empirical data, nor the artifacts involved in this work. The *Studies in the Structure*, for instance, hints only vaguely at "engineering data" as "a promising and accessible source of direct empirical information on the input-output structure of the individual industries" (Leontief et al. 1953, p. 14). Direct empirical information, so it seems to be suggested, could simply be collected, and could then provide ample access to the production structure of the national economy. Among the best sources that Leontief mentioned in an article in the early 1940s were engineering handbooks and other kinds of expert knowledge on production and consumption: "In analyzing the changing structure of the steel industry, we must get our information from the technical literature, from ironmasters and from rolling mill managers" (Leontief 1949, p. 225, cited in Boumans 2012, p. 4).

Behind the sparse hints in the literature lurk the many steps of research, which required a large part of the HERP's personal and financial resources. Most of the so-called "technical" and "engineering data" were gained from already available compilations such as industry accounts (i.e., balance sheet data), corporation reports, papers in trade journals, and reports by government agencies. One of the progress reports, issued regularly to inform patrons about research advancements, lists the most important sources of capital data: the Bureau of Internal Revenue's Statistics of income, Moody's company data, and the War Production Board's data on authorized war facilities. The rest of the data were provided by various administrative agencies such as the Bureau of Agricultural Economics and the Surplus Property Administrator, and magazines such as *Aviation Facts and Figures*, the *Minerals Yearbook*, and others. With regard to the interviews that were intended to disclose "direct information", it mentioned that numbers were compiled by consulting production officials, engineers, and technicians. However, written in 1950, after two years of empirical research, the report had to admit that while the endeavor to create such direct information was a "new departure for economics", it had brought about several unexpected difficulties. Not only was it time- and cost-intensive, it also confronted the researchers with the constraints of their ignorance. Under the heading "We need to know", the report registered the problems of creating research material and mentioned all the categories of the input–output scheme for which no sources could be found. While the advances in the construction of models, the development of industrial classification schemes, and the handling of computing techniques were easily praised, the goal of creating technical data for the economy as a whole was eventually deemed to be "utopian". Not only was little information gained from experts in production, but the numbers had also been shown to be unreliable (all: "Preliminary Report" 1950).

We can only speculate about the form and appearance of the (scarce) newly compiled research – whether the content of telephone conversations with production engineers was filled into standardized forms, whether interviews were recorded on the ground, on which documents the information given by interviewees were based, which questions were asked, and how all of these factors shaped the answers. In the end, only little of this research material remained: the HERP looked for very specific data with regard to concrete research questions. And the artifacts, which were supposed to disclose the information, had to be brought into the right shape in order to fit the other components of input–output research. Investigators were simply interested in the "information" that could be gained from the material: it could be easily matched with the object of research (in this case, the capital structure of the US economy), its specific problematization within a theoretical frame (input–output flows between sectors, static and dynamic), and the existing research infrastructure (mathematical models, computing techniques).

It is common for practitioners to speak of their material as if it was readymade and easily available, even though they spent much of their time on the (often futile) attempt to catch a piece of "direct information" describing the realities of production processes. The whole point of the language of "direct" was to differentiate the HERP's research from the "preponderantly deductive" partial equilibrium analysis at the Cowles Commission (Leontief et al. 1953, pp. 4–5). While econometricians such as Tjalling Koopmans or Trygve Haavelmo advocated probability-based techniques, the HERP held the view of economic accounting. Its researchers pursued a specific empirical approach that they strategically situated, in rather broad brushes, between econometric measurement practices and "radical empiricist" national income statistics (cf. Boumans 2012; Biddle 2017). Still, the HERP's researchers aimed at getting at the organizing "structure" of the national economy invoking the *tableau économique* as well as Walrasian general equilibrium. This did not mean, however, that mathematical models of a general equilibrium were used to interpret already-existing data (as would become standard econometrics from the 1970s on). In contrast, the HERP's notion of a balance basically referred to an accounting framework and its work depended on close collaboration with the BLS as a large-scale data creation project. For one, it took arduous efforts to create the data. Second, the scheme itself was not simply taken from a theoretical body of economic theory but had to be designed in a way that allowed for the material to be fitted in. In this sense, the HERP was not a place where ready-made mathematical formulae were merely filled with data, but provided a site for the mutual shaping of both concepts and artifacts, the desires of economic governance, and not least the expectations and intentions of researchers.

Filling tables

An artifact, the anthropologist Annelise Riles says, is "something one treats as if it were simply a found object in the world" (2006, pp. 16–17). Against the notion of "raw data" that input–output researchers seemed so keen on collecting, however, the existing material had to be cooked before it was included in input–output tables (cf. Gitelman 2013). The data from the various sources had been created for different purposes and questions, with different instruments of measurement, and under contingent circumstances. The work of creating tables required specific techniques and procedures of data homogenization, consistent with the guidelines, incorporating conventional and personal judgment of researchers interpreting and valuing data, checking the records, comparing the different infrastructures that created them, and finally bringing the different data into line with specific standards. As Anne Carter recalls, it took decades to develop "meaningful and consistent conventions" for creating input–output tables, i.e., the very rules of classification and definitions that would turn into a standard procedure: "Should transactions be measured in producers' or purchasers' prices? What about transportation costs? How should inconsistencies in reporting best be treated?" (2012, p. 54).

A major, more basic step in the process of homogenizing the data was to bring them into the same unit of measurement, i.e., to deal with the problem of valuation. Some of the numerical material provided counts of inputs and outputs in terms of physical units such as tons, bushels, ton miles, or man–hours. Other sources in turn provided the monetary value of inputs to production. The latter served as the means of homogenization: different materialities and measuring units were turned into the monetary quantity of their wholesale prices. Similar to measurement practices of national accountants, treating prices as the main measuring rod meant assuming that the market acted as a "unifying mechanism" combining heterogeneous things into one single value entity (Kuznets 1933, p. 208). When lumping together inputs and outputs of various industries, it was assumed that prices would be proportional to their marginal significances. This idea, rooted in marginal utility theory, amounted to saying that the price of the product said something about its relation to other products. Firms adjusted the quantities of production so that the marginal product of capital would (it was assumed) equal the price of capital, and the marginal product of labor was equated with the price of labor, i.e. the wage rate. The relation between inputs and outputs was therefore given in terms of prices and wages, which meant interpreting the data as stemming from a state of competitive equilibrium.

Once homogenized in terms of monetary value, data were still inaccurate and incomplete, and researchers brought them into a form that fit the empirical scheme. It was necessary to subdivide industries into several sub–industries such that the detailed data gathered on sub–industries could be "collapsed" into a single aggregate industry, "so as to reduce the amount of necessary computations" ("Preliminary Report" 1950). The division of the economy into sectors was somewhat arbitrary. One of the four fold-in tables inserted in the back of *Studies in the Structure* contains a comparison of eight different schemes of industrial classifications that had been used. The number of sectors seems to have been a trade-off between computability and complexity: the more sectors taken into account, the more detailed the analysis, but also the more complex the required computation. About 50 percent of the classified industrial groups were based on complete coverage; whether the collected data were sufficient to count for the remaining industries as well was a matter of researchers' judgment. The progress report of 1950, for instance, mentions that the available data for those industries with only a minor coverage of their plants "were felt to be typical of the industries which they represented".

As an accounting system the industrial scheme provided rules for correcting, interpolating, and completing the collected data in order to create a determinate system of interrelated variables. Input–output tables were basically a double-entry table charting "transactions" between different industries. For a specific year, the table tracked what each sector supplied to every other industrial sector and to final demand (households, government, "foreign countries", and gross private capital formation). The variables were related to each other in an unambiguous way, which provided a means to cross-check the consistency of the data and triangulate missing variables. Seen in this way, and akin to national accounting, input–output figures brought together several kinds of measurements and connected them into an overarching accounting framework (cf. Morgan 2011a, pp. 307–308). New measurements were created both by aggregating, i.e., summing up, the numbers found in existing records and by imputing missing data. The readymade tables portrayed a closed system of capital flows: everything that went into production was actually used for production; everything that was produced was either used in production or consumed by households.

What were the artifacts of input–output research at the HERP? In the first instance perhaps it was interview transcripts, newspaper excerpts, telephone notes, balance sheets of firms as well as tables with accounting data as compiled by the BLS. Merging various kinds of artifacts, input–output tables materialized the economy in a new form, which in turn brought about additional conceptual content. The HERP created displays of the national economy as viewed from above, looking at what flowed between industries. Brought into the right shape to fit the circular flow of capital, whatever flowed had hardly any resemblance with the research material that had been initially compiled. In this sense, input–output tables do bear traces of their history – think of the visualization of the tableau économique – but, due to their new shape, provided a new reification of the economy, opened up a new way of seeing this entity, and nurtured new actions to steer it.

Computers

New computational techniques and equipment were essential for the HERP's work. At the beginning of the 1930s, when Leontief compiled the first US input–output table, slide rules and electric calculators were still an essential part of the relevant office equipment for quantitative research. After his aim to calculate a system of 44 input–output equations had failed because it exceeded contemporary computing capacities, Leontief cooperated with his MIT colleague John B. Wilbur. The "Wilbur Machine", a mechanical analogue computer that was the size of a small car and weighed half a ton, allowed the calculation of a system with ten sectors (Leontief to Harvey 1948). Ten years later, in the year in which the BLS and Leontief founded the HERP, a group of researchers around the computing pioneer Howard Aiken finished the Harvard Mark II. Financed by and built for the US Navy, the electromechanical computer had built-in hardware for several mathematical functions (among them the logarithm, the square root, and the exponential). Leontief and Herb F. Mitchell, who was Aiken and Leontief's PhD student, used this large relay computer to solve a static system of 38 simultaneous linear equations – another boundary object that would prove useful to both economists (as it obtained numerical results on an unprecedented scale) and to computer scientists (developing improved calculation methods) (Iverson 1954, abstract). Answering questions of a journalist in 1948, Leontief explained that the satisfactory results of the application of a computer:

> To give you an idea about the magnitude of the computational job involved
> in inverting a 38×38 matrix, it is sufficient to state that in the process of this
> work, nearly 300,000 ten-digit numbers were punched into and read from
> tapes, and 1,500,000 digits were printed. Approximately 110,000 multi-
> plications and 350,000 additions were performed. The whole process took
> 59½ hours of uninterrupted machine time. This time should be doubled to
> include the time for set-up, tape-checking, trouble-shooting, etc.
>
> (Leontief to Harvey 1948)

In the mid-1950s, such operations had already become routine and the HERP's
computation of 1948 was repeated on the ENIAC (Electronic Numerical
Integrator and Computer) with a (pure) computing time of only 45 minutes
(Morgenstern 1954, pp. 495–496). The whole procedure of building up tables,
however, still took about two years (Golden 1959).

Parallel to the development of increasingly powerful computers, an artifact-
oriented history of input–output research could be told as a story of the ever-
better manageability of ever larger systems, which allowed for ever more
sophisticated techniques of managing the economy.[11] Computational techniques and equipment, however, were far more than a neutral enabling condition or a simple means for its calculations. For one, they essentially structured
the research practices of empirical workers. Apart from working with pen and
paper, the HERP's assistants operated mainframes, used electric calculators and
punching equipment to prepare cards, and waited for results. The computational routines also determined the composition, the division of labor, and the
skills required for the HERP's staff which, as well as many full- and part-time
researchers, included a professional computer programmer, a librarian, and
secretarial personnel (Carter 2012, pp. 55–56). In addition to these concrete
effects on the daily life of economic researchers, the introduction of computing
techniques afforded and nurtured the spread of a specific vision of the economy
materialized in input–output tables.

Merging frameworks of a circular flow, existing data with all the precon-
ceptions they contained, and the affordances and restrictions of contemporary
computing capacities, research at the HERP fabricated the first large-scale
input–output tables for the US. The related *mathematical* research object was
a thoroughly defined and internally consistent system of allocation of productive resources. While consumption and production of goods and services were,
specifically formatted, part of the system, all kinds of factors were excluded from
analysis. For instance, all tacit and non-plannable elements of production were
hidden in the black box of capital flows between sectors. And all aspects of
production that could not be assigned monetary value were likewise excluded.
Moreover, taking prices as representative of the relations between products
meant omitting all kinds of factors relevant to market prices such as oligopoly
and monopoly, cartels, dumping, subsidies, controls, etc. Input–output studies
excluded "land" as a factor of production, which was therefore neither part of
the tables nor of subsequent analysis; labor was treated as a homogenous factor,

meaning that there was no distinction, for instance, between manual and intellectual work. Everything unstable and contingent was described as being outside the production structure of technical coefficients and stable characteristics and was assumed as given, for instance, in the final demand, and thus taken to depend on "outside forces". Visualizing the inputs and outputs for all industries and sectors as "production flows" echoed the old metaphor of flowing liquid – money flowing like water, national wealth circulating like blood in the body, or national income as a hydraulic machine. Similar to these images, the economy input–output tables imagined was one of constant, unhampered circulation; there were, as Evsey Domar maintained, "whirlpools and cross currents where goods flow back and forth between industries" (Domar 1952, pp. 488–489). In such a balancing system, there was no slack, and no general over- or underproduction.

Similar to the way in which the HERP's publications spoke of a flow of empirical "information", which could simply be filled into tables without any further efforts being necessary, the tables visualized an immaterial and frictionless flow of information between industries about what and how much to produce. The invention of computing machines was not only crucial for the practical accomplishment of input–output research; they also contributed to perceiving the economy as an information system. In his appreciation of the Soviet economist L. Kantorovich's development of linear programming at the end of the 1950s, Leontief pointed out that this technique afforded a perspective on the "entire national economy as a kind of gigantic computer" (Leontief 1959, p. 629), and a few years later he added that as a computing machine it "tirelessly grinds out the solutions of an unending stream of quantitative problems" (Leontief 1966, p 237, cited in Mirowski 2002, p. 539). It is not a coincidence that the HERP's focus on the structure of the economy as a productive system and its early, heavy use of computers is reminiscent of the new research endeavors of systems analysis, cybernetics, and game theory. The image of the whole economy as a functional scheme that could be solved as a system of linear equations was structurally akin to attempts to analyze, for instance, systems in communication engineering, as an anecdote by structuralist linguist and literary theorist Roman Jakobson illustrates:

> [Jakobson] entered a Harvard lecture hall one day to discover that the economist Vassily Leontief, who had just finished using the room, had left an economic diagram of production on the blackboard. As Jakobson's students moved to erase the board, he declared, "Stop, I will lecture with this scheme." As he explained, "the problems of output and input in linguistics and economics are exactly the same."
>
> (cited in Geoghegan 2011, p. 116)

Interpreting capital flows between industries as the underlying capital structure of the national economy, however, opened up new possibilities for investigating the character and the dynamics of the system. From a structural point of view, economies with corresponding input–output coefficients were "structurally identical" and the comparison of input–output tables over time visualized the "structural change" of the respective economy.

Following input–output artifacts

The HERP eventually dissolved in the 1970s, at a time when input–output had already become a standard technique for the creation of economic knowledge and an essential component, if not the very basis, for a variety of modeling endeavors. Adapted to local conditions (institutional embedding, statistical systems, specific questions), it was used for planning and forecasting purposes. And in the more analytical realms of the economics discipline, it merged with the new mathematical techniques of linear programming and what was seen as conventional neoclassical theory, resulting in numerical general equilibrium modeling. So far, we have looked at the practices and artifacts involved in the making of input–output tables; following an artifact like the input–output scheme would mean to look as well at its transformations, the artifacts it engages with, the projects it initiates, the concepts it urges, and the surprises it leads you to. This could involve its abstraction in growth modeling, and dynamic programming, its adaptation as an actual tool for policy-making, or the circulation of the terminology of "input–output" drawing from and spreading to a variety of fields outside economics.

Between the 1950s and 1970s, in almost all countries in which planning models were constructed, input–output analysis was part of the models' architecture, either in the form of a straight-forward input–output model or as one element in a more complicated build-up. Whether through national economic management, or more centralized planning, these models were intended to help to find the best strategies for bringing the national whole into balance and sustaining this balance over time. After World War II the Central Planning Bureau of the Netherlands and the Norwegian Ministry of Finance, for instance, developed input–output tables as part of their national accounting systems – though not necessarily with the HERP's blueprint (cf. Akhabbar, Antille, Fontela, and Pulido 2011 for a survey of the European developments of input–output analysis). There, input–output models were used for macroeconomic planning purposes with regard to those sectors more or less directly under the influence of the government. Another early example was the creation of an Italian input–output table, organized by Hollis B. Chenery, and financed under the Marshall Plan. The purpose of the project was to investigate "the entire Italian economy", in particular the relations of the "relatively underdeveloped" Italian South (Mutual Security Agency 1953). In the course of the 1960s, several South American countries employed input–output analysis for planning purposes, and in 1968, the United Nations integrated input–output tables in the UN system of national accounts (SNA) through making "social accounting matrices" (SAM) an integral part of national accounting strategies (cf. Vanoli 2005). From the mid-1970s on, input–output lost momentum as a primary policy tool but, redesigned and under the umbrella term of "computable general equilibrium" (CGE) models, remains today an essential policy evaluation tool for government offices, private institutions, and international organizations. Alongside ever more powerful computing capacities, these models afforded ever more quantitative "what-happens-if" questions and forecasts of the effects of policy changes, regarding a variety of policy issues (such as immigration, pension funds, or mineral discoveries).

Input–output provided the basis for a wider ensemble of models and measurements, which meshed with one another, and mutually stabilized each other's results. An example is the Norwegian multi-sector growth model, which – having been developed in the context of macroeconomic planning – forms the basis of growth simulations today. When Leif Johansen checked his input–output model's "ability to explain and forecast", he compared the numerical simulation results "with reality" (1960, p. 131). This meant a comparison with a different kind of visualization of economic growth, namely already existing growth, productivity, capital, and employment trends based on the national accounts. Leaving aside the (in itself) noteworthy premise that it was meaningful to entangle different temporal horizons – a supposedly well-described past with a foreseeable future – it thereby assumed that the structure of "the economy" remained constant. More relevant to the notion of artifacts and epistemic infrastructures for governance is that these time trends themselves relied on very similar notions as the input–output model – the idea of a circular flow, macroeconomic accounting balances, measurement in terms of monetary value, the exclusion of historical contingency and uncertainties, etc. Despite their different appearances, these visualizations of the economy shared a common code, and followed, at least partly, the same rules (cf. Halsmayer 2017).

Following up

Our extended example only hints at the role artifacts play in the epistemic infrastructures of policymaking. Input–output analysis visualized the structure of national economies and thereby made them objects for both economics and economic governance. Suggesting an almost literal grip on sectoral interrelations, the national economic whole and its parts became manipulable entities, which excluded those features that did not fit the modeling project and followed the rules that the input–output scheme had established. Input–output tables as well as their measurements and simulations turned into essential components of the discursive and material assemblages, which made the phenomena in question visible and, once stabilized as policy devices, essentially provided the entities that policymakers acted upon and decided about.

Coming back to the notion of boundary objects, the products of economists' research – whether theories, facts, ideas, instruments, etc. – have to be both plastic and coherent at the same time (cf. also Morgan 2011b). If they are to circulate widely, they have to be suitable for various heterogeneous purposes at different times and places on the one hand and, on the other, they nevertheless need to keep an overall identity. Boundary objects emerge through cooperation of different communities – for instance, policymakers, empirical workers, economists, etc. It remains an open question how, following these objects, we move from local cooperative work (such as at the HERP) to the establishment of less local standards at different places. We might see the building of infrastructures, where the power of economic concepts unfolds in interrelation with wider political and economic forces, or be puzzled by the "mangle of practice" of scientific and administrative processes, which might also thwart the logic of schemes, models, and blueprints. In order to better understand the ways in which economists' artifacts became part of the infrastructures, which formed the basis for political decision-making, and in which the difference between the two notions of "model of" and "model for" collapsed, it would be necessary to investigate records of political decision-making processes, the written notes of commission meetings, and the material remains of the knowledge that provided the basis for these decisions: punch-cards, curves, tables, software packages, and the bureaucratic devices of policymaking bodies. These artifacts might enable the historian to analyze the processes of reinterpretation and transformation of economists' artifacts, how these were adapted, translated, extended, reduced, and perhaps ignored altogether in relation to other techniques, practices, agendas, and specific local, institutional, and strategic arrangements.

Notes

1 I am very grateful to the editors for their feedback and support, and to Jeff Biddle and Marcel Boumans, who discussed parts of this paper.

2 Introductions into what it can mean to look at practices in the history of economics have been given by Maas, Mata, and Davis (2011), and Stapleford (2017). Despite relating to rather different theoretical frameworks, both focus more on the symbolic and social organization of economic research, i.e., the creation and working of communities, their knowledge-making, the identities of economists, their skills and crafts.

3 On the problems of situating the making of "the economy" in the middle of the 20th century, see Slobodian (2016), who refers to earlier concepts of the economy, and hints at Marxist traditions in problematizing the concept.

4 Closely related is the literature on the performativity of models in economic sociology, for instance the contributions to MacKenzie, Muniesa, and Siu (2007), and Callon (1998). For a brief survey, see Hirschman and Popp Berman (2014).

5 The literature on the circulation of knowledge has become quite extensive. See, for instance, Secord (2004) on the processes of movement, translation, and transmission as a form of communicative action, Kaiser (2005) on the circulation of theoretical tools, Howlett and Morgan (2011) on traveling facts, and Daston (2000) on the circulation of scientific objects.

6 On the history of the concept as well as Star's preceding work on boundary objects in the history of brain research and computer science, see Bowker, Timmermans, Clarke, and Balka (2016).

7 When the Cold War grew more intense, the Air Force was concerned with possible obstructions to repeated wartime mobilization. Marshall Wood, the chief of

the Planning Research Division of the Air Force, integrated the Bureau's input–output work into an interagency project, known as the Project for the Scientific Computation of Optimum Programs (Project SCOOP), that was formed to mechanize programming techniques for decision-making through the new electronic digital computers (Kohli 2001, p. 204; on Project SCOOP, see Erickson, Klein, Daston, Lemov, Sturm, and Gordin 2013, pp. 58–61).

8 Aside from the collection of data, the HERP's aims were the related development of industrial classification schemes and, listed third, the mathematical analysis of dynamic models. The project's official program described its overall objective as "an attempt to lay an elaborate and well-integrated foundation for the empirical study of long-run problems" (original statement of the Project's research program as issued in March 1948, printed in Leontief et al. (1953, p. v)).

9 Apart from Elizabeth W. Gilboy (vice-director of the HERP for many decades), Robert Solow (the growth economist and soon-to-be one of MIT's economics fame), and Benjamin Handler, who all received special acknowledgement, the *Structure*'s preface mentioned the following statistical workers: Robert L. Allen, Judith Balderston, Otto Bird, Nancy Bromberger, Carol Cameron, William Capron, Sara Clark, Bernadette Drolette, Fay Greenwald, Ruth Kahn, Lora Katz, Robert Kavesh, Elaine Kazanowski, Mary Kazanowski, Lohn Lansing, Irwin Leff, Richard Levitan, Dolores McJilton, Leon Moses, M. Janice Murphy, Margaret Oliver, Myer Rashish, Richard Rosenthal, Ira Scott, Martha Shoesmith, Burton Singer, Edith Soodak, Raya Spiegel, Carl Stevens, Tun Thin, and Ruth Winer.

10 For a conceptual view of Leontief's improvements against earlier formulations as well as the biographical and intellectual contexts of his work, see, for instance, Bjerkholt and Kurz (2006).

11 For a more sophisticated account of the history of the computer in economics, see Backhouse and Cherrier (2017).

References

Akhabbar, Amanar, Gabrielle Antille, Emilio Fontela, and Antonio Pulido (2011). "Input-Output in Europe: Trends in Research and Applications." *OEconomia* 1(1): 73–98.

Backhouse, Roger E., and Béatrice Cherrier (2017). "'It's Computers, Stupid!' The Spread of Computers and the Changing Roles of Theoretical and Applied Economics." In Roger E. Backhouse, and Béatrice Cherrier (eds). *The Age of the Applied Economist: The Transformation of Economics since the 1970s, History of Political Economy* 49 (supplement): 103–126.

Biddle, Jeff (2017). "2016 HES Presidential Address: Statistical Inference in Economics, 1920–1965: Changes in Meaning and Practice." *Journal of the History of Economic Thought* 39(2): 149–173.

Bjerkholt, Olav, and Heinz D. Kurz (2006). "Introduction: The History of Input–Output Analysis, Leontief's Path and Alternative Tracks." *Economic Systems Research* 18(4): 331–333.

Boumans, Marcel (2005). *How Economists Model the World into Numbers.* New York, Routledge.

Boumans, Marcel (2012). "Logical Positivism and Leontief." Working paper, University of Amsterdam.

Bowker, Geoffrey C., and Susan Leigh Star (1999). *Sorting Things Out. Classification and its Consequences.* Cambridge, MIT Press.

Bowker, Geoffrey C., Stefan Timmermans, Adele E. Clarke, and Ellen Balka (eds) (2016). *Boundary Objects and Beyond: Working with Leigh Star.* Cambridge, MIT Press.

Breslau, Daniel (2003). "Economics Invents the Economy: Mathematics, Statistics, and Models in the Work of Irving Fisher and Wesley Mitchell." *Theory and Society* 32: 379–411.

Buck-Morss, Susan (1995). "Envisioning Capital: Political Economy on Display." *Critical Inquiry* 21(2): 434–467.

Callon, Michel (ed.) (1998). *The Laws of the Markets.* London, Blackwell.

Carter, Anne P. (2012). "Leontief's 'Stuff': An Archeology of Input-output Material." *OEconomia* 1(1): 51–59.

Charles, Loïc (2003). "The Visual History of the Tableau Économique." *European Journal of the History of Economic Thought* 10(4): 527–549.

Charles, Loïc, and Christine Théré (2012). "The Economist as Surveyor: Physiocracy in the Fields." In Mary S. Morgan, and Harro Maas (eds), *Observing the Economy: Historical Perspectives. History of Political Economy* 44 (supplement): 71–89.

Daston, Lorraine (ed.) (2000). *Biographies of Scientific Objects.* Chicago, Chicago University Press.

Desrosières, Alain (2003). "Managing the Economy." In Theodore M. Porter, and Dorothy Ross (eds), *The Cambridge History of Science, VII: The Modern Social Sciences.* Cambridge, Cambridge University Press: 553–564.

Domar, Evsey D. (1952). "Economic Growth: An Econometric Approach." *American Economic Review* 42(2): 479–495.

Dommann, Monika, Daniel Speich Chassé, and Mischa Suter (2014). "Einleitung: Wissensgeschichte ökonomischer Praktiken." *Berichte zur Wissenschaftsgeschichte* 37: 107–111.

Dorfman, Robert (1995). "In Appreciation of Wassily Leontief." *Structural Change and Economic Dynamics* 6: 305–308.

Düppe, Till (2011). *The Making of the Economy: A Phenomenology of Economic Science.* Lanham, Lexington Books.

Düppe, Till (2017). "Gérard Debreu's Values: Axioms and Anecdotes." *Research in the History of Economic Thought and Methodology* 35A: 85–111.

Erickson, Paul, Judy L. Klein, Lorraine Daston, Rebecca Lemov, Thomas Sturm, and Michael D. Gordin (2013). *How Reason Almost Lost Its Mind: The Strange Career of Cold War Rationality.* Chicago, University of Chicago Press.

Geoghegan, Bernard Dionysius (2011). "From Information Theory to French Theory: Jakobson, Lévi-Strauss, and the Cybernetic Apparatus." *Critical Inquiry* 38: 96–126.

Gießmann, Sebastian (2015). "Der Durkheim-Test. Anmerkungen zu Susan Leigh Stars Grenzojekten." *Berichte zur Wissenschaftsgeschichte* 38: 211–226.

Gitelman, Lisa (ed.) (2013). *"Raw Data" is an Oxymoron.* Cambridge, MIT Press.

Golden, Soma S. (1959). "Leontief Relates Economic Theory to Fact. Professor's Research Project Perfects Input-Output Analysis." *The Harvard Crimson,* December 17, www.thecrimson.com/article/1959/12/17/loentief-relates-economic-theory-to-fact/?page=2 (accessed December 2, 2017).

Guillory, John (2004). "The Memo and Modernity." *Critical Inquiry* 31(1): 108–132.

Hacking, Ian (1999). *The Social Construction of What?* Cambridge, Harvard University Press.

Halsmayer, Verena (2017). "A model to 'Make Decisions and Take Actions': Leif Johansen's Multisector Growth Model, Computerized Macroeconomic Planning, and Resilient Infrastructures for Policymaking." In Roger E. Backhouse, and

Béatrice Cherrier (eds), The Age of the Applied Economist: The Transformation of Economics since the 1970s. *History of Political Economy* 49 (supplement): 158–186.

Halsmayer, Verena (2018). "Following Artifacts." *History of Political Economy* 50(3): 629–634.

Hirschman, Daniel and Elizabeth Popp Berman (2014). "Do Economists make Policies? On the Political Effects of Economics." *Socio-Economic Review* 12(4): 779–811.

Howlett, Peter, and Mary S. Morgan (eds) (2011). *How Well Do Facts Travel: The Dissemination of Reliable Knowledge.* Cambridge, Cambridge University Press.

Iverson, Kenneth E. (1954). "Machine Solutions of Linear Differential Equations: Applications to a Dynamic Economic Model." Thesis presented to The Division of Applied Science in partial fulfillment of the requirements for the degree of Doctor of Philosophy in the subject of Applied Mathematics, Harvard University, January, www.jsoftware.com/papers/MSLDE.htm (accessed January 15, 2018).

Johansen, Leif (1960). *A Multi-Sectoral Study of Economic Growth.* Amsterdam: North-Holland.

Kaiser, David (2005). *Drawing Theories Apart: The Dispersion of Feynman Diagrams in Postwar Physics.* Chicago, University of Chicago Press.

Kohli, Martin C. (2001). "Leontief and the U.S. Bureau of Labor Statistics, 1941–1954: Developing a Framework for Measurement." In Judy L. Klein and Mary S. Morgan (eds), *The Age of Economic Measurement. History of Political Economy* 30 (supplement): 190–212.

Kuznets, Simon (1933). "National Income." In Edwin R. A. Seligman (ed.), *Encyclopedia of the Social Sciences,* vol. 11. New York, Macmillan: 205–244.

Latour, Bruno (1990). "Visualisation and Cognition: Drawing Things Together." In Michael Lynch and Steve Woolgar (eds), *Representation in Scientific Practice.* Cambridge, London, MIT Press: 19–68.

Leontief, Wassily W. (1944). "Output, Employment, Consumption and Investment." *Quarterly Journal of Economics* 58(2): 290–313.

Leontief, Wassily W. (1949). "Recent Developments in the Study of Interindustrial Relationships." *The American Economic Review* 39(3): 211–225.

Leontief, Wassily W. (1959). "The Problems of Quality and Quantity in Economics." *Daedalus* 88(4): 622–632.

Leontief, Wassily W. (1966). *Essays in Economics.* New York, Oxford University Press.

Leontief, Wassily W. and members of the Harvard Economic Research Project (1953). *Studies in the Structure of the American Economy.* Oxford, Oxford University Press.

Leontief, Wassily to Clifford Harvey, editor of the Christian Science Monitor, May 6, 1948, Wassily Leontief Papers, Faculty Archives, Collections of the Harvard University Archives, Harvard University, HUG 4517.5, box 5, file C.

Lipartito, Kenneth (2016). "Review Essay: Reassembling the Economic: New Departures in Historical Materialism." *The American Historical Review* 121(1): 101–139.

Maas, Harro (2014). *Economic Methodology: A Historical Introduction.* London, Routledge.

Maas, Harro, Tiago Mata, and John B. Davis (2011). "Introduction: The history of economics as a history of practice." *European Journal for the History of Economic Thought* 18: 635–642.

MacKenzie, Donald, Fabian Muniesa, and Lucia Siu (eds) (2007). *Do Economists Make Markets? On the Performativity of Economics.* Princeton, Princeton University Press.

Mirowski, Philip (2002). *Machine Dreams: Economics Becomes a Cyborg Science.* Cambridge, Cambridge University Press.

Mitchell, Timothy (1998). "Fixing the Economy." *Cultural Studies* 12(1): 82–101.

Mitchell, Timothy (2005). "The work of economics: How a Discipline Makes its World." *European Journal of Sociology* 46: 297–320.

Mitchell, Timothy (2014). "Economentality: How the Future entered Government." *Critical Inquiry* 40: 479–507.

Morgan, Mary S. (2011a). "Seeking Parts, Looking for Wholes." In Lorraine Daston and Elizabeth Lunbeck (eds), *Histories of Scientific Observation*. Chicago, University of Chicago Press: 303–325.

Morgan, Mary S. (2011b) "Travelling Facts." In Peter Howlett and Mary S. Morgan (eds), *How Well Do Facts Travel: The Dissemination of Reliable Knowledge*. Cambridge, Cambridge University Press: 3–39.

Morgan, Mary S. (2012). *The World in the Model: How Economists Work and Think*. Cambridge, Cambridge University Press.

Morgan, Mary S. and Marcel Boumans (2004). "Secrets Hidden by Two-Dimensionality: The Economy as a Hydraulic Machine." In Soraya de Chadarevian and Nick Hopwood (eds), *Models: The Third Dimension of Science*. Stanford, Stanford University Press: 369–401.

Morgenstern, Oskar (1954). "Experiment and Large Scale Computation in Economics." In Oskar Morgenstern (ed.), *Economic Activity Analysis*. New York, Wiley: 484–549.

Mutual Security Agency (1953). *The Structure and Growth of the Italian Economy*, prepared by Chenery, Hollis B., Paul G. Clark, Vera Cao Pinna and others. Rome and New York, Oxford University Press.

"Preliminary Report of the Final Progress Report" (1950). Leontief Papers, Collections of the Harvard University Archives. Faculty archives, HUG 4517.5, box 8, folder: Progress Reports – A.F.

Riles, Annelise (ed.) (2006). *Documents: Artifacts of Modern Knowledge*. Ann Arbor, University of Michigan Press.

Rockman, Seth (2017). "Introduction, Forum: The Paper Technologies of Capitalism." *Technology and Culture* 58(2): 487–505.

Secord, James A. (2004). "Knowledge in Transit." *Isis* 95: 654–272.

Slobodian, Quinn (2016). "Which 'the Economy'? Complicating the Timothy Mitchell Thesis," Comment at Historicizing "the Economy" Workshop, Harvard University, September.

Speich Chassé, Daniel (2013). *Die Erfindung des Bruttosozialprodukts. Globale Ungleichheit in der Wissensgeschichte der Ökonomie (Kritische Studien zur Geschichtswissenschaft 212)*. Göttingen, Vandenhoeck & Ruprecht.

Stapleford, Thomas (2017). "Historical Epistemology and the History of Economics: Views Through the Lens of Practice." *Research in the History of Economic Thought and Methodology* 35A: 113–145.

Star, Susan Leigh (2010). "This is Not a Boundary Object. Reflections on the Origin of a Concept." *Science, Technology, & Human Values* 35: 601–617.

Star, Susan Leigh and James R. Griesemer (1989). "Institutional Ecology, 'Translations' and Boundary Objects: Amateurs and Professionals in Berkeley's Museum of Vertebrate Zoology, 1907–1939." *Social Studies of Science* 19(3): 387–420.

Tellmann, Ute (2014). "Kommentar: The Economic or the Economy? Reflections on the Objects of Historical Epistemology." *Berichte zur Wissenschaftsgeschichte* 37: 165–169.

Vanoli, André (2005). *A History of National Accounting*. Amsterdam, IOS Press.

Vogl, Joseph (2014). *The Specter of Capital*. Stanford, Stanford University Press.

Yates, JoAnne (1989). *Control through Communication: The Rise of System in American Management*. Baltimore, Johns Hopkins University Press.

10 Reading popular histories of economics

Tiago Mata

Uneducating historians of economics

How to train the next generation of historians of economics? The apprentice historian has in 2018 a wealth of resources to exploit. If she wants to get a head start on the themes and problems that might grip the field in 20 years, she might leaf through the yearly supplements of *History of Political Economy*. If she needs to get acquainted with the canon of economics, she might travel to summer schools coast to coast, Italy to North America, offering initiation into the interpretative arts. She might then join scholarly networks, of senior, junior, or mixed membership, and invite the critical exam of her peers on work in progress. The historian-in-training of today can scan the horizons of the discipline, be socialized in collective reading, and shape community. The opportunities have never been as numerous.

These resources accomplish an initiation into scholarship. While graduate programs in the history of economics are closed or thinned, they ensure the preservation of our field. They deserve to be commended. They are also narrow in outlook . . . At the end of this essay I aim to have convinced my reader that writings on the history of economics are more diverse, puzzling, and unruly than the literature that circulates in conferences, summer schools, and webinars. The essay re-opens simple historiographical questions: Who writes history, how is it written, for whom?

To address these questions I must delimit a corpus. All the titles I discuss are classified as histories of economics (or of economic thought) by booksellers and library catalogues. I exclude no titles on grounds of the credentials of their authors or the reputation and vocation of their publisher. I consider only titles appearing after 1949, date of the publication of Joseph Dorfman's monumental *The Economic Mind in American Civilization*. In an argument to expound elsewhere, I contend that histories of economics before that date were remarkable for establishing and celebrating national schools of thought.[1] The territorial and linguistic frames suited assertions of national character of established repute by the close of the 19th century (Stapleton 2001; Mandler 2006). National studies of economic thinking of course continued to be published beyond World War II, for instance Craufurd Goodwin's studies of Canadian (1958) and Australian (1966) economic thought, but these tended to be motivated by filling lacunas in the literature rather than discerning a cultural exceptionalism.

One explanation to the historiographical break c. 1950 might be postwar's cosmopolitanism. But if that explanation is too remote or faint, a more proximate one is that in the 1950s as the economics discipline gained eminence in policy analysis and newsworthiness (Mata and Medema 2013) that visibility changed the readers and stakes of the histories. It is then that we enter our era – a time when journalists, intellectuals, and scholars from all disciplines are readers and writers in the history of economics (for a recent survey of the latter see Fontaine 2016).[2] To my colleague the historian-in-training I propose that she allow herself to drift from the prescribed itineraries of the history of economics and follow me to explore this historiography that lays before us a wilder terrain.

This essay is organised along the deceptively trivial questions of who, how, and to whom history is written. My answers place narratives about economists and economics past at the borderlands between popular and scholarly media. I will show that it is not only difficult but likely also futile to attempt to demarcate content that is "popular" from that which is scholarly (with similar concerns as Topham 2009). Rather than setting out bibliographical criteria that might rescue texts from their disorder, I want to train our attention to the rich lives of histories when they successfully confound genres and reach out to publics (on the underlying conception of knowledge in transit see Mata forthcoming).

I consider only printed books and therefore my strategy has a whiff of antiquarianism. Most writing in economics is printed in scholarly article format, working paper, report ,or op-ed, not in books. The turn from books to articles occurred in the natural sciences as early as the 1840s (Frasca-Spada and Jardine 2000), for the social sciences in the last 50 years. In the past decade, economics has also figured regularly in podcasts, cable TV, and in a few but notable motion pictures, including two Oscar winners (*Beautiful Mind* and *Inside Job*). Similar observations apply to the history of economics, the preferred format is the peer-reviewed article. However, unlike economics, book publishing remains viable and sought after. Histories of economics are less regularly featured in audio-visual media, although every few years the BBC broadcasts a series on that subject, the most recent instance on the radio show/podcast *More or Less* in 2011.[3] The story of economics past has also appeared on screen as a result of a few cross media tie-ins. One notable example is *Commanding Heights* a book by Daniel Yergin and Joseph Stanislaw (1998) that in the heat of the pro-globalization, anti-globalization controversies of the 1990s promised to trace those antinomies to the (personal) rivalry between J. M. Keynes and F. Hayek. Soon after publication the story appeared as a series on USA's Public Broadcasting Service with the tag line of "How can a couple of cranky economists in their ivory towers change the world? Commanding Heights provides the answer, with a sweeping view of 20th century economic history" (Yergin 2002). The narrative thus inhabited a book, a TV broadcast, a DVD box set, and an award-winning website (now defunct) addressing high school students. Fully aware that examining books may offer only a partial view of the cultural landscape, I will show that books preserve the vitality to carry us across a vast and fascinating cultural terrain.

Who writes the history of economics?

In a celebrated essay on the history of books, Robert Darnton described the life of a book as running "from the author to the publisher . . . the printer, the shipper, the bookseller, and the reader" (Darnton 1982, p. 67).[4] Setting a book free onto the world is a circuitous and multi-agential process and in the 20th century an activity with a financial bottom-line. Acknowledging the commercial dimension of print culture calls for an analysis of the ways publishers structure publishing.

In 2017, the writings of university-based historians of economics appear predominantly under the imprint of Routledge, Cambridge University Press, Oxford University Press, M.E. Sharpe, Edward Elgar, and occasionally in some of the other university presses such as Princeton, Harvard, and Chicago. These titles share a familiar pattern of being studies in depth, with small print runs, (laxly) marketed to specialists and libraries. It is unusual to find these texts in bookstores not domiciled on university campuses. With expensive price tags they procure a small profit and only after several years. Look to the stands that line up airports hallways or to the recommendations on Amazon and you will find a different kind of book, with a different kind of author and a different imprint.

Recommended online and on bookstore stands, Sylvia Nasar's *Grand Pursuit* (2012) or David Warsh's *Knowledge and the Wealth of Nations* (2006) speak to us of the wondrous adventure of economic analysis and are as expansive in their timeframe and subject as some of the early and mid-century texts that once surveyed the history of the discipline (for instance, the many times updated and translated history by Eric Roll). Not all popular histories of economics sell by way of their comprehensiveness, and *Grand Pursuit* was commercially disappointing after the triumph of *Beautiful Mind*.[5] There is no sure formula for mass appeal, but there is today a correlation between scope and publisher. Stories of grand vistas and bold claims are to one side, to the other studies that are hyper-academic in motivation and language with strict constraints upon their length.

Until the 1980s the distinctions between the book markets of "trade" (for the mass public), "college" (for students), and "scholarly" remained fuzzy (as noted in Coser, Kadushin, and Powell 1982), they have since sharpened. The takeover of publishing companies by media conglomerates, the grip of retail chains over distribution, the changing habits of readers and the power of literary agents have together led to a polarization (Thompson 2013). To one side are the "best-sellers" (to which one might add textbooks) negotiated with fat advances and rolled out in major promotional campaigns, to the other small print runs with no expectation of commercial success. Several publishers hold multiple imprints to manage the presence in those few and well delimited markets. Gone are the markets in between, for instance the metropolitan (café) culture catered by independent publishers/ booksellers (Schiffrin 2001). My business history of publishing is necessarily brief and schematic but I hope sufficient to remind us that books are objects in markets and that markets change.

Darnton, a scholar of Early Modern France, answers the question "who writes" by noting that printers, shippers, and booksellers shape the materiality, personality, and reach of books. The name on the cover is never the only author. Today we must attend to retail chains, institutional subscription contracts, accountants, literary agents, and commissioning editors as silent authors. Once we think of historiography in the context of late 20th century publishing we can distinguish pathways lined with various actors that benignly edit the scope, language, and attitude of the historical imagination. Plotting a renewal of the history of economics requires cunningly engaging these pathways.

How is history written?

In that acclaimed essay, Darnton gives us another insightful steer when he remarks that authors are readers that "associat[e] with other readers and writers, they form notions of genre and style and a general sense of the literary enterprise, which affects their texts" (Darnton 1982, p. 67). The analysis of how writing about the economy has shadowed fictional genres has been a vibrant research topic of literary theory (see Poovey 1998, 2008), but to heed Darnton's plea one does not require a degree from an English department or to become an expert in the genealogies of genre. Instead, it requires that we attend to how writers associate and emulate.

Reflections on genre in the history of economics are unusual. The most sophisticated contribution comes from one of the editors of this volume (Weintraub 1999). In the 1990s at the instigation of Mark Blaug and others, ink and tempers were spilled over if history of economics should be written as "rational" or "historical reconstruction" (Blaug 1990, Backhouse 1992). Despite their differences the antagonists seemed to agree that genres must be justified and defined from first principles, preferably bearing philosophical credentials. My suggestion, following the trivial observation that writers read, is to trace out genres from expressions of admiration and evidence of emulation.

Among the top candidates for most successful books in the history of economics in the second half of the 20th century – in print since 1953 – is Robert Heilbroner's *Worldly Philosophers*. The book is a study of the "Great Economists" (its alternative UK title) including "a philosopher and a madman, a parson and a stockbroker, a revolutionary and a nobleman, an aesthete, a skeptic, and a tramp". Heilbroner has a novelist's care for characters and the chapters are packed with endearing anecdote and caricature. Marx was an "angry genius". Keynes was "politically devout" and exhibited the "curious combination of an engineering mind and a hopeful heart". Twenty years after the publication of *Worldly Philosophers*, Leonard Silk, once an editor of *Business Week* but at the time an editorial writer at the *New York Times*, wrote a collective study of living economists that resembled the Heilbroner vignettes. Silk (1974) motivated his book as hoping "that by exploring the ideas, careers, and, to a degree, the personalities of these five economists . . . I might give a picture of the present state of economics". Paul Samuelson was "Enfant Terrible Emeritus"; Milton Friedman was "Prophet of the Old Time Religion"; and J. K. Galbraith proposed "Socialism Without Tears". The chapters weave an intimate coherence between lives, temperaments, and ideas.

Neither Heilbroner nor Silk wrote standard biographies from cradle to grave and beyond, nor were their chapters patterned as profiles in the style of those weekly churned in the well-tested formulas of the *New Yorker* or of management magazines. These were studies of personality that required being assembled as a set to make each individual intelligible. The collective portraits established that the economics discipline was a lofty endeavour that carried the humanity of its makers. By literary device at different times with different political inclinations, Heilbroner and Silk opposed a common view that economics is narrow and consensual and replaced it with the alternative conception of heart warming pluralism.

These histories shared with science journalism a vocation to dignify economists. Economists were deserving of admiration (and reporting) for their intelligence, moral and civic commitment. However, popular science and campaigns aimed at enhancing the "public understanding of science" call for a devout and distant admiration of scientific lives (Lewenstein 1992), by contrast the *Worldly Philosophers* reaches out to the views of the public and assigns them champions within the economics pantheon. It compliments readers' intelligence, greeting them with arguments for the many parties of a democratic polity. It does not attempt to dampen controversy and re-inscribes it as legitimate discourse.

Sometimes credited, other times not, a book like Heilbroner's becomes a model to adopt and adapt. There are also instances when one expects conventions to form but they do not. A series of "Penguin histories of economics" would presumably exhibit some continuity, each title similarly designed to be didactic, portable, and entertaining. However the three titles that have appeared with that heading share little in their justifications, organization, or tone (Barber 1967; Galbraith 1987; Backhouse 2002). One (W. Barber's) is a study of the analytical achievement of four systems of thought (Classical, Marxian, Neo-classical, Keynesian) while another (J.K. Galbraith's) sets out to show how ideas are embedded in events of their times and how economists only reluctantly update their beliefs. Both texts review a similar core of writings and authors, but the third history (R. Backhouse's) opens up the field of view to a multitude of authors and ideas. All three were successful books of very different appeal.

The haunting phrases that conclude Keynes' (1936) *The General Theory of Employment, Interest and Money*, make regular appearances in popular writings on economics, unsurprisingly also in histories. The belief that the "ideas of economists and political philosophers, . . . are more powerful than is commonly understood", is followed by the invitation to examine how "[p]ractical men, who believe themselves to be quite exempt from any intellectual influences, are usually slaves of some defunct economist" (ibid., pp 383–384). Keynes gifts us a tantalising hypothesis and a ready format, the study of the economic prejudices of statesmen. Many authors use the Keynesian aphorism in their prefaces and introductions as if it was a direct endorsement, but few have subscribed to his simple political sociology.[6] Biographies that illuminate ideas with tales of a good life are a staple of the non-fiction section of bookstores and scores have been written for the history of economics. They are about the lives of economists (or philosophers), not of the great men that they reached from their graves, to name only a few J. M. Keynes (Moggridge, Skidelsky), T. Veblen (Tilman, Spindler, Jorgensen and Jorgensen, Edgell), J. Schumpeter (McGraw), J. M. Clark (Shute), A. Gershenkron (Dawidoff), I. Fisher (Allen), Fisher Black (Mehrling). When the same scholar is the subject of multiple biographies, a common occurrence, the new treatment must prove itself original enough and maybe superior to its predecessor. Albeit not one constitutive of genre, that is another dialogue between old and new.

Looking over these patterns of choice it seems that economists' lives matter. The key to make sense of how lives are composed into narrative is not to distil ideal types from the mass but to see the dialogues between texts and authors, of editorial projects diverging and intersecting over time.

How are histories of economics read?

Economists are seen as the primary readership of the history of economics. Historians are regularly urged to match language, themes, and problems with the interests of contemporary economists. Earlier I pondered whether academic historians' mild ambitions were less a matter of will than a manifestation of the structures of contemporary publishing. Next I argue that beyond our close peers in faculties of economics there is a numerous, thoughtful, and enthusiastic public for the history of economics. Upstream the history of economics has multiple authors, downstream it has even more readers.

It has been over 40 years since Stanley Fish urged scholars to abandon the notion that "meaning is embedded in the artifact". His invitation was to transfer the responsibility of interpretation away from texts and onto readers, looking for "interpretative communities" as "made up of those who share interpretative strategies not for reading (in the conventional sense) but for writing texts, for constituting their properties and assigning their intentions" (Fish 1976, p. 483). "Writers are readers" was my claim in the previous section, and now my claim is that "readers are writers". Pre-modern and Victorian scholars of the book thumb through marginalia in old books and decipher diaries and letters to interrogate the intimate experience of reading. Historians of the present have other resources.

One of the many communities of affinity that the worldwide web has empowered is book readers. Retail chains that want to add promotional momentum at least possible cost have encouraged these groups and bankrolled their online platforms. Goodreads.com was created in 2007 as a database of book reviews, scores, and recommendations submitted by its free subscription membership. At the time of writing it claims 65 million members, 68 million reviews of various lengths, and 2 billion books listed. In 2013 the company was bought by Amazon and its reviews, recommendations, and prizes now link to Amazon purchases; Amazon algorithmic recommendations and ads chase you to the Goodreads pages.

Anyone with an account on social media knows that in the late 2010s interactions online are often toxic. Book reviews on Amazon are notoriously so. The recommendations and reviews in Amazon.com of Nancy McLean's *Democracy in Chains*, an exposé of James Buchanan and public choice's participation in American right-wing politics, lists 508 reviews and several commentary threads (accessed February 2018). The reviewers are unequivocal and uncompromising in their appreciation and dismay, 74 percent of readers award the book 5 stars, 16 percent the lowest score of 1 star. Admirers and detractors volley accusations of intellectual crime. To them the book is either the cypher of our times, "magnificent" and "empowering", written by an eminent historian, or that same historian is failing the standards of scholarship and has produced a "intentionally misleading smearing job", "dishonest", a work of fiction. This vitriol is mostly absent from Goodreads where the book has 219 reviews and 875 ratings of a more balanced distribution.

Goodreads is an "interpretative community" (or even several communities) of readers sharing a passion for books and their interpretation. Setting Goodreads and Amazon side by side we must conclude that no forum can provide us with unfiltered access to the minds of the "average" reader. Every community (online or offline) has norms and recurring patterns of social interaction. Most reviews in Goodreads are casual and a paragraph long, the longer ones have structure and style, a bit of posturing, and emulate what book reviews look like in literary digests. The reviews repeat tropes and the repetition is in part a technical feature of writing one's thoughts crowded by dozens or even hundreds of other reviews of the same text. In Goodreads, unlike in Amazon, discussions are disabled, but members can "like" reviews which then move them up the list. The recognition through "likes" is the clearest social reward that encourages some affected argument. The limited scope of interaction indicates that the Goodreads format is a legacy from before Web 2.0 and social media.

Worldly Philosophers has been rated 4,935 times (average of 4.11 out of 5) and reviewed 326 times in Goodreads. Reading the reviews we glimpse at the book's field of circulation. One finds plenty of reviews by young college students who were offered or recommended the book by teachers or peers when they struggled with their motivation to study economics. In number and emphasis these compete with two other groups of readers/reviewers experiences. Some report re-encountering the book after decades of neglecting it on their shelves. Some come to it with goals of self-education in economics. Self-identified "humanists" are delighted by the book, Jeremy writes on June 28, 2016, that "Like many weepy humanists, I don't read many books that deal with economics in a sincere, deep way (too dry, too mathy, the usual wimpy criticisms.) Heilbroner's overview is wonderful" and Erik in October 9, 2011 that "[m]y estimation of economic science lies somewhere between where I rate astrology and phlogiston, but I'm giving this a chance to convince me otherwise", he was convinced. There is a fair amount of protest (but also admiration) directed at how Heilbroner introduces Marx, and a string of readers surprised by discovering Keynes and his extraordinary intellect (e.g. J. C. Keely, July 16, 2008; Bruce, September 8, 2008; Jazli, July 27, 2017). In Goodreads each book is experienced in both personal (idiosyncratic) and public (argumentative) ways without unifying plots or sentiment, yet over and over we read that *Worldly Philosophers* shines brightest because of the dreadful expectation that economics and economists must be dull. Reading the readers of *Worldly Philosophers* one encounters the history of economics as a moving and entertaining experience.

Academic books also get reviewed and rated. E. R. Weintraub and T. Düppe's *Finding Equilibrium* has 11 ratings (average of 4.36) and 1 review, P. Mirowski's classic *More Heat than Light* gets 32 ratings (average of 4.06) and 3 reviews, and his later and mass appeal *Never Let a Serious Crisis Go to Waste* gets 156 ratings (average of 4.15) with 15 reviews. The book whose reviews I want to probe in some depth is one of the most recommended and reviewed in "economics" lists with historical interest. Several of the top reviews of *Commanding Heights* (862 ratings, average of 4.04 and 65 reviews) recommend it as a companion, and counter, to Naomi Klein's *The Shock Doctrine: The Rise of Disaster Capitalism* published by Random House in 2007. As of this writing, *Shock Doctrine* has 27,435 ratings (average of 4.22) and has been reviewed 2,142 times.

Similarly engaged with the themes of *Commanding Heights*, Klein's book was discussed in all major newspapers, and she was profiled in magazines at the time of publication, the hallmarks of "best-seller" promotion (Macfarquhar 2008). Since the success of her 2000 book, *No Logo*, Klein has become a forceful voice in militant debates about globalization and corporate capitalism. *Shock Doctrine* was described as a piece of investigative achievement, "to the point of investing over $200,000 of her advance payments in research operations, building a virtual academic institute in order to get the goods on such unsexy freemarket gurus as the late University of Chicago economist Milton Friedman" (Allemang 2007). Thus in most media outlets, the book was represented principally as investigative, partisan journalism.

The message of the book is that under the cover of spontaneous or induced crises, because these are periods of mass disorientation and suspension of democracy, market ideologues push through anti-popular reforms of privatization and cuts in public services. As the *Washington Post* reviewer put it:

> [t]he imposition of radical, Milton Friedmanesque free-market capitalism, [Klein] claims, often takes place when the targeted population is reeling from some exogenous shock: either a foreign invasion, like the "shock and awe" takeover of Iraq in 2003, or a natural disaster, like the tsunami and Hurricane Katrina, or even an economic meltdown, as occurred in Southeast Asia in 1997 and Argentina in 2001.
>
> (Tharoor 2007)[7]

The centerpiece of Klein's book is the involvement of Milton Friedman and the University of Chicago's Economics Faculty in the regime of Augusto Pinochet in 1970s Chile. Economics, dictatorship, and corporate takeover blend in this narrative.

Goodreads reviewers found the book objectionable for many reasons. A scholar might review the book like Gordon (September 1, 2011) judging that:

> the fact that the book is well-crafted and well-researched does not make it a well thought-out piece of writing . . . It's neither good journalism nor a good piece of political/economic analysis. But it's a very good rant for those already in her camp.

Many among the critics found the analogy of "electric shock" and "economic shock" a semantic confusion (Manny, November 20, 2008). Many protested how Milton Friedman was portrayed, Justin Evans (December 11, 2013) writing:

> quite why she needs to find a Villain to pin it all on (i.e., Milton Friedman) is beyond me: . . . it often reads as if Milton Friedman pulled the strings in every major event of the late twentieth century, which, loathe his theories as I do, he did not do.

Yet, even among those that rejected the book's central conceit, there was admiration for the achievement of argument and synthesis.[8] Szplug (December 16, 2013) states that "[t]he evidence . . . is, at best, circumstantial and correlational, and it attempts to graft a veneer of evil onto the otherwise inflectionless economic policies" but she/he then concludes:

> there are plenty of volumes out there proclaiming the wonders of our recently erected globalized market system; those such as Klein's are a welcome tonic, sobering in their presentation, righteous in their outrage, and compelling in their urge for readers to question exactly how manipulable (sic) these recurrent financial crises are, both in the way they are brought-about and settled afterwards.

And Evan (October 8, 2007) suggests that "any intelligent person who has read Thomas Friedman and found his arguments somewhat persuasive, should read this book too, and decide what sounds most persuasive for themselves". These reviewers do not read or write about Klein in isolation but place her book in the range of arguments found in the opinion press and in non-fiction paperbacks. They respond to the implausibility of post-Cold War triumphalism, of "flat worlds" and "ends of history" (the likes of *Commanding Heights*).

Shock Doctrine gained a new lease of life with the crash of 2008, and several readers turned to the book seeking meaning to financial traumas of that Fall. Chloe (October 14, 2008) recommended it for "anyone curious as to why they are now unemployed". After the media fanfare was well over, the book continued to be reviewed, several of the most "liked reviews" are only a few years old. One finds reviews in English, predominantly, a handful in Spanish, and several in Arabic, all declaring the book "important", e.g. Amr Mohamed, September 1, 2013, deemed it "worth more than five stars". One finds lengthty reviews that are like school reading reports, giving a chapter by chapter account, but also open letters, a thank you note to the author (in arabic), and a few free-wheeling essays on how the ideas might be applied to new cases in the late 2010s.

Across this festival of subjectivities, two types of experience are reported frequently and with emphasis. The first speaks of the reader encountering the extreme events portrayed in the book. Reviewers call it "deeply disturbing" (Trevor, May 25, 2008); "so disturbing that I didn't even finish the book" (Greg Sedlacek, August 21, 2015); "chilling, writhing outrage of a book. A hideous, squealing beast of a book" (James, March 1, 2008). To some the disturbance is too difficult to bear and write only a note to record their trauma, to others the emotions resolve into a call to moral outrage. Trevor (the most "liked" review, with 212 "likes") concludes:

> [t]here are so many lessons in this book, but the major one is that if people stand up against these greedy lunatics then we can stop them. We can reclaim our dignity and redistribute some of what has (sic) plundered from us. The criminal waste of tax dollars by these corporations in both Iraq and New Orleans is almost beyond description.

The other salient experience only a bit less corporal and more intellectual in quality bears the tagline of "eye opener" (Peggy, January 4, 2009; Mosca, Dec 29, 2008; and many others), "eye opening" (Jenny, November 15, 2011; Steven Williams, November 6, 2015; and more), "a shocking eye-opener" (Tanja Berg, August 2, 2011), and on and on . . . What makes these readers describe the book as one of the most important books they have ever read (Ellie, August 2, 2014) are the surprising connections between Latin American elites and the University of Chicago, between corporate contracts and the aftermatch of war, richly described and documented. Some of this readership declares itself new to non-fiction, others express the confusion of not understanding the world around them, and in particular how political events, ideologies, and economic policies intertwine. The book is a revelation of understanding, as Riya (January 8, 2012) puts it "this book literally turned my world upside down and changed my views on politics and economics. Mind = blown". The reviews of Goodreads testify that *Shock Doctrine* elicited a broad spectrum of responses, that these were thoughtful, a few sophisticated.

The readers of *Worldly Philosophers* and *Shock Doctrine* reveal to us how difficult it is to imagine or second guess a readership. To presume Klein's public to be leftwing and like-minded conspiracy theorists is to miss out on how the book elicited emotional labours of indignation and intellectual labours of understanding, not a comforting reaffirmation of prior beliefs but an upsetting startling experience. It is impolitic but also wrong to conceive the mass public as a throng of uneducated and unpolished masses and to trivialize the act of reading by assuming readers to be passive receptacle of ideas. If the readers of *Worldly Philosophers* shows us that the history of economics can entertain, the readers of *Shock Doctrine* of histories' capacity to become tools for deep understanding. Readers used Klein's book to unify the spheres of politics and economy, to make events in distant lands intelligible, events in the book and long after its publication, and thus a vast and bewildering global world gained coherence and cohesion in their mind's eye.

Unpopular histories

What value is there for the university historian to study popular narratives? In popular histories the scholar encounters a different kind of writing making sense of a record the scholar knows well, and possibly mild amusement (or irritation) at its mythmaking, for instance, reading Nasar's portrayal of Alfred Marshall as a Russell Crowe blonde genius. For those of us who write about a very recent past, that remains in memory of retiring or working scholars, one discovers in mass print usable information. Scribes, with the reputation of a David Warsh or the accolades and portfolio of a Michael Lewis, will get reclusive characters to tell their stories. Warsh's *Economic Principals* – the *Boston Globe* column, the book anthology, the on-going online magazine – is packed with valuable source information. Lewis's latest book, *The Undoing Project*, contains insights into the lifelong partnership of D. Kahneman and A. Tversky that I have not seen in scholarly paper. These are the uncontroversial, utilitarian (fun! and data!) reasons to read pop histories.

In this essay I gestured to a bolder defence of why we should attend to popular print and how we might do it. For this collection of historiographical essays I rehearse a perspective that sees books as objects circulating in culture and inscribed many times, by many actors. Adopting this perspective would align discussions of the historiography of economics with themes of the history of science, where books have been incorporated into the "material turn" and high and low brow print meet as equals as objects of study. In the simplest of terms, we should not prejudge what books merit being followed around in culture and which must be put to rest.[9] One should not presume how texts are read, one should also not presume who reads them. Our disciplinary traditions, the philosophy of history, and most certainly our own assessment on the quality of a classic text are not to be trusted as judgments of the texts' social and historical importance.

What holds true for the great books of natural history and for the great books of political economy must also hold true for history books. As we learn to record how history books make their way in culture, we will be asked to reflect why some of them become objects of popular fascination. But more than seeking formulas for publishing success, the value of reading the history of economics amply is to exercise our imaginations and ambitions. When we set ourselves the goal of appealing to economists alone, when we commit to a vocation as guardians of disciplinary memory, we lose sight of the horizon of possible narratives that economic ideas and economic lives afford and the publics that they grip. Faced by the sublime (or anarchic) landscape of popular and learned cultures, we begin to ask novel questions about our work, its conditions of production and circulation.

The play of the historical imagination is not without rules and I have hinted at some of them. The business models of publishing edit the scope of historical writing and set it on alternate paths to pre-assigned publics. But the business models of publishing, like those of journalism, like those of most media, are always unravelling, again today, by force of digital consumption of content. What lies ahead for books and for their social lives remains uncertain. While publishers and ancillary professionals dictate limits, I have argued that authors look for companions and outlined how genres might be described through relationships of emulation between authors and texts. Finally, I have called attention to readers and to how they renew and extend histories by crafting emotional urgency to them and by enlarging them in argument. To think the practice of writing history is to remember that writing always begets more writing, that we are all readers among readers and writers among writers.

Rather than conclude by once more repeating Keynes' zombie proverb of 1936, I quote from one of Naomi Klein's reviewers, Shannon (Giraffe Days). On July 2, 2009 she wrote that:

> there is a kind of history that gets overlooked, that doesn't get taught in schools or universities aside from a fourth-year optional course that no one bothers to take. It's a history that is fundamental to understanding our world, both past and present and where the hell we're going. It's a history that touches everyone, regardless of class, gender, race or age, but that slips out the back door before anyone thinks to call it to account, put it on trial and expose its heinous crimes. I'm talking about economic history, the history of economics, and the power economics plays in everything that happens in the world.

Let's do that.

Notes

1 A notable contributor to this genre is Wilhelm Roscher's *Geschichte der Wissenschaft in Deustschland* of 1874, that through various translations ushered a greater appreciation for German economics which was often absent in the English and French surveys of earlier decades. For an earlier example of the national frame see Theodore Fix's entry "Economie Politique" for the *Dictionnaire du Commerce et des Marchandises*, 1855, Paris: Hachette.

2 One of the richest veins of popular writings on economics in America is magazines (Mata 2011), fitting my periodization see the remarkable "Economists" in *Fortune* (McDonald 1950).

3 If we observe that J. K. Galbraith's TV series *Age of Uncertainty* (a history of economics) preceded, indeed prompted, Milton Friedman's *Free to Choose* than one might say history of economics was televised before economics (Burgin 2013).

4 Darnton's 1982 essay was a culmination of a long trajectory in the analysis of books and reading that is usually said to have began with D. McKenzie's (1969) "Printers of the Mind", a challenge to the idea that there were fixed patterns to book production, and setting out a more erratic and complex process than previously assumed. Equally important was the literature from France that began even earlier, notably in Lucien Fevre and Henri-Jean Martin's *L'Apparition du Livre* of 1957.

5 The success of *Beautiful Mind* will forever be bound to the motion picture. One might observe the movie as echoing earlier representations of the genius and tormented mathematician, from *Good Will Hunting* (1997) to *Proof* (2005) and thus not speaking to popular conceptions of the economist but of the mathematician. Indeed, the movie never identifies Nash as an economist.

6 *Commanding Heights* is written in the style of the forgotten influence of dead economists, and in the next section we will encounter another title that lavishly attributes historical agency to economists. Of special note is also work on the history of finance, in particular that of Peter Bernstein, see Bernstein (1992).

7 Joseph Stiglitz reviewing for the *New York Times*, remarked "There are many places in her book where [Klein] oversimplifies. But Friedman and the other shock therapists were also guilty of oversimplification, basing their belief in the perfection of market economies on models that assumed perfect information, perfect competition, perfect risk markets. Indeed, the case against these policies is even stronger than the one Klein makes" (Stiglitz 2007). Christopher Hayes (2007) only complained that Klein was addressing the wrong economist and that she should have picked Hayek.

8 At least one reader trained in economics, expressed ambivalence. Riku Sayuj (October 25, 2011) felt "as strongly as the author that The Shock Doctrine is changing the world. But it runs in the face of all economics I have been taught and I find myself scorning and muttering 'alarmist'".

9 From a very different starting point, Kenneth Carpenter and the Reinert family working from the Foxwell-Goldsmiths collection are reclassifying the canon of political economy pre-1850 (Reinert, Carpenter, Reinert, and Reinert 2017). Their metrics are what books were most reissued and translated in that period. The surprising and disturbing finding is that the "most popular" book in political economy is not the *Wealth of Nations* or Say's *Traite* or his *Cours*, but Ben Franklyn's *Way to Wealth* (see the online exhibit at http://waytowealth.org/).

References

Allemang, J. (2007). "Shocked and Appalled; Shock Resistant: Naomi Klein, an Audacious Voice in a Discouraged Era." *The Globe and Mail*, September 1.

Backhouse, R. (1992). "How Should We Approach the History of Economic Thought, Fact, Fiction or Moral Tale?" *Journal of the History of Economic Thought* 14(1): 18–35.

Backhouse, R. (2002). *The Penguin History of Economics*. London, Penguin.

Barber, W. (1967). *A History of Economic Thought*. Harmondsworth, Penguin.

Bernstein, P. L. (1992). *Capital Ideas: The Improbable Origins of Modern Wall Street*. New York, Maxwell Macmillan International.

Blaug, M. (1990). "On the Historiography of Economics." *Journal of the History of Economic Thought* 12(1): 27–37.

Burgin, A. (2013). "Age of Certainty: Galbraith, Friedman, and the Public Life of Economic Ideas." *History of Political Economy* 45(5): 191–219.

Coser, L., Kadushin, C., and Powell, W. (1982). *Books: The Culture and Commerce of Publishing*. New York, Basic Books.

Darnton, Robert (1982). "What is the History of Books?" *Daedalus* 111(3): 65–83.

Dorfman, Joseph (1946–1959) *The Economic Mind in American Civilization*. New York: Viking Press.

Fish, S. E. (1976). "Interpreting the 'Variorum'." *Critical Inquiry* 2(3): 465–485.

Fontaine, P. (2016). "Other Histories of Recent Economics: A Survey." *History of Political Economy* 48(3): 373–421.

Frasca-Spada, Marina and Jardine, Nick (eds) (2000). *Books and the Sciences in History*. New York: Cambridge University Press.

Galbraith, J. K. (1987). *A History of Economics: The Past as the Present*. Harmondsworth, Penguin.

Goodwin, C. (1958). "Canadian Economic Thought: 1814–1914." Dissertation. Duke University. Durham, NC.

Goodwin, C. (1966). *Economic Inquiry in Australia*. Durham, Duke University Press.

Hayes, C. (2007). "The New Road to Serfdom." *In These Times*, November 9.

Heilbroner, R. L. (1953). *The Worldly Philosophers: The Lives, Times, and Ideas of the Great Economic Thinkers*. New York, Simon and Schuster.

Keynes, J. M. (1936). *The General Theory of Employment, Interest and Money*. London: Palgrave Macmillan.

Klein, N. (2007). *The Shock Doctrine: The Rise of Disaster Capitalism*. New York, Henry Holt.

Lewenstein, B. V. (1992). "The Meaning of Public Understanding of Science in the United States after World War II." *Public Understanding of Science* 1(1): 45–68.

Macfarquhar, L. (2008). "Outside Agitator; Naomi Klein and the new new left." *New Yorker*, December 8.

Mandler, P. (2006). *The English National Character: The History of an Idea from Edmund Burke to Tony Blair*. New Haven, Yale University Press.

Mata, T. (2011). "Trust in Independence: The Identities of Economists in Business Magazines, 1945–1970." *Journal of the History of the Behavioral Sciences* 47(4): 359–379.

Mata, T. (forthcoming). "Economics – and History – As Communicative Action." *History of Political Economy*.

Mata, T. and Medema, S. (2013). "Cultures of Expertise and the Public Interventions of Economists" *History of Political Economy* 45(5): 1–19.

McDonald, John A. (1950). "The Economists." *Fortune*, December.

McKenzie, D. (1969). "Printers of the Mind: Some Notes on Bibliographical Theories and Printing-House Practices." *Studies in Bibliography* 22: 1–75.

Nasar, S. (2012). *Grand Pursuit: The Story of Economic Genius*. New York, Simon & Schuster.

Poovey, M. (1998). *A History of the Modern Fact: Problems of Knowledge in the Sciences of Wealth and Society.* Chicago: Chicago University Press.

Poovey, M. (2008). *Genres of the Credit Economy: Mediating Value in Eighteenth- and Nineteenth-Century Britain.* Chicago, Chicago University Press.

Reinert, E. S., Carpenter, K, Reinert, F. A., Reinert, S. (2017). "80 Economic Bestsellers before 1850: A Fresh Look at the History of Economic Thought." *Working Papers in Technology Governance and Economic Dynamics* no. 74.

Schiffrin, A. (2001). *The Business of Books: How the International Conglomerates Took Over Publishing and Changed the Way We Read.* London, Verso Books.

Secord, J. A. (2004). "Knowledge in Transit." *Isis* 95(4): 654–672.

Silk, Leonard (1974). *The Economists.* New York: Basic Books.

Stapleton, Julia (2001). *Political Intellectuals and Public Identities in Britain since 1850.* Manchester, Manchester University Press.

Stiglitz, J. (2007). "Bleakonomics." *New York Times,* September 30.

Tharoor, S. (2007). "Doing Well by Doing Ill." *Washington Post,* November 25.

Thompson, J. B. (2013). *Merchants of Culture: The Publishing Business in the Twenty-First Century.* Cambridge, Wiley & Sons.

Topham, J. R. (2009). "Introduction." *Isis,* 100(2): 310–318.

Warsh, D. (1993). *Economic Principals: Masters and Mavericks of Modern Economics.* New York, Free Press.

Warsh, D. (2006). *Knowledge and the Wealth of Nations: A Story of Economic Discovery.* New York, W. W. Norton & Company.

Weintraub, E. Roy (1999). "How Should We Write the History of Twentieth-Century Economics?" *Oxford Review of Economic Policy* 15(4): 139–152.

Yergin, D. and Stanislaw, J. (1998). *The Commanding Heights: The Battle for the World Economy.* New York, Free Press.

Yergin, D. and Stanislaw, J. (2002). *The Commanding Heights: The Battle for the World Economy.* Revised and updated ed. New York, Simon & Schuster.

11 Detectives, storytellers, and hackers

Historians of economics in an age of social media

Beatrice Cherrier

Introduction

By all accounts, social media have thoroughly reshaped our networks, habits, and lives over the last 15 years.[1] So much so that they are currently experiencing a backlash. Articles in which former Facebook, Apple, and Google top executives regret building websites and applications that are ripping society apart are becoming a new literary genre. Social media has equally transformed business and professional practices, including scholarly ones. Surveys show that academic uses are unevenly distributed across countries, gender, and disciplines (see for instance Lupton 2014). The probability that you, reader, own at least one social media account regardless of your age or location, is 40 percent, 70 percent if you live in the United States. Yet, if you are a historian of economics, there is less than 10 percent chance that you use this account in your scholarly work. The purpose of this chapter is to convince you to rethink your resistance to or disinterest in using social media as a professional tool.[2]

This chapter is not intended as a "how to" guide. First, because tutorials specifically designed for historians already abound on the web.[3] So do discussions of opportunities and shortcomings, from trolling to abuse, limited impact, and ephemeral attention. Second, because each platform has its own set of interaction rules and technological constraints. These evolve constantly – see for instance the famous 140 characters limitation on Twitter, turned 280 in the fall of 2017. The survival of each social media company is never granted (see for instance Topolsky 2016). Nor is my goal to walk the reader through the menagerie of websites and applications. Though scope varies, the term social media (or social networks, as Boyd and Ellison 2008 call them) usually spans blogs, Facebook, Twitter, Instagram, Linkedin, Google+, Tumblr, Snapchat, sometimes YouTube, Wikipedia, podcast websites, ResearchGate, or Academia.edu (Staniland 2017). The Merriam Webster definition highlights their shared characteristics: they are "forms of electronic communication (such as websites for social networking and microblogging) through which users create online communities to share information, ideas, personal, messages, and other content (such as videos)". In this chapter, I will focus on what I have learned from years of blogging and tweeting.[4] I have little experience in Facebook interaction, though it is one of academics' preferred platforms.[5]

There are as many reasons to blog, tweet, and seek social media interaction as there are researchers online. The Scholar Stage blog, for instance, identifies four blogging styles: 1) "News Through the Long View" in which the historian highlights contemporary trends in society by recasting them in larger historical contexts; 2) "history as a mirror" which aims at drawing enduring lessons from the past; 3) "publishing without peer review" in which authors offer "extended historical narratives for an online audience"; and 4) "public research notes" meant at keeping the historian's work organized, but publicly. Some posts evoke reference lists, book reviews, surveys, or textbook chapters and are aimed at educating audiences; others are historical vignettes ripe with anecdotes from the archives. Some seek to spur historiographical debate, others are more executive summaries of completed research with a clear dissemination purpose.[6] The *History of Economics Playground*, founded by Loïc Charles, Tiago Mata, and Floris Heukelom in 2007, was largely intended as an online office for geographically dispersed graduate students. We used it to debate our objects and methods, to confront our historiographical perspectives. As we moved to the *INET blog* in 2010, our tone and purpose shifted. Our posts were aimed at covering conferences, publicizing new collective projects, and disseminating research results. I use my personal blog, *The Undercover Historian*, for various purposes: dissemination, thinking out loud, answering reference queries, surveying the existing literature, curating chronologies, and even as a writing workshop. Twitter can and does serve many functions as well.

Providing an exhaustive overview of how historians of economics could benefit from social media is thus impossible and doomed to be outdated by the time it goes in print. The present discussion therefore seeks to emancipate from the institutional and technical constraints associated with specific social media to focus on the new practices and questions they generate, and their significance for historians of economics. I do *not* believe that using social media fundamentally transforms historians' objects, research questions, or historiographies. They won't lead you to reclaim Fernand Braudel over Marc Bloch or Gordon Woods or Susan Leigh Star, or Hegel over Foucault. They won't shift your focus from forensic to narrative, from cultural to political, from intellectual to activist history. My claim, rather, is that using social media to write the history of economics *for* publics and *in* public alters our entire research process. It does so because social media bring a dose of interaction at every stage, from gathering data to writing, collaborating, sharing, and showcasing history, and interacting with publics. This interaction highlights that history is as much about *us* as about our *objects*. Social media may not change our identities as historians, but they make our epistemological commitments and underlying agendas more salient, through bringing key questions of processes and audiences to the fore (see Pinto and Taithe 2015).

Gathering new data

History of economics is an applied science, and as such feeds itself with data: textual, archival, oral, statistical, or else. What social media therefore first bring to the table are new types of qualitative and quantitative data. Platforms have enabled the observation, quantification, and measurement of all kind of social behaviors, interactions, and engagements. Twitter's Application Programming Interfaces (APIs) were initially open, so that social scientists have been able to scrap huge quantities of data, and the platform has quickly emerged as a valuable data repository (Ahmed 2015; Carpenter 2017). Scrapping and visualizing data have become standard practices in some branches of sociology. The word "digital ethnography" has been coined to designate a new set of practices whereby social behavior is being observed through Twitter. For instance, changing moods, anti-immigrants sentiments, contagion processes, responses to national disasters, sleep patterns, or voting behaviors have recently been investigated (McCormick, Lee, Cesare, Shojaie, and Spiro 2015).

Social media data are equally interesting for historians of economics, at least those working on a past recent enough so that its frontiers with the present are blurred.[7] Twitter can help us study, for instance, the success of Thomas Piketty's *Capital in the XXIth century*, and more generally, the dissemination of economic ideas. The birth and development of new ideas is also documented in blog posts and social media exchanges. Quantitative easing, for instance, moved into Federal Open Market Committee (FOMC) minutes and academic papers after months of online exchanges. Economists' growing engagement with social media also result in a constant flow of methodological jousting: What is a "good model"? What is an "acceptable proof"? Should models predict? Should they be realistic? Tracking those debates in a pre-web era required studying enduring correspondences or print exchanges between two scholars, or being lucky enough to find conference minutes in the archives. These kinds of data are now all over the place. It enables historians to identify changing and enduring patterns. Present debates are, in spite of the "empirical turn" and "age of big data" economics purportedly has entered, strikingly reminiscent of the Cowles vs National Bureau of Economic Research (NBER) "Measurement Without Theory" controversy and the induction vs deduction dispute.[8]

Social media also offer a way of interacting directly with our protagonists, one either alternative to or conceived as a new kind of oral history (see Chapter 3 by Jullien in this volume). It allows us to shift our focus away from those protagonists whom economists and Nobel committees designate as worthy object of studies. This handful of "hall of fame" characters are usually white, men, Western, theorists in the Cold War, or more recently empirical scientists. They have succeeded in developing "dominant" approaches to economics; they are "winners". Yet, with adequate tooling up in sociology and anthropology, social media allow us to observe and interact with the thousands of scientists and experts making the fabric of the discipline, from textbook writers to graduate students, teachers, programmers, journal editors, court witnesses, government economists, and all kind of publics.[9] They offer the opportunity to gather information that are difficult to extract from published materials or even archives: on departmental cultures, workshop interactions, the choice of a name for a famous model, the macroeconomics textbooks in use at Chicago, Minnesota, or MIT during the 1980s, the spatial organization of offices and computer equipment, all of which Haslmayer, Collier, and Giraud (Chapters 7, 8, and 9 in this volume) each argue are important clues to understand how economics practices have evolved in the past decades.[10] Millions of tweets, blog and online articles comments or customer book reviews can also be mined to study publics' understanding of economics (see Chapter 10 by Mata in this volume).

Twitter exchanges also highlight how economists understand, construct, and weaponize their own history. Canonical history is both an object of study and a set of narratives that compete with, often supersede, and sometimes influence ours. Blog posts and columns have been a privileged site where the notion that economics is having an "empirical turn" enabled by big data and computerization has developed and spread (Backhouse and Cherrier 2017). Since the 2008 financial crisis, Twitter has been buzzing with heated exchange on the state of macroeconomics, the status of Dynamic Stochastic General Equilibrium (DSGE) models, and the "way forward". The historian can both attend these debates and intervene, asking DSGE modelers what they believe is the value of their models, confronting both proponents and detractors with the visions of Milton Friedman, Robert Lucas, Don Patinkin, Franco Modigliani, Albert Ando, or Fed economists.

Writing

An often-overlooked characteristic of social media is that they inescapably involve writing. When I blog, tweet or comment on Facebook, I not only write *for* publics and *in* public but also for myself. I leave the discussion of the public aspect for the following sections, only pointing, at this stage, that latent publicity brings discipline to the endeavor: if writing is like going to the gym, and I believe it is, social media provide the windows that separate the running mill on which you're sweating from the visitors' corridor. At the same time, scholarly writing is highly personal. Some colleagues love it, words flow from their fingers, and they have no qualms rewriting their drafts endlessly. I loathe writing as much as I enjoy being immersed in archives. Oozing archive boxes usually leave me with a set of puzzle pieces, which I have no idea how to fit together. As a graduate student, I was told it would get better with experience, but agonizing over the present draft is evidence to the contrary. Many of us were educated as economists, meaning that we were not trained in writing scholarly articles whose "proofs" and "evidence" are not independent from the quality of the prose they are couched in.[11] Most of us do not write in our native language. And all of us need to practice anyway. Social media can be used as a writing workshop, a kind of gym. "In some people's eyes, I am less of a thinker, less of a historian, because I blog and tweet and post to Facebook . . . But at least I'm writing. You know? . . . writing begets writing," intellectual historian L.D. Burnett (2015) explains.

Blogging allows cutting a paper in smaller pieces so that can each be more easily refined, polished, and tested. It raises the quality of the "survey of the existing literature", since the unifying features of a body of papers need to be spelled out explicitly. I came up with the idea of researching the history of the *Journal of Economic Literature* (*JEL*) codes while writing a blog post on the (largely overlooked) history of applied economics.[12] When drafting the paper a year later, I faced a recurring dilemma. Should I embed the various topics I wanted to tackle into a chronological framework, or should I instead choose a topical structure, providing chronological elements in one or several subsections? I thus drafted a series of topical blog posts: classifying economics during the war; should theory be an independent category? Why was the microeconomics category much easier to frame than the macroeconomics category? There were enough redundance for me to settle on a chronological structure, but the exercise sharpened my outline of cross-cutting themes in the introduction.

Twitter offers even more challenging writing opportunities. It allows *threading*, aka writing a series of 5, 10, or 30 tweets to summarize one or several papers, outline a narrative, or elaborate an opinion. The thread has to be structured and consistent enough so as to catch the reader's attention and convince him to jump from one tweet to the next, down the whole series; 280 characters do not allow subtle logical articulation and transitions, so that overall consistency requires shaping a kind of *flow*, a simple yet compelling narrative arc, possibly a chronological one. Doing so forces the writer to weed her story until its spinal chord is excavated and strengthened. Tweeting a set of ideas allowed Aurélien Goutsmedt and I to put together a set of ideas on the making and dissemination of Milton Friedman's 1968 presidential address. Our inconsistencies and missing data were highlighted by the thread structure. We subsequently wrote a post, itself pointing to the additional research necessary to write a full-fledged paper.[13] Tweeting is also a good way to train yourself to "pitch" better. History of economics editor Paul Dudenhefer (2017) emphasizes the importance of "making the reader care" by framing a paper in a meaningful yet economical way. This involves being able to challenge a shared context and lay out the paper's thesis in just two or three sentences, a Twitter format. Threading Roger Backhouse's (2017) biography of Paul Samuelson, for instance, forced me to explain why a 900-page book was worth a read in 280 characters catchy enough to draw the ephemeral attention of the reader.

Collaborating

Our first readers are our colleagues. The gradual marginalization of the history of economics since the 1970s has made places where several historians can interact and trade ideas scarce. Our community is scattered, with members often working alone in an intellectual and institutional environment that is at best curious, sometimes hostile, often indifferent. Restoring a sense of community is momentarily achieved through disciplinary conferences, and such was the justification for the establishment of the Societies for the History of Economics (SHOE) list in 1995 and of the young scholar's *Playground* blog in 2007. As Adam Kotsko (quoted in Charpentier 2014) noted in the early days of social media, blogging is "especially great for academics who would otherwise be quite isolated from other academics with similar interests". I believe that Twitter offers a less costly, more flexible, and more permanent infrastructure to support an online community. It allows researchers from various locations, disciplinary and institutional backgrounds to share news, call for papers, working papers, publications, PhD defenses, hires. The History of Economic Society and the European Society for the History of Economic Though have thus recently pooled together to set up a Twitter account.[14] It also allows conferences to be live-tweeted: if a paper is publicly available online, or if panelists feel confortable with social media, scholars in the audience tweet major ideas and the most significant questions. This helps those who could not attend keep track of the reception of new research and of ongoing debates.

Twitter thus works as an online "faculty lounge" (Priem, Piwowar, and Hemminger 2012). Since exchanges are 1) public and 2) searchable, these virtual lounges are less closed and exclusive than physical ones. They escape disciplinary boundaries, which is especially fit for a discipline whose survival is predicated on the reaffirmation of an identity, yet not a disciplinary one. What unites the Twitter community is its objects, not its institutional structure. It does not matter whether you come from an economics, history, history of science, sociology, or anthropology department, or elsewhere. The online structure of scholarly Twitter also eases bibliographic search and comparative study.[15] When I work on how economics is classified, why the American Economic Association has set up a prize system after World War II, or on changing notions of what make "good data", I systematically wonder what the situation is in other sciences. Querying a major history of science publication does not always yield a satisfactory outcome. Twitter allows to jump from account to account, from research program to research program, and to identify ongoing work on physics classification or on the social history of the Fields medal. It also eases the identification of those artifacts which stand in between big fundamental texts and archival traces of the daily lives of scientists, which happened to shape a generation's approach without being set in stone: an American Economic Association presidential address that was not so much cited but influenced a generation of graduate students; some exchange in which the naming of a new generation of macroeconomic models generated meaningful disagreement.[16]

Another collaborative endeavor is publishing, from the choice of a journal to processing comments by referees. As is now well understood, social media have brought new online science communities who seek to transform academic publishing. Websites like OpenUP Hub, PubMed Commons, or Pubpeer have institutionalized online open peer-review, that is, anonymous or signed unsolicited pre-publication or post-publication comments (Ross-Hellauer 2017). Posting online content on social media platforms likewise implies accepting unsolicited comments, whether via emails or through online comments or rejoinder posts. It is therefore a useful (though sometimes painful) way to get feedback. Social media can finally change relationships to editors, with some of them asking that a blog post is turned into a *bona fide* submission to their journal.

Sharing and hacking

Historians of economics are somewhat schizophrenic. On the one hand, they often complain that economists, journalists, and citizens ignore their work. On the other, they usually consider dissemination as a separate, secondary, and lower kind of activity. The problem we face is not one of contempt or disinterest anymore. It's one of invisibility. The 2017 economics graduate student or assistant professor does not hold history of economics in low esteem, she does not even know such scholarship *exists*, even less where to find it. Yet, the thirst for history has not disappeared. Students want to know why and how their discipline has become mathematized, how to define a model, or who this "Haavelmo" is. Interest is not restricted to recent history of economics. Many scholars yearn for the wisdom imparted by Adam Smith, Ricardo, Marx, or Keynes, or for the hundred ways economists have conceived interest rates, capital, labor, land, or prices in the past centuries.

Social media offer a low-cost way to solve this tension. Twitter affords research dissemination with a few clicks. It can be a substitute to now disappeared history courses. It allows economists' attention to be hacked, hooked, and channeled to a piece of history that they did not even know could become significant to them. "Social media platforms have *disintermediated* communication between scholars and publics", Healy (2017, p. 771) notes. Hacking attention however requires: 1) open, or at least easy, access (time is scare, attention is fledging, it is often a matter of now or never, of immediately accessing a paper) and 2) articulated content, overarching stories, and clear narrative arcs. Historians of economics are good at studying how Irving Fischer or Charles Kindleberger conceived debt, how Robert Solow produced his growth model or how Lawrence Klein thought individual behavior and macroeconomic aggregate related to one another. At providing broader narratives on how measurements, theories, and models of growth have changed throughout centuries or how they have managed to *predict* in the last 100 years, much less so. There is little incentive to write surveys, to hook pieces of research together. Twitter allows putting references together, discussing a set of papers together without the costs of writing a full-fledged survey.[17] But the demand for history of economics highlighted by social media points to the need for overarching surveys and textbooks. The reward system of our field needs to change.

The peculiar structure of online engagement however creates new types of challenges. Attention is low, ephemeral, and bouncing. This has several consequences. At first, attention is biased upward. If your post is messy, your English fledging, your purpose unclear, no one will hold it against you.

You will just be ignored. Chances are, you will be ignored even when the quality of your contributions is high. What will get you attention is regularity, resilience, and consistency. You need to build an identity, a voice, a style. This means shouting in the wild and failing to engage with the public most of the time. Hacking publics' attention is rewarding, but it creates new tensions: you don't choose who reads you, for what purpose, and how your work is used and cited. Granted, a blog post is a *work in progress* and is recognized as such. Approximations, imperfections, and corrections are allowed. A Twitter exchange is considered a live unpolished conversation.[18] Yet it does not mean you can write anything.

First, critical and snarky tweets can be screenshot and circulated around, anonymous Twitter users can troll.[19] Second, the development of the preprint system in economics has made scholars and journalists more comfortable with citing not-yet refereed working papers. The reputation gained through writing regularly acts as a gatekeeper (Jamali, Nicholas, and Herman 2016). Blog posts can therefore find their way into media outlets such as the *Financial Times* or *The Economist*, without journalists having to ask permission to quote.[20] Always keep in mind that the content fed into social media is, *by definition*, available for quoting. Those posts which are written as draft or research notes are also mentioned in scholarly papers. Seeing Maria-Christina Marcuzzo and Giulia Zacchia (2016) citing a post on the "quantitative turn" in history of economics or Matt Jackson (2018) using a post on the metaphors economists use to describe their practices as the basis to reflect on the status of market design theory was rewarding. Having a comment to a colleague's own blog post cited as an example of skepticism toward the potency of the term "neoliberalism" was more unsettling (Mirowksi 2018). I wrote that comment on the fly, without even thinking someone other than the blog author would read it. It was cited with care and benevolence, but I should have kept possible uses of social media content in mind. The researchers who populate our histories of recent economics are often alive, sometimes still active. As I learned over the years, writing about their intellectual development and commenting on their work will systematically yield a response, online or offline.[21] Writing about history of economics online thus paradoxically requires being prepared both to be ignored and to be noticed.

In short, the historian of economics engaging with social media has no control over audiences. Second-guessing readers always fails, and what gets attention may not be what you find more innovative. I wrote a few posts on the history of the *JEL* codes for an economics audience, who largely ignored them. They eventually found some echo among intellectual and business historians. My account of Al Roth's 2018 American Economic Association presidential address and of the ethical shyness of economists garnered attention from sociologists. The piece economists found most interesting dealt with the metaphors economists have used to describe their work since the 19th century. Yet it did not seem very original to me. That economists have compared themselves with philosophers, physicists, engineers, dentists, or physicians reflected a well-established consensus in my field. Healy (2017, p. 778) notes that his more successful posts are those which identify patterns and stylized facts rather than provide explanations. My own limited experience likewise suggest that descriptive posts are more successful than interpretative ones and that the more sweeping, the more successful at gathering attention. This observation is in line with Hans-Michael Trautwein's (2017) remark that historians of economists are "the last generalists".

Showcasing

According to Healy (2017, p. 775), social media "tend to move the discipline from a situation where some people self-consciously do 'public sociology' to one where most sociologists unselfconsciously do sociology in public". This, he explains, because "new social media platforms have made it easier to be *seen*", creating "a distinctive field of public conversation, exchange and engagement". Social media do not merely allow historians of economics to trade reference, discuss alternative "modeling" practices of monetary theories, or disagree on the influence of the Cold War and Civil Rights movements on the objects and methods of economists. It requires them to do so *in public*. It is often considered as a shortcoming – being challenged in public might highlight some weakness in the analysis and create a reputation of sloppiness.[22] Resistance to airing disciplinary dirty laundry online also derives from the notion that scientific credibility is tied to the ability to achieve and publicize some kind of disciplinary "consensus".[23]

I don't share this worry. Science is predicated on the belief that truth is not *sui generis*; it involves puzzles, trials, and errors. Doubting and arguing in public is a sign of individual soundness and disciplinary self-confidence. It is being comfortable with scientific method. As I wrote above, tweeting is "thinking in progress", and it is recognized as such. Researching the history of economics in public is also a way to help other scholars relate to our practices. Laying out a puzzle (why have subfields who most benefited from computerization, such as large-scale macroeconometrics or, computational general equilibrium become marginalized as the PC spread?), posting an exchange between Paul Samuelson and Milton Friedman or a figure representing a principal component analysis, a co-citation network, or the result of some *Newsweek* articles text-mining and arguing over interpretation, allow us to frame history as a process whereby some quantitative and qualitative data are gathered, exploited, and interpreted. Rough data – qualitative and quantitative – are put on display, suggesting both commonalities and specificities in the methods historians need to use to make them speak.[24] Finally, opening the narrative black box by writing history in public and circulating working papers allow fellow historians to engage in a sort of early online public referee process, and economists to react in a public and articulated way.

Showcasing our work also involves curating history. As history of economics is becoming invisible, so are our methods, the type of data we use. These are often material artifacts, and part of the credibility resides in this materiality. I believe telling stories via social media is not enough. These stories need to be fleshed-out with portraits, videos or audio recordings, pictures of computers, output reels, laboratories, classrooms, books, correspondence, curricula, grant applications.

Interacting

Audiences will not read what you put online passively. Colleagues and protagonists will ask questions, challenge you, yell, try to change your histories, to censor, and to troll you. The emotional and reputational costs of being on social media can be high. Reasons to expect pushback (and to enjoy it) are manifold. First, historians of economics do not own any monopoly over history. As put by Pedro Pinto and Betrand Taithe (2015, p. 2), citing Marxist historian Raphael Samuels:

> History is not the prerogative of the historian, nor even, as postmodernism contends, a historian's invention, it is rather a social form of knowledge; the work in any given instance, of a thousand different hands . . . This exponential production outside of academic circles and far from its own debates on the value of history or post modern theory is offering the most extraordinary Copernican challenge a profession could face.

Much history of economics is produced in economists' blogs and self-reflective papers on the state of macroeconomics, public economics, etc. Our histories may therefore compete with theirs. Unsettling memories can bring resistance. This issue is especially salient when economists' histories are instrumental, meant to settle credit issues. Choosing what is remembered is wielding power, and "the power to grant credit thus makes contemporary history vulnerable to the attempts of censorship", Düppe (this volume) warns, and "Economists cooperate with historians because they wish to influence the first sediments of history". Through social media interaction, whose protagonists our narratives serve becomes clearer, and economists cooperate with historians to influence them too. Even those narratives whose purpose is not to restore credit, but to unpack how ideas, models, and practices are developed and circulated, affect the relationships between protagonists or communities. By becoming historical objects in our hands, the sunspot literature, disequilibrium economics or contingent valuation become worthy of attention, and, in the end, distinct, consistent, and recognized scientific endeavors.[25]

Interacting directly with graduate students, government and think-thank economists, academics or central bankers may change our practice as much as we may want to change theirs. At the very least, it makes tensions over purpose, methods, and identities more salient. Over the past decades, we have evolved from being economists doing history to historians studying economics. We have become emancipated in terms of objects and methods. Archive oozing and interviews have spread, and the deployment of quantitative techniques more akin to digital humanities than econometrics or experiments are on the rise. Our disciplinary identity has expanded to the edges of sociology and history of science, sociology, and intellectual history. Yet, in spite of calls to move to history departments, I suspect that historians of economics are still overwhelmingly located in economics departments. Many of us teach economics, are evaluated according to economics rankings, and may define themselves as economists. Most important, all of us write history with a purpose, however latent: changing economists' theories and practices, providing facts to anchor current debates on the state of the dismal science, instilling more reflexivity into their intellectual and institutional practices, and improving policymakers', citizens', and journalists' ability to decipher and assess economics. We may have diverse audiences in mind, but we want to be relevant, and social media allow a better grasp at current debates and angst. Whether our research topics should be allowed to shift accordingly is a matter of debate, but Twitter cues may help us pitch our chosen stories to improve our outreach.

The economists we engage online are both our colleagues and our objects of study. Social media compel us to navigate our dual identity as economists and historians.[26] You might sometimes think and feel like an economist, an insider, someone who shares a culture. You might sometimes feel like a historian, oblivious to the "truth" of a theory or the suitability of a practice, only focused on the structure of a debate. Online discussions occasionally shift to the history battleground, which mean economists are entering your field. You become the one with more at stake, you may feel angered that history is distorted, that evidence is ignored. Social media therefore create a complex set of interlocking emotions. Navigating this web requires a good understanding of one's own motives and identity. Social media ultimately require a taste for historiography, as the historian of economics is compelled to rethink the "distance" between her and her subjects, one supposed to guarantee objectivity. Should it be a chronological distance, an emotional distance, a historiographical distance, and how to preserve it? Isn't Hans Gadamer and Paul Ricoeur's concept of "understanding" or C. Wright Mill's notion of "sociological imagination" most helpful here? Isn't the key how the historian links the past, the present, and the future? I often find myself reminding economists that our perspectives are essentially different: their baseline is the present, and when discussing with me, they look backward. As a historian, my baseline is what economists were doing decades and centuries ago, and my work is forward-looking.

Conclusion

In this chapter, I have attempted to convince you that while social media engagement can be costly, the benefits for historians of economics are potentially huge. This is a good reason for all historians who like a good economics argument to give it a try, and join their some 50 colleagues already registered.[27] I have also suggested that doing so raises important questions of research processes and audiences, some that will outlive existing technical platforms. It requires us to articulate our perspectives on the present state and future of their discipline, and to reconceive dissemination and public work. These are not separate lower activities to be performed after research is completed. Research questions, methodological quandaries, and blind alleys are for the public eye too. Doing research in public will make it stronger.

What social media afford should not be conceived as reconnecting to a lost audience. There are as many reasons to be interested in the history of economics as readers. Predicting what topic will "work" and what will not is bound to fail – except Friedman and the Chicago School, always a hit. And altering research interests to please a fantasized audience is the surest path to loose our hard-won intellectual independence. A suggestion, then, is to adopt Corey Robin's (2016) admonition: the public intellectual "is writing for an audience that does not yet exist . . . she is writing for a reader she hopes to bring into being". While Robin uses this idea to target fashionable and successful writers, it is also one useful as a guide for scholars working in a marginalized area: do not strive to regain a lost audience, but bring one into being. Because blogging and tweeting largely consist in shouting in the wild, they paradoxically dispense the historian with targeting a specific audience. Writing the history of economics in public and disseminating it in the end require a good deal of enthusiasm for the quality of what is being published and optimism in its possible social benefits.

Notes

1 The birth of social media is dated either 1997 or 2004, the year SixDegrees and Facebook, respectively, were created (see Boyd and Ellison 2008 for a history).
2 This article is largely based on Cherrier (2018), which discusses how historians of economics would benefit from tweeting more. Social media statistics are taken from the Social Media Fact Sheet of the Pew Research Center.
3 See Carrigan (2016) and Charpentier (2014) on academic blogging and tweeting, and the American Historical Association's guide to tweeting (http://blog.historians. org/2011/08/five-ways-for-historians-to-use-twitter/ [accessed July 3, 2017]). See Healy (2017) for a discussion of the shortcomings of social media plateforms and the limits of quantitative measures of success.
4 I have been blogging since 2007. My current blog can be found at https://beatri cecherrier.wordpress.com. I opened a Twitter account (@undercoverhist) in 2015.
5 The History of Economic Society set up its own Facebook account in 2016. Discussions of how the platform can foster fruitful exchanges can be found in Healy (2017).
6 For exemple, Etherwave Propaganda, curated by Will Thomas and Chris Donohue, ran extensive research notes and surveys; the collective blog US Intellectual History as well as the Scatterplot and Orgtheory.net sociology blogs combine various styles.
7 Doing the "history of the present" is, since Michel Foucault outlined its contours, an accepted endeavor (Garland 2014).
8 In a nutshell: https://twitter.com/Noahpinion/status/684418194300260352
9 These practitioners, often anonymous, have less-direct stakes in how our stories are told than high-profile economists. This allows us to avoid being embattled in those credit fights described in Düppe (Chapter 2 in this volume) and in this chapter.

10 The latter was a macroeconomist's response to a series of tweets in which I wondered loud about the origins of the term "Lucas Critique". See https://twitter.com/Undercoverhist/status/850869673390374913

11 The History of Economic Society set up a writing workshop during its annual 2017 conference, led by Paul Dudenhefer.

12 Throwing your ideas in the wild also makes you vulnerable to plagiarism or being scooped. This is a bigger real or imaginary threat for young scholars, those who would also benefit more from writing small texts more regularly. Solis (2013) has helped me debunk the imaginary part.

13 See https://twitter.com/Undercoverhist/status/932743061205061632 and https://twitter.com/AGoutsmedt/status/932663844111048705. Chari and Goldsmith-Pinkham (2017) likewise began as a series of exploratory tweets in May 2017, one that received feedback and was subsequently turned into a paper (see https://twitter.com/paulgp/status/862410435491975168).

14 Its account handle is @Societies_HET. Its tweets are visible at https://twitter.com/Societies_HET

15 Proposing a set of reference on the history of economic facts, observations, and data allowed me to get tens of additional references from sociologists, historians of accounting and insurance, etc.: https://twitter.com/Undercoverhist/status/784309163362955269

16 The latter was a macroeconomist's response to a series of tweets in which I wondered about the origins of the term "Lucas Critique". See https://twitter.com/Undercoverhist/status/850869673390374913

17 Here is an example, dealing with contingent valuation: https://twitter.com/Undercoverhist/status/879094178470387712

18 Though I never found any explicit scholarly social media etiquette, my understanding is that it is fair to cite tweets in blog posts, and blog posts in academic papers. This is why I chose to link to relevant examples of tweets rather than directly quoting from them in this article.

19 Several popular scholars and journalists therefore use algorithms that systematically delete their tweets after a few days. See Bruenig (2017).

20 Two examples of journal articles mentioning history of economics blog posts are Hartford (2017) and Avent (2018).

21 Here is an exemple: https://marketdesigner.blogspot.fr/2018/03/the-economist-discusses-repugnant.html

22 On the importance of online reputation, see Jamali et al. (2016).

23 This idea is widely spread among economists, as attested by the many publications by economists and methodologists. Economics is the only science (with climate) that has a "professional consensus" Wikipedia entry.

24 See for instance this thread by historian of computer science Marie Hicks on the joys and pains of doing archive work, and the associated comments: https://twitter.com/histoftech/status/868237344310251521

25 Proponents of self-called "heterodox" approaches have long understood this, which explains that there exist more histories of heterodox economics than mainstream ones.

26 This also applies to historians of economics coming from other backgrounds. A sociologist, for instance, will have to come to terms with the tense relationships and sometimes-perceived pecking order between the two disciplines.

27 Here is a list of scholars who tweet on topics related to the history of economics: https://twitter.com/Undercoverhist/lists/history-of-economics

References

Ahmed, W. (2015). "Using Twitter as a Data Source: An Overview of Current Social Media Research Tools." *LSE Impact Blog*, 07/10/2015, http://blogs.lse. ac.uk/impactofsocialsciences/2015/07/10/social-media-research-tools-overview/ (accessed 07/03/2017).

Avent, Ryan (2018). "Economists Cannot Avoid Making Value Judgements." *The Economist: Free Exchange*, 02/24/2018.

Backhouse, Roger (2017). *Founder of Modern Economics: Paul A. Samuelson. Volume 1: Becoming Samuelson, 1915–1948*. London, Oxford University Press

Backhouse, Roger and Cherrier, Beatrice (2017). "The Age of the Applied Economist." *History of Political Economy* 49(5): 1–33..

Boyd, Danah and Ellison, Nicholas (2008). "Social Network Sites: Definition, History, and Scholarship." *Journal of Computer-Mediated Communication* 13(1): 210–230.

Bruenig, Elizabeth (2017). "Why (and How) I Delete All my Tweets Every Day." *Medium*, 06/28/2017, https://medium.com/@ebruenig/why-and-how-i-delete-all-my-tweets-every-day-93282d0d38fa (accessed 02/28/2018).

Burnett, L. D. (2015). "The Other Side of the River." *Saved by History, blog post*, 12/05/2015, http://savedbyhistory.blogspot.fr/2015/12/the-other-side-of-river. html (accessed 02/28/2018).

Carpenter, E. (2017). "Using Twitter for Sociological Research." *Shifting Paradigms Blog*, 03/06/2017, https://rampages.us/efcarpenter/2017/03/06/using-twitter-for-sociological-research/ (accessed 07/03/2017).

Carrigan, Mark (2016). *Social Media for Academics*. London, Sage.

Chari, Anusha and Goldsmith-Pinkham, Paul (2017). "Gender Representation in Economics Across Topics and Time: Evidence from the NBER Summer Institute." NBER Working Paper no. 23953.

Charpentier, Arthur (2014). "Blogging in Academia, A Personal Experience." 18/02/2014. Available at SSRN: https://ssrn.com/abstract=2398377

Cherrier, Beatrice (2018). "Why Historians of Economics Should Tweet." *History of Political Economy* 50(3), forthcoming.

Dudenhefer, Paul (2017). "Motivating and Framing A Paper." *Paul Dudenhefer Blog*, 06/21/2017, https://www.pauldudenhefer.net/news/2017/6/21/motivating-and-framing-a-paper (accessed 07/03/2017).

Garland, David (2014). "What Is 'History of the Present'? On Foucault's Genealogies and their Critical Preconditions." *Punishment and Society* 16(4): 365–384.

Hartford, Tim (2017). "Why Economists Should Be More Like Plumbers." *Financial Times*, 01/18/2017.

Healy, Kieran (2017). "Public Sociology in the Age of Social Media." *Perspective on Politics* 15(3): 771–780.

Jackson, Matt (2018). "The Role of Theory in an Age of Design and Big Data." In Jean-Franois Laslier, Hervé Moulin, Remzi Sanver, and William S. Zwicker (eds), *The Future of Economic Design*. Forthcoming.

Jamali, H. R., Nicholas, D., and Herman, E. (2016). "Scholarly Reputation in the Digital Age and the Role of Emerging Platforms and Mechanisms." *Research Evaluation* 25(1): 37–49.

Lupton, Deborah (2014). "'Feeling Better Connected': Academics' Use of Social Media." Working paper, News & Media Research Center, University of Canberra.

Marcuzzo, Maria-Cristina and Zacchia, Giulia (2016). "Is History of Economics What Hisorians of Economic Thought Do? A Quantitative Investigation." *History of Economic Ideas* 24(3): 29–46.

McCormick, T. H., Lee, H., Cesare, N., Shojaie, A., and Spiro, E. S. (2015). "Using Twitter for Demographic and Social Science." *Sociological Method and Research*, 1–32.

Mirowksi, Philip (2018). "Hell is Truth Seen to Late." *Zilsel* 3: 146–180.

Pinto, Pedro Ramos and Taithe, Bertrand (2015). "History in Public? Historians in the Age of Impact." In Pinto, P. R. and Taithe, B. (eds), *The Impact of History: Histories at the Beginning of the 21th Century*. London, Routledge: 1–11.

Priem, J., Piwowar, H., and Hemminger, B. (2012). "Altmetrics in the Wild: Using Social Media." *arXiv*: 1203.4745v1 [cs.DL].

Robin, Corey (2016). "How Intellectuals Create a Public." *The Chronicle Review*, 01/22/2016, www.chronicle.com/article/How-Intellectuals-Create-a/234984 (accessed 07/03/2017).

Ross-Hellauer, Tony (2017). "What Is Open Peer Review? A Systematic Seview." *F1000Res* 6: 588.

Solis, Daniel (2013). "What If Someone Steals Your Idea." *Daniel Solis Blog*, http://danielsolisblog.blogspot.fr/2013/07/what-if-someone-steals-your-idea.html (accessed 02/28/2018).

Staniland, Mark (2017). "How Do Researchers Use Social Media and Scholarly Collaboration Networks (SCNs)?" *Of Schemes and Memes Nature Blog*, 06/15/2017, http://blogs.nature.com/ofschemesandmemes/2017/06/15/how-do-researchers-use-social-media-and-scholarly-collaboration-networks-scns (accessed 02/28/2018).

The Scholar Stage (2016). "How to Be a History Blogger." *The Scholar Stage* blog, 02/06/2016, http://scholars-stage.blogspot.fr/2016/02/how-to-be-history-blogger.html

Topolsky, Joshua (2016). "The End of Twitter." *The New Yorker*, 01/29/2016, https://www.newyorker.com/tech/elements/the-end-of-twitter (accessed 02/28/2018).

Trautwein, Hans-Michael (2017). "The Last Generalists." *European Journal in the History of Economic Thought* 24(6): 1134–1166.

Afterword

Till Düppe

This project started out as "The historiography of contemporary economics". We initially thought the authors shared a common interest in the contemporary, also called recent, period of economics, a period which is often loosely tagged "post-World War II". We thought that both the historical vicinity and the different character of economics of this period posed historiographical issues that were different from those of preceding periods. There were good reasons for this. Historical vicinity implies that there are more sources available compared to earlier periods since the historical actors, or those who knew them personally, are still among us. The first part of this volume on memories, and their use in interviews and witness seminars, is in fact to a large extent limited to the historiography of the contemporary period. Even without sharing the notion of the history of the 20th century as particularly special, as in my own contribution, these contributions share a sense of urgency based on the fact that living memories pass away with their subjects.

But as discussions at the meeting in Lausanne continued, this remained the only essential characteristic of the contemporary period. Though the authors do share an interest in recent economics, none of them wished to limit their historiographical reflections to the contemporary. It is true that the number of sources available to historians is considerably higher due to the increased size of the profession and its documentation techniques, but this only gives occasion to the use of alternative methods, which in principle could be equally applied to earlier periods. Network analysis and prosopography are a case in point. They are easier to apply in a contemporary context, but are surely applicable as well to preceding periods, particularly considering that data from earlier centuries become more and more accessible (think of how economic historians can now scroll down centuries of data!). It is also true that the technical character of economics as a modelling science *gives occasion* to choose strategies for representing ideas and their contexts that are different from the traditional interpretive or survey-oriented modes of writing. But the resulting historiographical framework, such as that of "artefacts" proposed by Halsmayer, is in no way exclusive to the kind of models used today. Several works in the recent history of economics (such as Charles 2003; Maas 2011; and of course Morgan 2012) have shown that what I have labelled "material historiographies" can be easily applied to preceding centuries. Inversely, however, it is also true that writing the history of older economics gives occasion to, but does not require limiting the writer to, reading and interpreting books in the canon. In short, while the contemporary period invites a heightened awareness of the historian's place, role, and task, the resulting historiographies are to a large extent not limited to this period. The preceding chapters might be of interest to the entire community of historians of economics. This is why we agreed to change our working title to "Contemporary historiography of economics".

Another consensus that emerged from our discussion was that this collection of essays covers only examples of various contemporary historiographies, plural, rather than "the" contemporary historiography of economics. That is, the preceding essays do not try to create a new canon that replaces other kinds of interpretive or textual-based historiographies. There is no doubt that this kind of work will continue to exist since the world of ideas has the power to transcendent its contingent origins, the power to draw us into it by re-enacting these ideas in the here and now. Without questioning the scholarly value of such works, this collection of essays nevertheless helps to consciously choose what kind of stories we tell. While the economist's soul of historians of economics might bless us with appreciation and, if you wish, admiration for economic ideas, it is the historian's soul that grants us scholarly ethos. In this sense, this collection is indeed a plea, as Margaret Schabas put it years ago (1992), for more autonomy of the history of economics as part of the history of science.

These results of our discussions might be viewed against the background of the generational character of this book that is mentioned in the introduction. Many of the authors had the opportunity for some kind of collaboration with E. Roy Weintraub, and for many a research stay at Duke's Center for the History of Political Economy was formative for their becoming historians of economics and committing to this precarious field. Certainly for me, the field became attractive because I wanted to know more about "How Economics Became a Mathematical Science". What Roy's work, and his 2002 book in particular, did was to open up the literature in the history of science; it helped us to understand the odd world of the current practices of economists on a background that is invisible when going from text to text. As a pioneer of his own genre of writing, as he described in the introduction to this book, Roy had many fewer allies in the history of economics; the rhetorical fineness of his judgement, as apparent in his many review articles or interventions in the SHOE list, can be seen as a result of this generational change in the history of economics from which we profit today. Thanks to Roy's ardent support, and the opportunities he created at the Center for the History of Political Economy and the Economists' Papers Archive of the Rubenstein Library, there is now a growing generation of historians who can do their research without the need to delineate their work against economists who think of history as the sermonizing of brown and blue leather-bound books of Böhm-Bawerk, Gide, and Rist. And so there was a third consensus among the authors in Lausanne that, without "negative theology" of criticizing others, we wish to provide a positive image of our work as an invitation for others to extend, examples of what can be done – while treasuring in our book-shelves the blue softcover jacket of *How Economics Became a Mathematical Science*.

References

Charles, Loïc (2003). "The Visual History of the Tableau Economique." *European Journal of the History of Economic Thought* 10(4): 527–549.

Maas, Harro (2011). "Sorting Things Out: The Economist as an Armchair Observer. In Daston, L. (ed.), *Histories of Scientific Observation*. Chicago, University of Chicago Press: 207–229.

Morgan, M. S. (2012). *The World in the Model: How Economists Work and Think*. New York, Cambridge University Press.

Schabas, Margaret (1992). "Breaking Away: History of Economics as History of Science." *History of Political Economy* 24(1): 187–213.

Weintraub, E. Roy (2002). *How Economics Became a Mathematical Science*. Durham, Duke University Press.

Index

Page numbers: Tables are given in **bold**; figures in *italics*; notes denoted by [page number] 'n' [note number].

For Product Safety Concerns and Information please contact our EU
representative GPSR@taylorandfrancis.com
Taylor & Francis Verlag GmbH, Kaufingerstraße 24, 80331 München, Germany

www.ingramcontent.com/pod-product-compliance
Ingram Content Group UK Ltd.
Pitfield, Milton Keynes, MK11 3LW, UK
UKHW020957180425
457613UK00019B/731